PRAYER *Lifestyle*

NAVIGATING DAILY CHALLENGES WITH FAITH AND PRAYER

APOSTLE IVON VALERIE

Prayer Lifestyle: Navigating Daily Challenges with Faith and Prayer
Copyright ©2023 by Ivon Valerie
All rights reserved. No part of this book may be reproduced, stored in a retrieval system, or transmitted in any form or by any means, electronic, mechanical, photocopying, recording, scanning, or otherwise, without the publisher's prior written permission.

New International Version (NIV) copyright © 1973, 1978, 1984, 2011 by Biblica, Inc.®
Used by permission. All rights reserved worldwide.
King James Version (KJV) public domain
New Living Translation (NLT) are taken from the Holy Bible, New Living Translation, copyright ©1996, 2004, 2015 by Tyndale House Foundation. Used by permission of Tyndale House Publishers, Carol Stream, Illinois 60188. All rights reserved.
ESV® Bible (The Holy Bible, English Standard Version®), copyright © 2001 by Crossway, a publishing ministry of Good News Publishers. Used by permission. All rights reserved. The ESV text may not be quoted in any publication made available to the public by a Creative Commons license. The ESV may not be translated in whole or in part into any other language.

Printed in the United States of America
ISBN: **978-0-9974655-1-8**
SAPIENTIAL PUBLISHING
Cover design by Ivon Valerie
Interior design by Ivon Valerie
First edition: February 2023
10 9 8 7 6 5 4 3 2 1

Table of Content

Dedication --- 7
Introduction --- 9

Worship and Adoration --- 13
Praise and Worship --- 14
Adoration of God --- 17
Acknowledging God's Sovereignty --- 20
Expressing Gratitude to God --- 24

Personal Growth and Transformation --- 29
Spiritual Growth --- 30
Emotional Healing --- 33
Physical Healing --- 36
Overcoming Negative Patterns --- 39
Breaking free from Addictions --- 42

Relationships and Connections --- 47
Marriage and Family --- 48
Friendships and Community --- 51
Reconciliation and Forgiveness --- 54
Building Healthy Relationships --- 57
Protection for Loved Ones --- 60

Finances and Provision --- 65
Financial Blessings --- 66
Abundance and Prosperity --- 69
Debt Elimination --- 72
Job and Career Opportunities --- 76
Increase in Income --- 80

Faith and Trust --- 85
Building Faith --- 86
Overcoming Fear and Doubt --- 89
Trusting in Difficult Times --- 93
Building a Deeper Relationship with God --- 97

Protection and Safety --- 101
Protection from Harm and Danger --- 102
Protection from Negative Influences --- 105
Safety in Travel --- 108
Safety in the Workplace --- 111

Protection for Loved Ones --115
Wisdom and Discernment --**119**
Wisdom for Daily Living --120
Wisdom for Decision Making ---123
Discernment for Relationships ---126
Discernment for Opportunities ---129
Government and Authority ---**133**
Leaders and Government Officials------------------------------------134
National and International Issues --------------------------------------137
Peace and Justice---140
Protection of Religious Freedom --------------------------------------144
Protection of Human Rights --148
Community and Outreach ---**153**
Local Communities--154
Poor and Marginalized ---158
Sick and Suffering --161
Missions and Outreach --164
Unity and Harmony Among Different Groups ---------------------167
Healing and Deliverance ---**171**
Physical Healing --172
Emotional and Mental Healing --176
Spiritual Healing --180
Deliverance from Addiction and Negative Patterns -----------183
Protection Against Spiritual Attacks------------------------------------186
Success and Prosperity ---**191**
Success in Business and Career-------------------------------------192
Academic Success--195
Financial Prosperity---198
Abundance and Blessings ---201
Favor and Promotion ---204
Protection and Guidance ---**209**
Protection Against Physical Harm-----------------------------------210
Protection Against Negative Influences-----------------------------213
Guidance in Decision Making ---216
Guidance in Relationships ---219
Guidance in Personal Growth and Development-----------------222
Strength and Courage ---**227**
Inner Strength ---228

Emotional Strength ---232
Physical Strength ---235
Courage to Face Difficult Situations ---238
Courage to Take Action ---241
Purity and Holiness ---**245**
Purity of Heart ---246
Purity of Mind ---249
Purity of Body ---252
Holiness in Daily Living ---255
Personal Sanctification ---258
Grace and Mercy ---**263**
Grace in Times of Need ---264
Mercy in Times of Failure ---267
Grace and Mercy for Others ---270
Grace and Mercy for the World ---273
Increase of Grace and Mercy in the Church ---276
Mental Health and Emotional Well-being ---**281**
Relief from Anxiety ---282
Relief from Depression ---285
Emotional Stability ---289
Self-Care and Self-Compassion ---293
Inner Peace and Calm ---296
Financial Freedom ---**301**
Debt Elimination ---302
Financial Stability ---305
Increase in Income ---309
Wise Financial Management ---312
Provision and Abundance ---316
Overcoming Obstacles ---**321**
Overcoming Fear and Doubt ---322
Overcoming Self-Doubt ---326
Overcoming Negative Thoughts ---329
Overcoming Difficult Circumstances ---332
Overcoming Addiction and Negative Patterns ---335
Career and Business ---**341**
Job Opportunities ---342
Successful Business Ventures ---346
Promotions and Advancements ---350

Wisdom and Guidance in Career Decisions --- 354
Financial Stability and Success in Business --- 357
Education and Learning --- 361
Academic Success --- 362
Wisdom and Understanding --- 366
Guidance in Choosing a Career or Field of Study --- 369
Success in Professional Development --- 373
Success in Continuing Education --- 377
Children and Family --- 381
Children's Well-being --- 382
Children's Protection --- 386
Children's Spiritual Growth --- 390
Guidance in Parenting --- 393
Family Unity and Harmony --- 397
Travel and Safety --- 401
Safe Travels --- 402
Protection While Away from Home --- 405
Guidance in Travel Decisions --- 409
Provision During Travels --- 412
Protection While Traveling with Loved Ones --- 415
Creativity and Arts --- 419
Inspiration and Creativity --- 420
Success in the Arts --- 423
Wisdom and Guidance in Artistic Decisions --- 426
Increase in Artistic Talents --- 429
Protection for Artists and Creators --- 432
World Peace and Justice --- 437
Peace in the World --- 438
Peace in War-Torn Countries --- 441
Justice for the Oppressed --- 444
Safety for Humanitarian Workers --- 447
End to Human Trafficking --- 450
Natural Disasters and Relief Efforts --- 455
Safety During Natural Disasters --- 456
Protection of Homes and Properties --- 459
Provision During Times of Crisis --- 462
Guidance in Disaster Relief Efforts --- 465
Wisdom for Leaders in Times of Crisis --- 468

Dedication

This book is dedicated to my brother, **Stanford Junior Valerie**, whom God has used as my rock and guiding light on many occasions. Junior, your strength and determination have inspired me and helped me navigate some of life's many challenges.

You have saved my life many times, and I will always be grateful for your unwavering love, support, and protection. You have taught me the power of resilience, and I have learned much from you about beating the odds.

I honor and respect you for the man you are, and I love you. Thank you for being my brother and for ALWAYS being there.

With love and gratitude,
- Apostle **Ivon Valerie**

Introduction

With **Prayer Lifestyle: Navigating Daily Challenges with Faith & Prayer**, you can experience the transformative power of prayer and positive declarations. As an author and believer, I recognize just how critical prayer is in our lives - it has the potential to alter our daily life profoundly! Combining prayers and declarations into your daily life can provide tranquility and comfort during trying times.

We've all been through tough times, but we can reclaim the courage and serenity to get through them with prayer. This book was specifically put together to grant you this power! As you make your way through these prayers and confirmations, you will gain enthusiasm and insight that will help guide your life's journeys armed with faithfulness and prayer. It is also important to note that each prayer's wording has been crafted so it can be easily tailored around any special needs or predicaments that may arise.

This book is organized into chapters that explore several topics and help build a connection with God, such as personal growth, relationships, finances, career, health, and protection. Each chapter provides different prayers for specific needs and scriptural references so individuals can find the courage they need in uncertain times. The inspiring words of this manual give an all-encompassing approach to praying over various aspects of one's life journey.

As you read through each chapter, we want to help you connect profoundly with God's word while meditating on His promises. To do this, we have gathered an assemblage of empowering quotes and scriptures that are carefully tailored to match the themes in each chapter; these inspiring words will provide insight into the Lord's will for you, no matter what you're facing.

As you make your way through this book, take some time to read and truly internalize each prayer and declaration. For added impact, declare the prayers aloud as if they are yours; I am certain that when done with intention, you will feel a transformation like never before - from experiencing inner peace and hope to forming a deep bond of trust with God.

My prayer for you is that as you immerse yourself further in your faith and learn to apply prayer and trust in God, He will come through on your behalf, granting you the desires of your heart. I hope this book will provide a valuable resource. Let it be the map that leads you to a deeper connection with our Creator while discovering peace, hope, and purpose through adversity. May these pages bring forth blessings upon all who read them! Put faith into action with this unique collection of prayers and declarations that will help guide you through any challenge!

Ivon Valerie

Worship and Adoration

Worshiping and adoring God is a fundamental part of our association with Him. It involves displaying admiration, homage, and profound respect toward the divine power. Worshiping and showing devotion to God helps us comprehend His supreme characteristics and enriches our appreciation for Him, strengthening our relationship. Through worship and adoration, we can effectively communicate how much we love He who has gifted us life!

Prayer Lifestyle

Praise and Worship

Praise and worship express reverence, adoration, and devotion to God through song, prayer, and other forms of expression. It is an act of humility and submission to God's sovereignty, acknowledging His power and majesty.

Scripture References

Psalm 95:6 - "Come, let us bow down in worship, let us kneel before the Lord our Maker"

Psalm 100:4 - "Enter his gates with thanksgiving and his courts with praise; give thanks to him and praise his name."

Isaiah 12:5 - "Sing to the Lord, for he has done glorious things; let this be known to all the world."

Inspirational/Motivational Quotes

"Praise is the language of heaven, and it is also the language of victory on earth." - Smith Wigglesworth

"Worship is the fuel and fire of our spiritual journey." - Rick Warren

"True worship is not about us and our feelings; it is about God and His greatness." - Charles Stanley

Prayer

Dear Lord,
I stand before you with reverence and gratitude, recognizing your power and greatness. I am eternally thankful for the many incredible things you have done in my life due to the grace you continuously give me. I offer you appreciation and admiration as I stand humbly in front of You.

With my voice of praise, I implore that you fill me with your presence. Letting go of all self-interests and selfishness, I intend to worship you in truthfulness and genuine reverence to honor your name alone. Lead me by Your will so my heart may overflow with love for You above all else.

In this time of reverence, I humbly submit my worries, hesitations, and anxieties to you. With utmost trust in your goodness and reliability, I am conscious that You are constantly with me. From the depths of my heart, I thank You for Your unwavering love and mercy. Amen.

Declaration

I make a bold declaration today, with conviction in my heart, that I will wholeheartedly and unreservedly praise and worship the

Prayer Lifestyle

Lord with every aspect of my being. I will enter His gates with a heart full of thanksgiving, acknowledging all He has done for me and all He continues to do. I will approach His courts with praise on my lips, giving Him the honor and glory that is due to His holy name.

I understand that true worship is not just about singing songs or saying prayers but about offering my entire self to the Lord in a spirit of humility and obedience. I will worship Him in spirit and in truth, allowing His holy presence to fill me and permeate every part of my being. I will let go of my desires and preferences and seek only to please Him and glorify His name.

As I sing His praises, I will let my voice be a vessel of worship, lifting the name of Jesus and declaring His greatness. I will let my heart be filled with adoration for my Lord and my Savior, and I will let my mind be focused on Him and His greatness. I will use all my strength to serve Him and glorify His name. This is my declaration, vow, and commitment to the Lord, now and always. I trust in His goodness and faithfulness and know He is always with me. I am eternally grateful for His love and grace.

Adoration of God

Adoration of God shows deep love, reverence, and devotion to God. It expresses awe and wonder at His greatness and acknowledges Him as the source of all things.

Scripture References

Psalm 8:1 - "O Lord, our Lord, how majestic is your name in all the earth! You have set your glory above the heavens."

Psalm 96:9 - "Worship the Lord in the splendor of his holiness; tremble before him, all the earth."

Isaiah 6:3 - "And they were calling to one another: "Holy, holy, holy is the Lord Almighty; the whole earth is full of his glory."

Inspirational/Motivational Quotes

"Adoration is the highest form of worship, for it recognizes God's worth above all else." - A.W. Tozer

"Adoration is the language of the heart, expressing the deep love we have for God." - Rick Warren

"Adoration is not just a feeling; it is a choice to focus on the greatness of God." - Charles Stanley

Prayer

Dear Lord,
I come before you with an open and submissive heart, adoring your importance and worth. You are the source of all things, and I identify that nothing in this world likens to your splendor and holiness. I want to express my deep love for you and admit that you are above all else.

I am in awe of your grandeur and the brilliance of your holiness as I worship you. I tremble before you, admitting my smallness and insignificance compared to your importance. I give you all the glory and praise, for you alone are worthy of it. You are the originator and sustainer of all things, and I am thankful for how you have blessed me and directed me throughout my life.

Your grace and mercy humble me, and I rely on your goodness and faithfulness. Please continue to fill me with the consciousness of your presence and that my heart has always adored you. I am committed to worshiping and serving you with all my heart, soul, mind, and strength. Amen.

Declaration

I boldly declare today that I will value the Lord with all my spirit, conveying my deep love and affection for Him. I identify that He is the origin of all things and that His worth transcends all else. I realize His superiority and sovereignty and worship Him in the majesty of His righteousness. I will tremble before Him in wonderment and marvel, remembering my insignificance compared to Him.

Ivon Valerie

I understand that worshiping God is not just a one-time action but a daily routine. I will make it a priority to concentrate on His excellence and decide to love Him always. I will convey my devotion to Him through prayer, song, and all other forms of manifestation. I will devote myself to a lifestyle of worship, where my heart and mind are constantly immersed in Him. I will take the time to meditate on His word and to reminisce on His love, grace, and mercy.

I know that this is not always effortless, but with the support of the Holy Spirit, I am committed to making it an everyday practice to adore the Lord. I depend on His goodness and loyalty and understand He is always with me, directing and upholding me. I am forever appreciative of His love and grace.

Acknowledging God's Sovereignty

Acknowledging God's sovereignty is to accept and submit to His divine authority over all. It means understanding that He steers the destiny of every soul and situation and always sees his plans brought to fruition.

Scripture References:

Psalm 47:2 - "For the Lord Most High is awesome; he is a great King over all the earth."

Isaiah 40:28 - "Do you not know? Have you not heard? The Lord is the everlasting God, the Creator of the ends of the earth. He will not grow tired or weary, and his understanding no one can fathom."

Daniel 4:35 - "All the peoples of the earth are regarded as nothing. He does as he pleases with the powers of heaven and the peoples of the earth. No one can hold back his hand or say to him: "What have you done?"

Inspirational/Motivational Quotes

"To acknowledge God's sovereignty is to understand that He is in charge of everything and that His plans and purposes will always prevail." - Charles Stanley

"God's sovereignty means that He is in control of everything, even when it doesn't make sense to us." - Rick Warren

"When we acknowledge God's sovereignty, we can find peace in knowing that He is working everything out for our good and His glory." - John Piper

Prayer

Dear Lord,
With the utmost humility and respect, I bow before you to acknowledge your supreme authority. You are the reigning sovereign of all things, controlling every aspect of my life and creation. Your plans will prevail no matter how dire a situation may be; for it is through your hand that sustains us with grace.

Embracing faith in your divine plans, I entrust my dreams and expectations to you. Your infinite wisdom and compassion comfort me in knowing that all is working out for the best, no matter how perplexing the journey may be. I am confident you are taking me down a path of success toward a greater destiny —a pathway filled with delight and surprises ahead!

When life feels hard and unpredictable, I remind myself that You are in ultimate control. Your plan for my life is much bigger than anything I could ever create, which comforts me! Plus, since You are good and faithful through it all, I never need to worry about being abandoned.

I commit myself to follow and trust your authority with complete faith. I will strive to harmonize my wishes with yours, allowing Your plans for me to carry out in fullness. Gratitude fills my heart for the steadfast aid of your presence that accompanies me throughout life's journey; Amen!

Declaration

I recognize and honor God's supremacy over me and the entire universe with profound conviction. He is the source of all life, our sustainer in times of need, and His authority encompasses every corner of our lives. Today, I humbly acknowledge this truth with the utmost respect for His methodical control in my journey through life.

I willingly align with His plans and purposes since I am confident that the results will always work in my favor and bring Him glory. Regardless of whether or not I can comprehend why certain events occur, I choose to believe in His goodness, wisdom, and sovereignty without fail.

I find solace in the thought that He is always working out all things for my benefit and His honor. I have faith that He is guiding me, leading me on the journey He has chosen specifically for me, and will never leave my side.

I passionately commit to making it a priority to surrender and submit to God's rulership in my life. I will strive earnestly to align my desires with His divine plan, trusting that He knows what is best for me and stewarding the outcomes of my life for His glory alone. To better understand who He is and how He works, I shall study the scripture faithfully daily and commune with Him through prayerful conversation, relying on the wisdom of the Holy Spirit.

Struggling to submit is not always easy, but with the help of the Holy Spirit, I am unwavering in my commitment. I believe in His goodness and loyalty and that He will accompany me wherever I go, guiding and caring for me unconditionally. For this infinite love and grace displayed by God each day, eternally grateful could never even begin to describe how thankful I truly am.

Prayer Lifestyle

Expressing Gratitude to God

Expressing gratitude to God shows appreciation and thankfulness for all the blessings He has given us. It is recognizing that everything we have is a gift from Him and acknowledging His faithfulness and provision in our lives.

Scripture References

Psalm 100:4 - "Enter his gates with thanksgiving and his courts with praise; give thanks to him and praise his name."

Colossians 3:15 - "Let the peace of Christ rule in your hearts, for as members of one body you are called to peace. And always be thankful."

1 Thessalonians 5:18 - "give thanks in all circumstances; for this is God's will for you in Christ Jesus."

Inspirational/Motivational Quotes

"Gratitude is the heart's memory." - French Proverb

"Gratitude is the healthiest of all human emotions. The more you express gratitude for what you have, the more likely you will have even more to express gratitude for." - Zig Ziglar

"Expressing gratitude to God is not only a duty but a privilege, for it acknowledges the many blessings He has bestowed upon us." - A.W. Tozer

Prayer

Dear Lord,
I come before you with a heart full of gratitude, expressing my deepest thanks for all the blessings you have given me. I recognize that everything I have is a gift from you, and I am constantly reminded of your faithfulness and provision in my life.

I am grateful for your grace, mercy, and love, which you have freely given me despite my imperfections and shortcomings. I am filled with peace and joy, knowing that you are always with me and that your love endures forever.

I give you all the glory and praise, for you alone are worthy of it. Your love and goodness surround me, and I am grateful for how you have blessed and sustained me. Your grace and mercy humble me, and I trust in your faithfulness.

I commit to expressing my gratitude for your blessings in my daily life and to be mindful of all the good things you provide for me, big and small. I will strive to give back to you through worship, service, and obedience.

I am thankful for your constant presence and guidance in my life, and I trust your goodness and faithfulness. I am eternally grateful for your love and grace. Amen.

Declaration

Today, I boldly declare that I will express my gratitude to God for all the blessings He has given me. I will recognize that everything I have is a gift from Him, and I will acknowledge His faithfulness and provision in my life. I understand that being thankful in all circumstances is God's will for me, and I commit to making it a daily practice to express my gratitude to Him.

I will strive to be mindful of all the blessings in my life, big and small, and to recognize them as gifts from God. I will reflect on His goodness and provision and express my gratitude through prayer, song, and other forms of expression. I will strive to show my gratitude by serving others, being kind and generous, and obeying His will.

I understand that expressing gratitude is not just a one-time act but a daily practice. I will make it a priority to focus on God's blessings and choose to be thankful always. I will remind myself that God is in control and that everything happens according to His plan, even when I may not understand the reasons behind it.

I trust in God's goodness and faithfulness and know He is always with me, guiding and sustaining me. I am eternally grateful for His love and grace and always commit to expressing my gratitude to Him.

Ivon Valerie

Prayer Lifestyle

Personal Growth and Transformation

As human beings, we are constantly developing and evolving. It is essential to strive for personal growth and transformation in our lives, particularly when it comes to strengthening our bond with God. In this chapter, readers will explore prayers and declarations that can be used in identifying areas that require improvement within ourselves and setting goals for positive changes. By delving deeper into the importance of self-growth through a spiritual perspective, we can all aspire towards creating more meaningful connections between us and divinity.

Prayer Lifestyle

Spiritual Growth

Spiritual growth is becoming more like Christ, growing in knowledge and understanding of God's word, and developing a deeper relationship with Him. It is the process of being transformed by renewing our minds and growing in righteousness, holiness, and love.

Scripture References

2 Peter 3:18 - "But grow in the grace and knowledge of our Lord and Savior Jesus Christ. To him be glory both now and forever! Amen."

Colossians 1:10 - "so that you may live a life worthy of the Lord and please him in every way: bearing fruit in every good work, growing in the knowledge of God,"

1 Corinthians 14:20 - "But in your hearts revere Christ as Lord. Always be prepared to give an answer to everyone who asks you to give the reason for the hope that you have. But do this with gentleness and respect"

Inspirational/Motivational Quotes

"Spiritual growth is not about being a perfect person, but about becoming more like Jesus." - Rick Warren

"The key to spiritual growth is consistency in reading and obeying God's Word." - Charles Stanley

"Spiritual growth is about becoming more like Christ, not about having more experiences." - John Piper

Prayer

Dear Lord,
I come to you today with a humble and open heart, seeking spiritual growth. I desire to become more like you, to grow in my knowledge and understanding of your word, and to develop a deeper relationship with you. I ask that you would transform me from the inside out, renewing my mind and helping me grow in righteousness, holiness, and love.

I understand that this is not a one-time event but a lifelong journey, and I am willing to put in the effort to grow spiritually. I ask for your guidance and wisdom as I seek to understand your word and apply it to my life. I pray that you would give me the strength and the wisdom to live a life worthy of you and that I would be prepared to answer anyone who asks me to give the reason for my hope.

I want to grow in my faith and deepen my relationship with you, to know you more fully, to trust in your provision, to obey your commands, and to be conformed to your image. I ask that you help me be sensitive to your leading and obedient to your will.

I trust your goodness and faithfulness and know you are always with me, guiding and sustaining me. I am eternally grateful for your love and grace, and I commit to seeking spiritual growth, to be like you, and to honor you in my life. Amen.

Declaration

I declare today that I am committed to spiritual growth. I desire to become more like Christ, to grow in my knowledge and understanding of God's word, and to develop a deeper relationship with Him. I understand this is a lifelong journey, and I am willing to put in the effort to grow spiritually.

I will seek to be transformed by renewing my mind and growing in righteousness, holiness, and love. I will make it my daily practice to read and obey God's word so that I may be equipped to live a life worthy of Him. I will seek to apply His teachings to my life and to be sensitive to His leading and obedient to His will.

I will also be prepared to answer anyone who asks me to give the reason for my hope. I know that my faith is not just a personal belief but something that can impact others and inspire them to seek the same transformation.

I understand that this is not always easy, but with the help of the Holy Spirit, I am determined to make it a daily practice to grow spiritually. I trust in God's goodness and faithfulness and know He is always with me, guiding and sustaining me. I am eternally grateful for His love and grace and am committed to honoring Him.

Ivon Valerie

Emotional Healing

Emotional healing addresses and resolves negative emotions and past traumas that may prevent us from living fulfilling lives. It includes seeking forgiveness and letting go of pain, anger, and resentment.

Scripture References

Psalm 147:3 - "He heals the brokenhearted and binds up their wounds."

Isaiah 61:1 - "The Spirit of the Sovereign Lord is on me, because the Lord has anointed me to proclaim good news to the poor. He has sent me to bind up the brokenhearted, to proclaim freedom for the captives and release from darkness for the prisoners,"

2 Corinthians 1:3-4 - "Praise be to the God and Father of our Lord Jesus Christ, the Father of compassion and the God of all comfort, who comforts us in all our troubles, so that we can comfort those in any trouble with the comfort we ourselves receive from God."

Inspirational/Motivational Quotes

"The greatest healing therapy is friendship and love." - Hubert H. Humphrey

Prayer Lifestyle

"Healing takes courage, and we all have courage, even if we have to dig a little to find it." - Tori Amos

"Emotional healing is not about forgetting the past; it's about accepting it, understanding it, and learning from it." - Brené Brown

Prayer

Dear Lord,
I come to you today with a heavy heart, seeking emotional healing. I acknowledge the pain and negative emotions I have been carrying, and I ask for your forgiveness for any ways I have held onto them. I understand that these emotions and past traumas have been holding me back and preventing me from living a fulfilling life.

I ask that you help me let go of past traumas and negative feelings such as anger, resentment, and pain. I ask that you heal my broken heart and bind up my wounds. I know only you can bring true and lasting healing, and I trust your power.

I ask that you fill me with your peace and give me the strength to move forward. I understand that this may not happen overnight, and I am willing to take the time and effort to process and heal. I ask that you give me wisdom and guidance and surround me with loving and supportive people.

I trust in your goodness and faithfulness, and you are always with me, guiding and sustaining me. I am eternally grateful for your love and grace, and I commit to allowing you to heal me emotionally and allow me to live a fulfilling life. Amen.

Declaration

I make a bold declaration today that I am committed to emotional healing. I acknowledge the negative emotions and past traumas holding me back and preventing me from living a fulfilling life. I understand that addressing and resolving these issues is crucial for my overall well-being, and I am willing to put in the effort to heal.

I will actively seek forgiveness and let go of pain, anger, and resentment that I may have been holding onto. I will trust in the Lord's healing power, knowing that He is the ultimate source of healing and that He can bring true and lasting healing to my emotional wounds. I will trust in His power to heal my broken heart, bind up my wounds, and give me the strength and peace to move forward.

I will make it my daily practice to seek emotional healing through prayer, self-reflection, and seeking help if needed. I will be open to guidance and support from others and strive to take care of my emotional well-being just as I do for my physical well-being.

This process may not be easy, but I trust the Lord's goodness and faithfulness. I know He is always with me, guiding and sustaining me, and I am eternally grateful for His love and grace. I am committed to allowing Him to heal me emotionally and to live a fulfilling life.

Physical Healing

Physical healing is addressing and recovering from illnesses or injuries. It also involves taking care of our physical bodies through exercise, a healthy diet, and proper rest.

Scripture References

Isaiah 53:5 - "But he was pierced for our transgressions, he was crushed for our iniquities; the punishment that brought us peace was on him, and by his wounds, we are healed."

James 5:14-15 - "Is anyone among you sick? Let them call the church elders to pray over them and anoint them with oil in the name of the Lord. And the prayer offered in faith will make the sick person well; the Lord will raise them. If they have sinned, they will be forgiven."

Matthew 8:17 - "This was to fulfill what was spoken through the prophet Isaiah: "He took up our infirmities and bore our diseases.""

Inspirational/Motivational Quotes

"The best medicine in the world is a mother's kiss." - Anonymous

"Healing is a matter of time, but it is sometimes also a matter of opportunity." - Hippocrates

"The natural healing force within each one of us is the greatest force in getting well." - Hippocrates

Prayer

Dear Lord,
I come to you today with a heart full of hope, seeking physical healing. I acknowledge any illnesses or injuries that I am currently facing, and I ask for your healing power to be at work in my body. I understand that healing is physical, spiritual, emotional, and mental, and I trust in your ability to heal me completely.

I also ask for wisdom and guidance in taking care of my physical body through exercise, a healthy diet, and proper rest. I know these things are important for maintaining good health, and I ask your help making them a regular part of my life.

I also thank you for your promise of healing through your son Jesus Christ, and I trust in your faithfulness to fulfill it. I know that through Jesus, your healing power is available to me, and I believe that you can and will heal me in your perfect time and according to your will.

I trust in your goodness and faithfulness, and you are always with me, guiding and sustaining me. I am eternally grateful for your love and grace, and I commit to allowing you to heal me physically and take care of my physical body. Amen.

Declaration

I declare I am committed to physical healing. I acknowledge any illnesses or injuries I may have, and I am determined to address and recover from them. I understand that healing is physical, spiritual, emotional, and mental, and I trust the Lord's ability to heal me completely.

I will make it a daily practice to take care of my physical body through exercise, a healthy diet, and proper rest. I understand that these things are important for maintaining good health, and I will strive to make them a regular part of my daily routine. I will also seek medical help if necessary and trust the Lord to guide me in the right direction.

I trust in the Lord's promise of healing through His son Jesus Christ, and I declare that I am healed in His name. I believe that through Jesus, the Lord's healing power is available to me, and I trust that He can and will heal me in His perfect time and according to His will.

This process may not be easy, but I trust the Lord's goodness and faithfulness. I know He is always with me, guiding and sustaining me, and I am eternally grateful for His love and grace. I am committed to allowing Him to heal me physically and to take care of my physical body.

Ivon Valerie

Overcoming Negative Patterns

Overcoming negative patterns is recognizing and breaking free from harmful habits and behaviors that prevent us from living fulfilling lives. It involves making conscious choices to replace negative and positive patterns.

Scripture References

Romans 12:2 - "Do not conform to the pattern of this world, but be transformed by the renewing of your mind. Then you will be able to test and approve what God's will is—his good, pleasing and perfect will."

Galatians 5:16 - "So I say, walk by the Spirit, and you will not gratify the desires of the flesh."

Philippians 4:13 - "I can do all things through Christ who strengthens me."

Inspirational/Motivational Quotes

"Your only limit is the one you set for yourself." - Anonymous
"The greatest prison people live in is the fear of what other people think." - David Icke

"The first step towards change is awareness. The second step is acceptance." - Nathaniel Branden

Prayer

Dear Lord,

I come to you today with a heart full of humility, acknowledging the negative patterns holding me back. I understand that these patterns may be harmful habits and behaviors that have become ingrained in my life, and I ask your help in recognizing and breaking free from them.

I ask for your strength and wisdom as I make conscious choices to change these negative patterns and replace them with positive ones. I understand that this process may not be easy, but I am willing to put in the effort to transform. I ask that you would renew my mind and help me live according to your good, pleasing and perfect will.

I trust in your power to help me overcome, and I thank you for the victory in advance. I understand this is a process, and I will not give up, but I will keep seeking your help to overcome these negative patterns holding me back.

I trust in your goodness and faithfulness, and you are always with me, guiding and sustaining me. I am eternally grateful for your love and grace, and I commit to allowing you to help me transform and live a life in accordance with your will. Amen.

Declaration

I make a bold declaration today that I am committed to overcoming negative patterns in my life. I acknowledge the harmful habits and behaviors holding me back and am determined to break free from them. I understand that these negative patterns have become ingrained in my life, and it will take effort and determination to change them.

I will make conscious choices to change and replace these negative patterns with positive ones. I will actively seek the Lord's help in recognizing these patterns and making the necessary changes. I trust in the Lord's power to help me overcome, and I declare victory over these negative patterns in Jesus' name.

I will make it a daily practice to seek the Lord's help in overcoming negative patterns through prayer, self-reflection, and seeking help if necessary. I will be open to guidance and support from others, and I will strive to take care of my emotional, mental and spiritual well-being just as I do for my physical well-being.

This process may not be easy, but I trust the Lord's goodness and faithfulness. I know He is always with me, guiding and sustaining me, and I am eternally grateful for His love and grace. I am committed to allowing Him to help me overcome these negative patterns and live a fulfilling life.

Prayer Lifestyle

Breaking Free From Addictions

Breaking free from addictions is overcoming the power of addiction, whether it be to drugs, alcohol, or any other substance or behavior. It involves recognizing the problem, seeking help, and committing to change.

Scripture References

1 Corinthians 6:12 - "'Everything is permissible for me'—but not everything is beneficial. 'Everything is permissible for me'—but I will not be mastered by anything."

Philippians 4:13 - "I can do all things through Christ who strengthens me."

1 Corinthians 10:13 - "No temptation has overtaken you that is not common to man. God is faithful, and he will not let you be tempted beyond your ability, but with the temptation, he will also provide the way of escape, that you may be able to endure it."

Inspirational/Motivational Quotes

"The greatest step towards a life of simplicity is to learn to let go." - Steve Maraboli

"The only way out of the labyrinth of suffering is to forgive." - John Green

"You have within you right now everything you need to deal with whatever the world can throw at you." - Brian Tracy

Prayer

Dear Lord,
I come to you today, humbly acknowledging the power of addiction in my life. I understand that this problem has taken control of my life, and I ask for your help recognizing and overcoming it. I know this is not something I can do alone, and I ask for your strength and wisdom as I seek help and commit to change.

I trust in your power to set me free from addiction, and I thank you for the victory in advance. I understand that this may be a difficult journey, but I trust that with your help, I can overcome it. I ask for your guidance in finding the right support and resources to help me in this journey. I know many options are available, and I ask that you lead me to the best option. I will be open to guidance and support from others and strive to take care of my emotional, mental, and spiritual well-being just as I do for my physical well-being.

This process may not be easy, but I trust the Lord's goodness and faithfulness. I know He is always with me, guiding and sustaining me, and I am eternally grateful for His love and grace. I am committed to allowing Him to help me overcome addiction and live a fulfilling life. Amen.

Declaration

I boldly declare today that I am committed to breaking free from addiction. I understand its hold on my life, and I am determined to overcome it. I acknowledge that this is not something I can do alone, and I will seek help and commit to change.

I trust the Lord's power to free me from addiction and declare victory in Jesus' name. I will make it a daily practice to seek the Lord's help and guidance in this journey. I will actively seek support and resources, such as counseling, support groups, and professional help, to aid me in breaking free from addiction.

I understand this process may not be easy, but with the Lord's help and guidance, I am confident I can overcome addiction. I will be open to guidance and support from others and strive to take care of my emotional, mental, and spiritual well-being just as I do for my physical well-being.

I understand that this process may not be easy, but I trust the Lord's goodness and faithfulness. I know He is always with me, guiding and sustaining me, and I am eternally grateful for His love and grace. I am committed to allowing Him to help me overcome addiction and live a fulfilling life.

Ivon Valerie

Prayer Lifestyle

Ivon Valerie

Relationships and Connections

Relationships and connections form the bedrock of our lives, offering us a sense of belonging, support, and camaraderie. This chapter sheds light on how to build strong relationships with others to create robust communities. It provides readers with prayers and declarations that can be used to deepen their current ties as well as develop new ones.

Marriage and Family

Marriage and family are foundational relationships God has created and ordained. They provide a sense of love, security, and support. A strong marriage and family can be a source of joy and blessings, while a weak one can cause pain and suffering.

Scripture References

Ephesians 5:25 - "Husbands, love your wives, just as Christ loved the church and gave himself up for her"

Proverbs 22:6 - "Start children off on the way they should go, and even when they are old they will not turn from it."

Colossians 3:18-19 - "Wives, submit yourselves to your husbands, as is fitting in the Lord. Husbands, love your wives and do not be harsh with them."

Inspirational/Motivational Quotes

"A happy marriage is the union of two good forgivers." - Ruth Bell Graham

"The most important thing in a marriage is to be committed to it and to make it work." - Dr. Phil McGraw

Ivon Valerie

"A successful marriage requires falling in love many times, always with the same person." - Mignon McLaughlin

Prayer

Dear Lord,
I come to you today filled with gratitude for the gift of marriage and family. I understand the importance of these relationships in my life, and I ask for your guidance and wisdom as I work to build a strong and healthy marriage and family.

I pray for love, respect, and understanding in my relationships with my spouse and family. I ask that you help us be a source of joy and blessings to each other and those around us. Building a strong and healthy family takes effort and commitment, and I ask for your help in making that happen.

I ask for your protection and provision for my loved ones, and I trust your faithfulness to meet our needs. I know that you are a loving and caring God, and I am confident that you will be with us every step of the way.

I will make it a daily practice to pray for my marriage and family, to seek guidance and wisdom from the Lord, and to nurture my relationships with them. I will strive to be a good spouse, parent, and family member and to create a loving, peaceful, and harmonious home environment.

I understand that this process may not be easy, but I trust the Lord's goodness and faithfulness. I know He is always with me, guiding and sustaining me, and I am eternally grateful for His love and grace. I am committed to allowing Him to help me build a strong and healthy marriage and family and to live a fulfilling life. Amen.

Declaration

I declare today that I am fully committed to building a strong and healthy marriage and family. I understand the importance of these relationships in my life, and I am determined to invest time and effort in building a successful marriage and family. I will strive for love, respect, and understanding in my relationships with my spouse and family. I will make it a daily practice to communicate effectively, listen attentively and practice empathy, forgiveness, and gratitude toward them.

I will seek guidance and wisdom from the Lord in building a successful marriage and family. I will make it a daily practice to pray for my marriage and family, to seek guidance and wisdom from the Lord, and to nurture my relationships with them. I will strive to be a good spouse, parent, and family member and to create a loving, peaceful, and harmonious home environment.

I declare that my marriage and family will be a source of joy and blessings to each other and to those around us. I trust in the Lord's protection and provision for my loved ones, and I declare that He will meet our needs. I understand that this process may not be easy, but I trust the Lord's goodness and faithfulness. I know He is always with me, guiding and sustaining me, and I am eternally grateful for His love and grace. I am committed to allowing Him to help me build a strong and healthy marriage and family and to live a fulfilling life.

Ivon Valerie

Friendships and Community

Friendships and community are important connections that provide support, encouragement, and accountability in our lives. God calls us to build relationships with others and to love and care for one another.

Scripture References

Proverbs 17:17 - "A friend loves at all times, and a brother is born for a time of adversity."

Ecclesiastes 4:9-12 - "Two are better than one, because they have a good return for their labor: If either of them falls down, one can help the other up. But pity anyone who falls and has no one to help them up. Also, if two lie down together, they will keep warm. But how can one keep warm alone? Though one may be overpowered, two can defend themselves. A cord of three strands is not quickly broken."

1 John 4:7-8 - "Dear friends, let us love one another, for love comes from God. Everyone who loves has been born of God and knows God. Whoever does not love does not know God, because God is love."

Inspirational/Motivational Quotes

"A friend is someone who knows all about you and still loves you." - Elbert Hubbard

"Friendship is the hardest thing in the world to explain. It's not something you learn in school. But if you haven't learned the meaning of friendship, you really haven't learned anything." - Muhammad Ali

"The greatest gift of life is friendship, and I have received it." - Hubert H. Humphrey

Prayer

As I come before you today, Lord, I am grateful for the friendships and community surrounding me. I know these relationships are a gift from you, and I want to make the most of them. I ask for your guidance and wisdom as I navigate the ups and downs of building and maintaining healthy relationships with others.

I pray for the strength and grace to be a supportive and encouraging friend to those around me and to show love and care for my community. I know I will not always get it right, but I trust your goodness and faithfulness to guide me and help me grow in love and compassion.

I also lift my friends and community to you, Lord, asking for your protection and provision for them. I trust that you are always watching over them and that you will meet their needs in your perfect way and at your perfect timing. Thank you, Lord, for the privilege of friendship and community and the joy and fulfillment that comes from loving and being loved by others. Amen.

Declaration

I declare that I am committed to building healthy relationships with friends and my community. I understand the importance of these relationships in my life, and I am determined to invest time and effort in building and maintaining them. I will strive to be a supportive and encouraging friend to others and to show love and care for my community. I will make it a daily practice to communicate effectively, listen attentively, and practice empathy, forgiveness, and gratitude toward them.

I will seek guidance and wisdom from the Lord in building and maintaining healthy relationships with friends and the community. I will make it a daily practice to pray for my friends and community. I will strive to be a good friend and member of my community and to create a loving, peaceful, and harmonious environment for them.

I understand that friendships and community are a source of support, encouragement, and accountability in my life. I will try to be there for my friends and community and allow them to be there for me. I trust in the Lord's protection and provision for my friends and community, and I declare that He will meet their needs. With the Lord's help, my friendships and community will be a positive and uplifting aspect of my life.

Prayer Lifestyle

Reconciliation and Forgiveness

Reconciliation and forgiveness are crucial in maintaining healthy relationships. It involves taking responsibility for one's actions, asking for forgiveness, and granting forgiveness to others. It is an important aspect of living in accordance with God's will and showing love and compassion to others.

Scripture References

Matthew 6:14-15 - "For if you forgive other people when they sin against you, your heavenly Father will also forgive you. But if you do not forgive others their sins, your Father will not forgive your sins."

Colossians 3:13 - "Bear with each other and forgive one another if any of you has a grievance against someone. Forgive as the Lord forgave you."

Ephesians 4:32 - "Be kind to one another, tenderhearted, forgiving one another, as God in Christ forgave you."

Inspirational/Motivational Quotes

"Forgiveness is not an occasional act, it is a constant attitude." - Martin Luther King Jr.

"The weak can never forgive. Forgiveness is the attribute of the strong." - Mahatma Gandhi

"Forgiveness is the final form of love." - Reinhold Niebuhr

Prayer

Dear Lord,
I come before you today humbly acknowledging my human nature that can lead to mistakes and hurt others. I ask for your forgiveness for any actions or words that may have caused harm to those around me. I ask for your guidance and wisdom in taking responsibility for my actions and asking for forgiveness when necessary.

I also ask for your grace and strength in granting others forgiveness and letting go of resentment and bitterness that may be holding me back from true reconciliation. Help me to see others through your eyes of love and compassion and to follow your will in all my relationships.

I ask for your continued guidance and wisdom as I navigate the complexities of relationships and the importance of forgiveness and reconciliation. I trust in your goodness and faithfulness to help me in this journey, and I thank you in advance for the healing and restoration that will come through your love and grace. Amen.

Declaration

I declare that I am committed to reconciliation and forgiveness in my personal and professional relationships. I understand that as a human being, I am prone to make mistakes and am willing to take responsibility for my actions and ask for forgiveness when necessary. I will be honest, sincere, and humble in my apologies and take the necessary steps to make amends.

I will also make it a daily practice to reflect on my relationships and strive to grant forgiveness to others, and let go of resentment and bitterness that may be holding me back. I trust the Lord's guidance and strength in this process and seek his wisdom in difficult situations. I declare that I will live by His will and show love and compassion to those around me, even when challenging.

I will prioritize maintaining healthy relationships and committing to being a peacemaker and a channel of reconciliation wherever I am. I will be a good listener and communicate effectively with those around me. I trust that God will help me to be a person of forgiveness and reconciliation in my relationships.

Ivon Valerie

Building Healthy Relationships

Building healthy relationships involves cultivating trust, honesty, and understanding in our connections. It requires effort and commitment, but the reward is a sense of love, support, and fulfillment.

Scripture References

Proverbs 3:5-6 - "Trust in the Lord with all your heart and lean not on your own understanding; in all your ways submit to him, and he will make your paths straight."

1 Corinthians 13:4-8 - "Love is patient, love is kind. It does not envy, it does not boast, it is not proud. It does not dishonor others, it is not self-seeking, it is not easily angered, it keeps no record of wrongs. Love does not delight in evil but rejoices with the truth. It always protects, always trusts, always hopes, always perseveres."

James 1:19 - "My dear brothers and sisters, take note of this: Everyone should be quick to listen, slow to speak and slow to become angry"

Inspirational/Motivational Quotes

"The greatest thing in family life is to take a hint when a hint is intended—and not to take a hint when a hint isn't intended." - Robert Frost

"The most important thing in communication is hearing what isn't said." - Peter Drucker

"The best index to a person's character is how he treats people who can't do him any good, and how he treats people who can't fight back." - Abigail Van Buren

Prayer

Dear Lord,
I come before you today, acknowledging the importance of healthy relationships. I ask for your guidance and wisdom in cultivating trust, honesty, and understanding in my connections with others. I know healthy relationships are built on mutual respect, open communication, and a willingness to work through challenges.

I ask your help in being patient, kind, and understanding with those around me. I will strive to listen actively and communicate effectively and make it a daily practice to be compassionate and empathetic toward others.

I trust in your provision and protection for my relationships, and I ask for your guidance in identifying the right people to have in my life and letting go of those who are not beneficial to me. I

trust in your faithfulness and goodness to bring the right people into my life and to surround me with positive influences.
Thank you in advance for your blessings in my relationships and the joy and fulfillment they bring to my life. Amen.

Declaration

I declare that I am committed to building healthy relationships in my life. I will actively cultivate trust, honesty, and understanding in my connections with others. I understand that healthy relationships are built on mutual respect, open communication, and a willingness to work through challenges.

I will make it a daily practice to be patient, kind, and understanding with those around me. I will listen actively and communicate effectively, striving to be compassionate and empathetic toward others. I know that these practices will help to build strong and lasting relationships.

I trust in the Lord's provision and protection for my relationships, and I ask for His guidance in identifying the right people to have in my life and letting go of those who are not beneficial to me. I believe that with God's help, I will be able to surround myself with positive influences and build relationships that bring joy and fulfillment to my life.

I thank God for his blessings in my relationships and for the joy and fulfillment they bring to my life. I will make it a daily practice to seek the Lord's guidance and wisdom in building healthy relationships, and I trust in his faithfulness and goodness to bring the right people into my life.

Prayer Lifestyle

Protection for Loved Ones

Protection for loved ones involves seeking the Lord's protection and provision for our family and friends. It involves trusting in God's faithfulness and love for our loved ones and asking for his protection in times of need.

Scripture References

Psalm 91:1-2 - "He who dwells in the secret place of the Most High shall abide under the shadow of the Almighty. I will say of the Lord, "He is my refuge and my fortress; My God, in Him I will trust.""

Isaiah 54:17 - "No weapon that is formed against you shall prosper, and every tongue that shall rise against you in judgment you shall condemn.""

Psalm 121:3-4 - "He will not let your foot slip— he who watches over you will not slumber; indeed, he who watches over Israel will neither slumber nor sleep."

Inspirational/Motivational Quotes

"The greatest good you can do for another is not just to share your riches, but to reveal to him his own." - Benjamin Disraeli

"Love is not something you go out and look for. Love finds you, and when it does, ready or not, it'll be the best thing to ever happen to you." - Unknown

"The greatest gift you can give someone is the gift of love and support." - Unknown

Prayer

Dear Lord,
I come before you today with a heart full of love and concern for my loved ones. I ask for your protection and provision so that your love and grace may surround them. I ask for your guidance and wisdom so they may make wise decisions and follow your will. I trust in your faithfulness and love for them, and I ask for your protection in times of need, whether physical, emotional, or spiritual. I thank you for the gift of love and support I can give them, and I ask for your guidance in showing them love and support in practical ways. Please help me be a source of encouragement and strength for them and always put their needs before mine. I pray for unity and peace within my family and for my loved ones to grow in their relationship with you. Amen.

Declaration

I come before you today, dear Lord, with a heart full of love and concern for my loved ones. I ask for your protection and provision for them, knowing that you are a faithful and loving God. I trust in your ability to protect and provide for them, especially in need. I ask for your guidance and wisdom in showing them love and support, and I thank you for the gift of love you have given me.

I commit myself to seek your protection and provision for my loved ones, and I trust in your faithfulness to meet their needs. I will make it a daily practice to pray for them and ask for your protection, knowing that you are always watching over them. I also commit to showing them love and support by being patient, kind, and understanding towards them. I ask for your guidance, knowing you are the source of all love.

I declare that my loved ones will be protected and provided for by you, dear Lord. They will experience your love and faithfulness in their lives, and your provision and protection will bless them. I trust in you to bring the right people into their lives and help them let go of those not beneficial to them. I ask for your blessings on my loved ones and thank you for the gift of family and friends. Amen.

Ivon Valerie

Prayer Lifestyle

Finances and Provision

Finances and provisions have a great influence over our lives. They are essential for us to be able to take care of ourselves, as well as those we love. To help readers gain more control over their finances, achieve financial independence and obtain greater stability in this area of life, this chapter offers prayers and affirmations to aid them on the path toward prosperity.

Financial Blessings

Financial blessings refer to God's provision and abundance in our financial lives. It includes financial stability, an increase in income, and overall financial well-being. Trusting in God's provision and believing in His promises for abundance can lead to a sense of peace and contentment in our financial lives.

Scripture References

Proverbs 3:9-10 - "Honor the Lord with your wealth, with the firstfruits of all your crops; then your barns will be filled to overflowing, and your vats will brim over with new wine."

Philippians 4:19 - "And my God will meet all your needs according to the riches of his glory in Christ Jesus."

Deuteronomy 28:8 - "The Lord will command the blessing on you in your barns and in all that you put your hand to. And he will bless you in the land that the Lord your God is giving you."

Inspirational/Motivational Quotes

"If you want to know your past, look into your present conditions. If you want to know your future, look into your present actions." - Unknown

"Money is a terrible master but an excellent servant." - P.T. Barnum

"Money is not the most important thing in the world. Love is. Fortunately, I love money." - Jackie Mason

Prayer

Dear Lord,
I come before you today, acknowledging the importance of financial stability in my life. I thank you for your provision and abundance in my past and ask for your continued blessings on my financial life. I ask for an increase in income, financial stability, and overall financial well-being. I trust in your promises of abundance and ask for your guidance in managing the resources you have given me.

I understand that money and material possessions should not be my ultimate goal but rather a tool to serve you and others. I will use it in a way that honors you and helps others. I will be a good steward of my resources and use them to glorify you and build your kingdom. I look forward to the future with confidence in your faithfulness, knowing that you will provide for all my needs according to your riches in glory in Christ Jesus. I trust your provision and abundance and will give you all the glory and praise. Amen.

Declaration

I declare that I trust God's provision and abundance in my financial life. I recognize that He is the source of all blessings and has promised to meet all my needs according to His riches in glory. I will have faith in His ability to provide for me and my family, and I will trust His faithfulness to bless me financially. I will make it my daily practice to seek the Lord's guidance and wisdom in managing the resources He has given me. I will be a wise steward of the resources God has provided and use them to further His kingdom.

I will also give thanks for the blessings He has provided in the past and look forward to the future with confidence in His faithfulness. I will remember that my trust in God's provision does not mean that I will not face challenges, but I will trust that He will use those challenges to teach me the valuable lessons I need to learn and to give me the strength and wisdom to overcome them.

I will also be a giver and will give back to the community and those in need, knowing that in doing so, I am sowing seeds that will reap a harvest of abundance. I will trust in the Lord's provision, and I will be grateful for the blessings that He has already given me and the blessings that are yet to come. Amen

Ivon Valerie

Abundance and Prosperity

Abundance and prosperity refer to having more than enough things we need and desire. It's about living a life of abundance, not scarcity, and trusting in God's provision for our needs. It's about having a mindset of abundance and not just focusing on lack and shortage.

Scripture References

Psalm 35:27 - "Let them shout for joy and be glad, who favor my righteous cause; And let them say continually, "The Lord be magnified, Who has pleasure in the prosperity of His servant.""

3 John 1:2 - "Beloved, I pray that you may prosper in all things and be in health, just as your soul prospers."

Deuteronomy 8:18 - "But remember the Lord your God, for it is he who gives you the ability to produce wealth, and so confirms his covenant, which he swore to your ancestors, as it is today."

Inspirational/Motivational Quotes

"The more you have, the more you are occupied. The less you have, the more free you are." - Mother Teresa

"The more you praise and celebrate your life, the more there is in life to celebrate." - Oprah Winfrey

"The greatest wealth is to live content with little." - Plato

Prayer

Dear Lord,
I come before you today with a grateful heart for your provision in my life. I thank you for the abundance you have already placed in my life, and I ask for your continued blessings of abundance and prosperity in every area of my life. I choose to release my old mindset of scarcity and lack and focus on abundance. I trust your provision and know you are always faithful to meet my needs.

I ask for your guidance and wisdom in managing the resources you have given me. I pray for discernment in making financial decisions and the wisdom to handle my finances in a way that brings glory to you. I pray for financial stability, an increase in income, and overall financial well-being. I know that you are the source of all blessings and that everything I have comes from you.

I also want to thank you for your provision in the past, and I look forward to the future with confidence in your faithfulness. I know you have a plan for my life, and I trust you. I know that you will continue to bless me, and I will be able to bless others. I pray for financial breakthroughs and opportunities that will allow me to be a blessing to others. Thank you, Lord, for your provision and abundance in my life. Amen.

Declaration

Today, I declare that I am grateful for the abundance God has bestowed upon me, and I trust that His blessings will continue to flow in my life. I will not be held back by the lies of scarcity and lack; instead, I will focus on the abundance available to me through God's provision. I will not be consumed by worries or fears about my finances but will trust the Lord's faithfulness. I will use the resources God has given me to bless others and to further His kingdom. I declare that I am living in prosperity and abundance, and I thank God for His provision in my life. I will make it my daily practice to seek God's guidance in managing my resources and to trust in His provision for my needs. I will focus on abundance, not scarcity, and share my blessings with others. I declare that I am blessed, highly favored by God, and will live in prosperity and abundance.

Debt Elimination

Debt elimination refers to paying off debts and becoming financially free. It requires a plan, discipline, and persistence, but with God's help, it is possible to eliminate debt and achieve financial freedom.

Scripture References

Proverbs 22:7 - "The rich rule over the poor, and the borrower is slave to the lender."

Romans 13:8 - "Let no debt remain outstanding, except the continuing debt to love one another, for whoever loves others has fulfilled the law."

1 Timothy 6:6-10 - "But godliness with contentment is great gain. For we brought nothing into the world, and we can take nothing out of it. But if we have food and clothing, we will be content with that. Those who want to get rich fall into temptation and a trap and into many foolish and harmful desires that plunge people into ruin and destruction. For the love of money is a root of all kinds of evil. Some people, eager for money, have wandered from the faith and pierced themselves with many griefs."

Inspirational/Motivational Quotes

"The greatest step towards a life of simplicity is to learn to let go." - Steve Maraboli

"The first step towards getting somewhere is to decide that you are not going to stay where you are." - Unknown

Prayer

Dear Lord,
I come before you today with a heavy heart, acknowledging that I have let my finances get out of control. I confess that I have been careless with the resources you entrusted me, and I ask your forgiveness. I know I cannot do this alone, and I humbly ask for your help eliminating my debt.

I ask for your wisdom and guidance as I work towards becoming financially free. This will not be easy, but I trust your provision and blessings. Please help me to have a clear understanding of my finances and give me the knowledge and skills I need to make wise financial decisions.

I ask for discipline and persistence as I work towards my goal. I know that sticking to a plan will be difficult, but I trust that with your help, I will be able to do it. Please help me to stay focused on my goal and not get discouraged when progress is slow.
I also ask for your protection from the temptations that lead to more debt. I know I am weak and will be faced with many temptations to spend money on things I don't need. I ask for

your strength to resist these temptations and to be content with what I have.

I trust your faithfulness to provide for my needs as I work towards debt elimination. I know you have a plan for my life and will not abandon me on this journey. I trust that you will provide for me, and I will give you all the glory as I become financially free. Amen.

Declaration

I declare that I am on a journey to debt elimination and financial freedom. I am taking responsibility for my finances and am confident that I will achieve my goal with God's guidance and provision. I trust in God's provision and blessings as I work towards becoming financially free. I know He has a plan for my life, and I trust that He will provide for me in all the ways I need. I will work hard and be diligent in my efforts, but I also know that God's hand will ultimately lead me to success.

I will exercise discipline and persistence in sticking to my plan. I understand that this journey will not be easy, and there will be times when I will be tempted to give up, but I will not let those moments discourage me. I will stay focused on my goal and remain determined to achieve debt elimination and financial freedom.

I will avoid temptations that lead to more debt. I know there will be temptations to spend money on things I don't need, but I will resist them. I will be content with what I have and make wise financial decisions that align with my goal.

Ivon Valerie

I trust God's faithfulness to provide for my needs as I work toward debt elimination. I know He is always with me and will not abandon me on this journey. I trust that He will provide for me in all the ways I need, and I will give Him all the glory as I achieve debt elimination and financial freedom. I declare this confidently and boldly, knowing that with God's help, I will succeed.

Job and Career Opportunities

Job and career opportunities refer to finding the right job or career path that aligns with one's skills, passions, and calling. It's about trusting in God's guidance and provision in finding the right job or career opportunity.

Scripture References

Proverbs 16:3 - "Commit to the Lord whatever you do, and he will establish your plans."

Isaiah 55:8-9 - "For my thoughts are not your thoughts, neither are your ways my ways," declares the Lord. "As the heavens are higher than the earth, so are my ways higher than your ways and my thoughts than your thoughts."

Colossians 3:23-24 - "Whatever you do, work at it with all your heart, as working for the Lord, not for human masters, since you know that you will receive an inheritance from the Lord as a reward. It is the Lord Christ you are serving."

Inspirational/Motivational Quotes

"The best way to predict your future is to create it." - Abraham Lincoln

"The only way to do great work is to love what you do." - Steve Jobs

"Your work is going to fill a large part of your life, and the only way to be truly satisfied is to do what you believe is great work. And the only way to do great work is to love what you do." - Steve Jobs

Prayer

Dear Lord,
I come before you with a heavy heart and a confused mind, asking for your guidance and provision in finding the right job or career opportunity. I know you have a plan for my life, and I trust you will lead me to the right path.

I ask for wisdom in making decisions as I search for the right job or career opportunity. I know many options and opportunities will come my way, but I pray that you let me discern which ones align with my skills, passions, and calling. I trust that you will guide me to make the right choices.

I also ask for your protection from opportunities not aligned with my skills, passions, and calling. I know these opportunities may seem tempting, but I pray you will give me the strength to resist them. I know you have a better plan for my life, and I want to align myself with that plan.

I trust in your faithfulness to guide me toward the right path. You will not abandon me on this journey and will always be with me, leading me to the right opportunities.

Thank you for the provision and blessings with the right job or career opportunity. I know that with the right job or career, I will be able to provide for myself and my loved ones and that I will be able to use my skills, passions, and calling to serve others. I trust that you will lead me to the right job or career opportunity to bring fulfillment, joy, and purpose to my life. Amen.

Declaration

I declare that I trust God's guidance and provision in finding the right job or career opportunity. I know He has a plan for my life, and I trust He will lead me to the right path. I will make decisions with wisdom and will seek His guidance every step of the way. I also declare that I will be protected from opportunities not aligned with my skills, passions, and calling. I declare that with the right job or career, I will use my God-given talents and abilities to serve others and positively impact the world. I also trust that the right job or career will bring provision and blessings to my life.

I understand that finding the right job or career is about earning a living, fulfilling my life purpose, and serving others. I will approach this journey with a servant's heart, knowing that whatever I do, I do it for the glory of God.

I also declare that I will have a positive attitude and a growth mindset toward this journey. I will not be discouraged by rejections or setbacks but see them as opportunities to learn and grow. I will remain patient and persistent, knowing God's perfect timing. I trust that with God's guidance and provision, I will find the right job or career opportunity to bring fulfillment, joy, and purpose to my life.

Increase in Income

An increase in income refers to having more money coming in, whether through a raise, a promotion, a new job, or a business venture. It's about trusting in God's provision and faithfulness in providing for our financial needs and believing that He can bring increase and abundance.

Scripture References

Malachi 3:10 - "Bring the whole tithe into the storehouse, that there may be food in my house. Test me in this," says the Lord Almighty, "and see if I will not throw open the floodgates of heaven and pour out so much blessing that there will not be room enough to store it."

2 Corinthians 9:8 - "And God is able to bless you abundantly, so that in all things at all times, having all that you need, you will abound in every good work."

Philippians 4:19 - "And my God will meet all your needs according to the riches of his glory in Christ Jesus."

Inspirational/Motivational Quotes

"The only limit to our realization of tomorrow will be our doubts of today." - Franklin D. Roosevelt

Ivon Valerie

"If you want to achieve something, you need to put in the work. And if you want to increase your income, you need to learn how to make more money." - Grant Cardone

"The more you make, the more you can give away, and the more good you can do in the world." - Mark Zuckerberg

Prayer

Dear Lord,
I come before you with an open heart and an open mind, asking for your provision and faithfulness in increasing my income. I trust in your promises of abundance, and I believe you can increase my finances. I know that you can do more than I can ask or imagine, and I ask for your provision in this area of my life.

I ask for your guidance and wisdom in making decisions leading to more money coming in. I know there are many ways to increase my income, but I pray that you will guide me to the right opportunities and decisions that will lead to financial growth. Please help me to have a clear understanding of my finances and give me the knowledge and skills I need to make wise financial decisions.

I also thank you for your provision in the past. I am grateful for the ways you have provided for me and my loved ones, and I know that your provision has been enough. I trust that your provision in the past guarantees your faithfulness in the future.

I look forward to the future with confidence in your faithfulness to provide for my needs. I know you are always with me and will not abandon me on this journey. I am confident I will give you all the glory as I experience financial growth.

I ask for your protection from temptations that lead to financial irresponsibility and the enemy's lies that try to convince me that you cannot or will not provide for me. I trust your goodness and faithfulness to guide me and help me grow in wisdom and abundance. Amen.

Declaration

I declare today that I trust God's provision and faithfulness in increasing my income. I believe in his promises of abundance, and I know He can do more than I can ask or imagine. I am open to the opportunities that He may bring to increase my finances, and I will make decisions with wisdom, knowing that He guides me toward the right path.

I declare that I am blessed and highly favored. I know God has a purpose for my life and plans to prosper and not harm me, giving me hope and a future. I am confident that as I align myself with His will, He will open the doors of blessings and abundance in my life.

I will work towards increasing my income by utilizing my skills and talents and by taking advantage of opportunities that come my way. I will be diligent in my efforts and approach this journey with a positive attitude and a growth mindset. I will not be discouraged by rejections or setbacks but see them as opportunities to learn and grow.

I also declare that I will be a faithful steward of the resources that God provides. I will use my finances to bless others and support His kingdom's work. I will not hoard or waste the resources He gives me but will use them in a way that honors Him.

I declare that I will experience an increase in my finances. I know that God's promises are true and that He is faithful to provide for my needs. I trust that as I align myself with His will, He will bless me with abundance, and I will experience a financial increase that will bring joy, fulfillment, and blessings to my life and the lives of others.

Prayer Lifestyle

Faith and Trust

Faith and trust are vital aspects of our relationship with the Almighty. Faith is believing in something unseen, while trust involves having confidence that those promises will be fulfilled. This chapter explores how essential faith and trust are to live a meaningful life filled with prayers and declarations. It helps readers grow their faith even more deeply in God's endless love and unfailing protection as they rely completely on Him.

Building Faith

Building faith refers to growing and strengthening one's belief in God and in His promises. It's about learning to trust God's word and plan for our lives.

Scripture References

Hebrews 11:1 - "Now faith is the substance of things hoped for, the evidence of things not seen."

2 Corinthians 5:7 - "For we walk by faith, not by sight."

Romans 10:17 - "So faith comes from hearing, and hearing through the word of Christ."

Inspirational/Motivational Quotes

"Faith is taking the first step even when you don't see the whole staircase." - Martin Luther King Jr.

"Faith is not the belief that God will do what you want. It is the belief that God will do what is right." - Max Lucado

"Faith is not something to grasp, it is a state to grow into." - Mahatma Gandhi

Ivon Valerie

Prayer

Dear Lord,

I come before you with a humble and open heart, asking for your help in building my faith. I know my faith is not where it should be, and I want to trust your word and plan for my life. I want to have a deeper understanding of your word and to be able to apply it to my life in a meaningful way.

I ask for your wisdom in understanding your word. I know that your word is alive and active, and I pray that you will open my eyes to the truth and revelation it contains. I also ask for your guidance in applying it to my life so that I can live in a way that is pleasing to you.

I pray for the strength to take the necessary steps to grow my faith. I know that growing in faith requires effort and sacrifice, and I pray that you will give me the strength to persevere in the face of difficulties. I pray that you will give me the courage to act on my faith, even when it is hard or uncomfortable.

I also ask for your protection from the temptations and distractions that can lead me away from you. I know that the enemy will try to hinder my growth in faith, and I pray that you will give me the strength to resist his lies and temptations.

Thank you for your faithfulness in leading me and guiding me throughout my life. I trust your goodness and love for me, and I know that you will never leave or forsake me. I trust you will help me grow my faith and trust in you more. Amen.

Declaration

I declare today that I am building my faith in the Lord. I know my faith is not where it should be, and I am determined to grow it. I will trust in His word and in His plan for my life. I will not let doubts and fears cloud my mind but will hold onto His promises and character.

I will seek wisdom in understanding His word and guidance in applying it to my life. I understand that God's word is a powerful tool to change my life. I will read, study, and meditate on His word daily and ask for His guidance to apply it to my life. I will take the necessary steps to grow my faith and trust in the Lord.

Growing in faith requires effort and sacrifice, and I am willing to work to grow my faith. I will intentionally develop a deeper relationship with God through prayer, worship, and fellowship with other believers. I also declare that I will be open to the guidance and leading of the Holy Spirit. I understand that the Holy Spirit is my helper and guide and will assist me in growing my faith. I will listen to His voice and follow His guidance.

I declare that I will not let my circumstances or the opinions of others dictate my faith. I will trust in the Lord and will not be swayed by the doubts and fears that may come my way. I know that with God's help, I will be able to build my faith and trust in Him more and more each day.

Ivon Valerie

Overcoming Fear and Doubt

Overcoming fear and doubt refers to facing and overcoming the feelings of fear and doubt that can hold us back from living the life God has planned for us. It's about trusting in God's promises and His ability to protect and guide us, even when we feel afraid or uncertain.

Scripture References

Isaiah 41:10 - "So do not fear, for I am with you; do not be dismayed, for I am your God. I will strengthen you and help you; I will uphold you with my righteous right hand."

2 Timothy 1:7 - "For God has not given us a spirit of fear, but of power and of love and of a sound mind."

Philippians 4:13 - "I can do all things through Christ who strengthens me."

Inspirational/Motivational Quotes

"Fear is just an illusion. It's the absence of faith." - Unknown

"You gain strength, courage and confidence by every experience in which you really stop to look fear in the face." - Eleanor Roosevelt

Prayer Lifestyle

"Faith is taking the first step, even when you can't see the whole staircase." - Martin Luther King Jr.

Prayer

Dear Lord,
I come before you with a heavy heart, asking for your help overcoming my fears and doubts. I know you are with me, and I trust you will strengthen and guide me in this journey. I ask for your wisdom in understanding that fear and doubt are illusions and do not come from you.

I ask for your help recognizing that fear and doubt are not from you but from the enemy, who wants to steal my peace, joy, and trust in you. I know that you have given me a spirit of power, love, and a sound mind, and I pray that you will help me to walk in that spirit and overcome my fears and doubts.

I pray for the strength to overcome my doubts and trust in you. I know that trusting in you requires effort and sacrifice, and I pray that you will give me the strength to persevere in the face of difficulties. I pray that you will give me the courage to act on my faith, even when it is hard or uncomfortable.

I also ask for your protection from the temptations and distractions that can lead me away from you. I know that the enemy will try to hinder my growth in faith, and I pray that you will give me the strength to resist his lies and temptations.

Thank you for your faithfulness in leading me and guiding me throughout my life. I trust your goodness and love for me, and I know that you will never leave or forsake me. I trust that you will help me overcome my fears and doubts and trust in me more each day. Amen.

Declaration

I declare today that I am overcoming my fears and doubts with the Lord's strength and guidance. I know that with God's help, I can face any challenges and overcome any obstacle that comes my way. I trust in His promises and ability to protect and guide me. I understand that fear and doubt are illusions and do not come from the Lord.

I declare that I will not allow fear and doubt to influence me. I will not let them control my thoughts, emotions, or actions. Instead, I will choose to trust in the Lord and in His promises. I will remind myself that He is always with me and will never leave or forsake me.

I also declare that I will be mindful of my thoughts and emotions and not entertain thoughts of fear and doubt when they arise. I will replace them with thoughts of truth and trust in the Lord. I will remind myself that I have been given a spirit of power, love, and a sound mind by the Lord, and I will walk in that spirit.

I further declare that I will be intentional in my spiritual growth and development. I will make an effort to read, study, and meditate on the word of God daily and to pray and communicate with the Lord regularly. I understand that by growing closer to Him, I will be able to overcome my fears and doubts with His strength and guidance.

Prayer Lifestyle

I declare that I will encourage others struggling with fear and doubt. I will share my own experiences and the lessons I have learned in overcoming them, and I will pray for and support those who are also on this journey. I trust in the Lord's ability to overcome any fear and doubt, and I will walk in faith and trust in Him.

Ivon Valerie

Trusting in Difficult Times

Trusting in difficult times means trusting God's plan and purpose, even when facing challenges and hardships. It's about having faith that God is in control and will work everything for our good.

Scripture References

Psalm 56:3 - "When I am afraid, I put my trust in you."

Isaiah 26:3 - "You will keep in perfect peace those whose minds are steadfast, because they trust in you."

Romans 8:28 - "And we know that in all things God works for the good of those who love him, who have been called according to his purpose."

Inspirational/Motivational Quotes

"Faith is not the belief that God will do what you want, it is the belief that God will do what is right." - Max Lucado

"In times of great stress or adversity, it's always best to keep busy, to plow your anger and your energy into something positive." - Lee Iacocca

Prayer Lifestyle

"The greatest test of faith is when you don't get what you want but still you are able to say Thank You Lord." - Unknown

Prayer

Dear Lord,

I come before you with a heavy heart, asking for your help in trusting you in difficult times. I know you are in control and will work everything for my good, but it can be hard to keep that perspective when I am going through tough times. I want your wisdom and guidance in understanding your plan and purpose for my life, especially in times of adversity.

I pray for the strength to maintain my trust in you, even in adversity. I know that trusting in you requires effort and sacrifice, and I pray that you will give me the strength to persevere in the face of difficulties. I pray that you will give me the courage to act on my faith, even when it is hard or uncomfortable.

I also ask for your protection from the temptations and distractions that can lead me away from you. I know the enemy will try to hinder my trust in you, and I pray that you will give me the strength to resist his lies and temptations.

Thank you for your faithfulness in leading me and guiding me throughout my life. I trust your goodness and love for me, and I know that you will never leave or forsake me. I trust that you will help me to maintain my trust in you, even in adversity, and to understand your plan and purpose for my life.

I also pray for the grace to see the bigger picture, to understand that this difficult moment is temporary, and that you have a greater purpose for me in this situation and will use it for my growth and your glory. I ask for your peace and comfort in being with me during this difficult time, to help me to trust in you, and to have faith that you are always with me, working everything for my good. Amen.

Declaration

I declare today that I trust the Lord even in difficult times. I understand that challenges and adversity are a part of life, but I trust the Lord's plan and purpose. I know He is in control and will work everything for my good. I will not let doubts and fears cloud my mind but will hold onto God's promises. I declare that I will maintain my trust in the Lord, even in the face of adversity. I understand that trusting in the Lord requires effort and sacrifice, and I am willing to work to trust in him. I will remind myself that He is always with me and will never leave or forsake me.

I will seek wisdom and guidance in understanding His plan and purpose for my life. I will pray for guidance and wisdom to understand the bigger picture, that this difficult moment is temporary, and that the Lord has a greater purpose for me. I will also seek guidance and wisdom to understand the lessons and growth that come with difficult times. I also declare that I will be mindful of my thoughts and emotions and not entertain thoughts of fear and doubt when they arise. I will replace them with thoughts of truth and trust in the Lord. I will remind myself that the Lord is in control and will work everything for my good.

Prayer Lifestyle

I declare that I will encourage others struggling with trust in the Lord during difficult times. I will share my experiences and the lessons I have learned in trusting the Lord during challenging times, and I will pray for and support those who are also on this journey. I trust in the Lord's ability to guide me and work everything for my good, and I will walk in faith and trust in Him even in difficult times.

Ivon Valerie

Building a Deeper Relationship With God

Building a deeper relationship with God means strengthening our connection through prayer, reading scripture, and worship and meditation. It's about developing a personal and intimate relationship with God.

Scripture References

James 4:8 - "Come near to God and he will come near to you." Matthew 6:6 - "But when you pray, go into your room, close the door and pray to your Father, who is unseen. Then your Father, who sees what is done in secret, will reward you."

Psalm 63:1 - "O God, you are my God; earnestly I seek you; my soul thirsts for you; my flesh faints for you, as in a dry and weary land where there is no water."

Colossians 3:16 - "Let the word of Christ dwell in you richly, teaching and admonishing one another in all wisdom, singing psalms and hymns and spiritual songs, with thankfulness in your hearts to God."

Inspirational/Motivational Quotes

"The more you seek God, the more you find of Him, and the more of Him you find, the more you love Him." - St. John of the Cross

"A deeper relationship with God is not just about knowing Him more, but about loving Him more." - Unknown

"Prayer is not asking. It is a longing of the soul. It is daily admission of one's weakness. It is better in prayer to have a heart without words than words without a heart." - Mahatma Gandhi

Prayer

Dear Lord, I come before you with an open and humble heart, asking for your help in building a deeper relationship with me. I know my relationship with you is not where it should be, and I want to strengthen my connection through prayer, reading scripture, and spending time in worship and meditation. I want to grow closer to you and understand you more.

I ask for your guidance in understanding your word. I know that your word is alive and active, and I pray that you will open my eyes to the truth and revelation it contains. I also ask for your wisdom in applying it to my life so that I can live in a way that is pleasing to you.

I pray for the strength to develop a personal and intimate relationship with you. I understand that developing a deep and meaningful relationship with you requires effort and sacrifice, and I am willing to work to grow closer to you. I will be intentional in my spiritual growth and development, and I will make an effort to read, study, and meditate on your word daily and to pray and communicate with you regularly. I also ask for your guidance in finding ways to worship and meditate on you. I know that there are many ways to do this, and I pray that you will show me the ways that will help me to connect with you more deeply.

Thank you for your faithfulness in leading me and guiding me throughout my life. I trust your goodness and love for me, and I know that you will never leave or forsake me. I trust you will help me build a deeper relationship with you and understand you more each day. Amen.

Declaration

I declare today that I am building a deeper relationship with God. I am committed to strengthening my connection with Him through prayer, reading scripture, worship, and meditation. Having a deeper relationship with God requires effort and sacrifice, and I am willing to work to grow closer to Him.

I also declare that I will be intentional in my spiritual growth and development. I will try to spend time in worship and meditation to connect with God more deeply. I will seek wisdom and guidance from God in understanding His word, and I will make an effort to read, study, and meditate on it daily so that it can become more alive in my life. I will seek to understand His will and ways and align my life with His purpose.

I also declare that I will be mindful of my thoughts and emotions and not entertain thoughts that may hinder my growth in my relationship with God. I will replace them with thoughts of truth and trust in Him, reminding myself that God is always with me and that He will never leave or forsake me.

I declare that I will encourage others struggling in their relationship with God. I will share my own experiences and the lessons I have learned in building a deeper relationship with God, and I will pray for and support those who are also on this journey. I trust in God's ability to guide me and help me to build a deeper relationship with Him, and I will walk in faith and trust in Him.

Ivon Valerie

Protection and Safety

Protection and guidance are key to our health, happiness, and prosperity. They offer us a sense of assurance and give us the confidence to conquer fear, uncertainty, or any other potential obstacle that may arise in life. This chapter emphasizes the significance of protection and guidance within our lives by offering prayers to protect ourselves from danger and seeking direction in wise decisions. With these empowering tools at your disposal, you can feel secure knowing nothing will stand between you and finding peace through faith.

Prayer Lifestyle

Protection From Harm and Danger

Protection from harm and danger refers to being safe from physical harm and dangerous situations. It's about trusting God's protection and guidance to protect us from harm.

Scripture References

Psalm 91:9-11 - "If you make the Most High your dwelling— even the Lord, who is my refuge— then no harm will befall you, no disaster will come near your tent. For he will command his angels concerning you to guard you in all your ways."

Isaiah 54:17 - "No weapon forged against you will prevail, and you will refute every tongue that accuses you. This is the heritage of the servants of the Lord, and this is their vindication from me," declares the Lord."

Proverbs 18:10 - "The name of the Lord is a strong tower; the righteous run to it and are safe."

Inspirational/Motivational Quotes

"The best defense is a good offense." - Unknown

"The man who can drive himself further once the effort gets painful is the man who will win." - Roger Bannister

"The only way to do great work is to love what you do." - Steve Jobs

Prayer

Dear Lord,
I come before you today with a heart full of gratitude and faith. I thank you for your constant presence in my life and the protection you have provided me with in the past. I ask that you continue to guide and protect me in all my ways.

I pray for your protection from harm and danger, both physically and spiritually. I trust in your faithfulness to keep me safe from any harm that may come my way. I ask for your wisdom and guidance in making decisions that will lead to safety and peace.
I pray for protection for my loved ones as well. I ask that you watch over them and keep them safe from harm or danger. I pray for your protection for my home, possessions, and all that is important to me.

I also ask for your protection from the unseen forces of evil. I pray for your protection from the enemy's attacks and for your guidance in standing firm in my faith. I am grateful for your loving protection and trust in your faithfulness. Please continue to watch over me and guide me in all my ways. Amen.

Declaration

I declare that I am protected by the Lord, the almighty and all-powerful God. I trust in His faithfulness and love for me, and I know He is always with me, watching over me and guiding me. I declare that I am protected from harm and danger, both physically and spiritually. I trust in the Lord's protection and guidance to keep me safe from any harm that may come my way. I declare that I will make wise decisions, knowing that the Lord is always with me and that He will guide me in the right direction.

I declare that I am protected in all circumstances, good or bad. I know the Lord is always with me and will never leave or forsake me. I trust in His protection and guidance and know He will always lead me to safety. I declare that the Lord also protects my loved ones. I trust that He will watch over them and keep them safe from harm and danger. I declare that the Lord protects my home and all that's important to me, and I trust in His protection for all I hold dear.

I declare that I will not be afraid, for the Lord is with me, and I trust His protection and guidance. I declare that I will walk in faith, knowing that the Lord is always with me, watching over me and guiding me.

Ivon Valerie

Protection From Negative Influences

Protection from negative influences refers to being safe from people, situations, or things that can lead to negative thoughts, behaviors, or actions. It's about trusting in God's protection and guidance to keep us from negative influences and help us surround ourselves with positive ones.

Scripture References

Romans 12:2 - "Do not conform to the pattern of this world, but be transformed by the renewing of your mind. Then you will be able to test and approve what God's will is—his good, pleasing and perfect will."

Proverbs 4:23 - "Above all else, guard your heart, for everything you do flows from it."

1 Corinthians 15:33 - "Do not be misled: "Bad company corrupts good character."

Inspirational/Motivational Quotes

"Surround yourself with people who make you better." - Unknown

"You are the average of the five people you spend the most time with." - Jim Rohn

"Hang out with people who are going to lift you higher." - Oprah Winfrey

Prayer

Dear Lord,
I come before you today with a humble heart and a deep desire for your protection. I ask for your guidance in recognizing and avoiding negative influences in my life. I am constantly surrounded by people, situations, and things that can lead to negative thoughts, behaviors, and actions. I want your wisdom on navigating these challenges.

I ask that you protect me from the influence of negative people, those who seek to bring me down or lead me astray. I ask that you give me the discernment to recognize when I am around negative people and situations and the courage to remove myself from those people and situations.

I pray for your protection from toxic environments or unhealthy relationships. I ask that you guide me in making wise decisions that will lead me away from these negative influences and towards positive, uplifting experiences.

I also ask for your protection from negative thoughts and behaviors. I know that my mind and heart can be a battlefield, and I ask that you help me to recognize negative thoughts and behaviors and to replace them with positive, uplifting ones. I pray that you will lead me to people, situations, and things that will lift me, help me grow, and bring me closer to you. I trust in your protection and guidance to protect me from negative influences and to guide me toward positive ones. I am grateful for your loving protection and trust in your faithfulness. Please continue to watch over me and guide me in all my ways. Amen.

Declaration

I declare that I am protected from negative influences by the Lord, the almighty and all-knowing God. I trust in His guidance and wisdom to recognize and avoid people, situations, or things that can lead to negative thoughts, behaviors, or actions. I know that with His help, I can choose my surroundings and the people with whom I interact.

I declare that I will surround myself with positive influences that will lift me, help me grow, and bring me closer to the Lord. I will seek out people who encourage and support me and avoid those who seek to bring me down. I declare that I will be protected from negative thoughts and behaviors. I will recognize when my mind and heart are being pulled toward negativity, and I will actively choose to replace those thoughts with positive, uplifting ones. I will consciously surround myself with positivity, from the media I consume to the music I listen to.

I also declare that God's wisdom will guide me in all my interactions. I will listen to the voice of the Lord and follow His guidance in all my decisions. I trust in His protection and guidance to shield me from negative influences and to guide me toward positive ones. I will listen to the voice of the Lord and follow His guidance in all my interactions.

Prayer Lifestyle

Safety in Travel

Safety in travel refers to being safe, whether for business or leisure. It's about trusting in God's protection and guidance to keep us safe on the road, in the air, or on the water.

Scripture References

Psalm 121:7-8 - "The Lord will keep you from all harm— he will watch over your life; the Lord will watch over your coming and going both now and forevermore."

Proverbs 3:23 - "Then you will go on your way in safety, and your foot will not stumble."

Psalm 91:11 - "For he will command his angels concerning you to guard you in all your ways."

Inspirational/Motivational Quotes

"Travel far, travel often. Life is not meant to be lived in one place." - Unknown

"The world is a book, and those who do not travel read only one page." - Saint Augustine

"Travel is the only thing you can buy that makes you richer." - Unknown

Ivon Valerie

Prayer

Dear Lord,
I come before you today with a heart full of gratitude and faith as I prepare to travel. I trust your faithfulness to keep me safe on the road, in the air, or on the water. I ask for your protection and guidance as I embark on this journey, and I pray that you will watch over me and keep me safe from harm and danger.

I ask for your wisdom in making decisions during my travels. I pray that you will guide me in choosing the right routes, the best accommodations, and the safest modes of transportation. I ask that you give me the discernment to recognize potential dangers and the courage to make wise decisions that will lead to safety.

I thank you for the opportunities to see new places and experience new things. I am grateful for the chance to expand my horizons and learn more about the world and its people. I pray that you will use my travels for your glory and that I will positively influence those I encounter on my journey.

I also ask for your protection for my loved ones while I am away. I pray you will watch over them and keep them safe from harm and danger. I pray for your protection of my home and possessions while I am away and that everything will be safe. I pray that you go before me, make every crooked path straight, subdue all evil under my feet, and open doors of divine opportunities so I can walk into them. I am grateful for your loving protection and trust in your faithfulness. Please continue to watch over me and guide me in all my ways as I travel. Amen.

Declaration

I declare that I am under the Lord's protection and guidance during my travels and that I trust His faithfulness to keep me safe on the road, in the air, or on the water. I will make wise decisions guided by the Lord's wisdom, and I will be protected from harm and danger. I trust the Lord to guide me through any challenges that may arise during my travels, and I will rely on His strength and guidance to overcome them.

I declare that my travels will bring opportunities to see new places and experience new things, and I will use them for the glory of God. I will be open to new experiences and perspectives and use the knowledge and understanding I gain to serve others and bring honor to the Lord. I declare I will be a light and an example of the Lord's love and grace to all I encounter during my travels.

I will also use my travel to grow closer to God by reflecting on His word, meditating on His promises, and praying for His guidance. I declare I will return home from my travels with a renewed sense of purpose, direction, and love for God. I am grateful for the Lord's protection and guidance during my travels, and I trust His faithfulness to keep me safe and guide me toward opportunities that will bring glory to His name.

Ivon Valerie

Safety in the Workplace

Safety in the workplace refers to being safe in the environment where one works, whether it is an office, a factory, or a construction site. It's about trusting in God's protection and guidance to keep us safe in our work and help us be productive.

Scripture References

Psalm 91:1-2 - "He who dwells in the secret place of the Most High shall abide under the shadow of the Almighty. I will say of the Lord, "He is my refuge and my fortress; My God, in Him I will trust.""

Proverbs 3:5-6 - "Trust in the Lord with all your heart and lean not on your own understanding; in all your ways submit to him, and he will make your paths straight."

Ephesians 6:10-18 - "Finally, be strong in the Lord and in his mighty power. Put on the full armor of God, so that you can take your stand against the devil's schemes. For our struggle is not against flesh and blood, but against the rulers, against the authorities, against the powers of this dark world and against the spiritual forces of evil in the heavenly realms. Therefore put on the full armor of God, so that when the day of evil comes, you may be able to stand your ground, and after you have done everything, to stand. Stand firm then, with the belt of truth buckled around your waist, with the breastplate of righteousness in place, and with your feet fitted with the readiness that comes from the gospel of peace. In addition to all this, take up the shield of faith, with which you can extinguish all the flaming arrows of the evil one. Take the helmet of salvation and the sword of the Spirit, which is the word of God."

Inspirational/Motivational Quotes

"The best way to predict your future is to create it." - Abraham Lincoln

"The only way to do great work is to love what you do." - Steve Jobs

"The future depends on what you do today." - Mahatma Gandhi

Prayer

Dear Lord,
I come before you with a humble heart, seeking your guidance and protection in my workplace. I trust your faithfulness to keep me safe and help me be productive. I ask for your wisdom in making decisions and discernment to know when to speak and remain silent. I ask for your protection from any harm or danger, both physical and emotional.

I pray for your strength and courage to face any challenges that may come my way and for the wisdom to know how to handle difficult situations with grace and integrity. I ask for your guidance in my interactions with colleagues and superiors to positively influence the workplace and exemplify your love and grace.

I thank you for the opportunity to use my skills and talents for your glory and for the provision of my needs. I pray that my work will bring you honor and be a blessing to those around me. I trust in you and know that you are always with me, guiding me every step of the way. I ask for your continued blessings and protection in my job and life. Amen.

Declaration

I declare that I am safe and productive in my work through the Lord's protection and guidance. I trust in His faithfulness to keep me safe and to help me be productive. I will make wise decisions and be protected from any harm or danger, both physical and emotional. I declare that my work is a way for me to use my skills and talents for the glory of God.

I declare that I will approach my work with a positive attitude and a servant's heart, always striving to do my best and positively influence those around me. I will be a model of integrity and honesty in the workplace and a source of encouragement and support to my colleagues and superiors.

I declare that I will stay focused on my goals and use my time and resources wisely, always striving to be efficient and productive. I will be a good steward of the opportunities and resources given to me, and I will use them to impact the world around me positively.

Prayer Lifestyle

I declare that I will trust in the Lord and know that He is always with me, guiding me every step of the way. I will have faith in His plan for my life and be open to His leadership and direction. I declare that I will be a light in the darkness, a beacon of hope, and a shining example of the love and grace of God in my workplace.

Protection for Loved Ones

Protection for loved ones refers to asking for God's protection for the people we care about, whether our family members, friends, or acquaintances. It's about trusting in God's protection and guidance to keep our loved ones safe and to help them grow and prosper.

Scripture References

Psalm 91:14-15 - ""Because he loves me," says the Lord, "I will rescue him; I will protect him, for he acknowledges my name. He will call on me, and I will answer him; I will be with him in trouble, I will deliver him and honor him. With long life I will satisfy him and show him my salvation."

Proverbs 11:21 - "Be sure of this: The wicked will not go unpunished, but those who are righteous will go free."

1 Peter 5:7 - "Cast all your anxiety on him because he cares for you."

Inspirational/Motivational Quotes

"The greatest gift you can give someone is your own personal development." - Jim Rohn

"I can't change the direction of the wind, but I can adjust my sails to always reach my destination." - Jimmy Dean

"You can't change the people around you, but you can change the people that you choose to be around." - Unknown

Prayer

Dear Lord,
I'm asking for your protection for my loved ones. I trust your faithfulness to keep them safe and help them grow and prosper. I ask for your wisdom in their decisions and protection from any harm or danger, both physical and emotional. I pray for their well-being, happiness, and provision of all their needs. I ask for your guidance in their lives so that they may follow your path and fulfill the purpose you have for them.

I pray for their relationships, that positive and supportive people may surround them, and that they may be a source of love and joy to those around them. Thank you for the loved ones you have placed in my life and the love and support they provide. I pray that you will use them for your glory and that their lives will be a testament to your love and grace.

I trust in you and know that you are always with them, guiding them every step of the way. I ask for your continued blessings and protection for my loved ones and our lives. Amen.

Declaration

I declare that the Lord protects my loved ones and that His love and grace surround them at all times. I trust in His faithfulness to keep them safe and to help them grow and prosper in every aspect of their lives. I declare that I will continuously pray for their wisdom, guidance, and protection from any harm or danger, both physical and emotional.

I declare that I will pray to them daily, asking for the Lord's blessings and guidance in their lives. I will pray for their health, relationships, work, and future. I will pray for their spiritual growth and ability to follow the path the Lord has laid for them.

I declare that I will be a source of love and support for my loved ones and be there for them in good times and in bad. I will be a listening ear, a shoulder on which they can cry, and a helping hand. I will encourage them in their dreams and support them in their goals. I declare that I will trust in the Lord's plan for their lives and that I will have faith that He is always with them, guiding them every step of the way.

Prayer Lifestyle

Ivon Valerie

Wisdom and Discernment

Navigating life's trials and tribulations relies heavily on both wisdom and discernment. Wisdom is the capacity to make sound judgments, while discernment involves recognizing good from bad. This chapter dives into how essential these two attributes are in our lives; it contains prayers and declarations that allow readers to intuitively craft wise decisions, comprehend their effects, and hone great judgment skills.

Prayer Lifestyle

Wisdom for Daily Living

Wisdom for daily living refers to applying God's wisdom in our everyday decisions and actions. It's about understanding God's will and way for our lives and making choices that align with God's will.

Scripture References

Proverbs 3:5-6 - "Trust in the Lord with all your heart and lean not on your own understanding; in all your ways submit to him, and he will make your paths straight."

James 1:5 - "If any of you lacks wisdom, you should ask God, who gives generously to all without finding fault, and it will be given to you."

Colossians 3:23-24 - "Whatever you do, work at it with all your heart, as working for the Lord, not for human masters, since you know that you will receive an inheritance from the Lord as a reward. It is the Lord Christ you are serving."

Inspirational/Motivational Quotes

"The only true wisdom is in knowing you know nothing." - Socrates

"The wisdom of the wise and the experience of the ages is preserved into perpetuity by a nation's proverbs, fables, folk sayings and quotations." - William Feather

"The greatest wisdom is in simplicity. Love, respect, tolerance, sharing, gratitude, forgiveness. It's not complex or elaborate. The real knowledge is free. It's encoded in your DNA." - Charles Eisenstein

Prayer

Dear Lord,
I come before you today with a humble heart, seeking your wisdom in my daily living. I desire to understand your will and way for my life and to make choices that align with that. I ask for your guidance in understanding your word and for your wisdom in applying it to my life. I pray for the strength to live a life that honors you.

I pray for the wisdom to make sound decisions and discernment to know when to speak and remain silent. I ask for your guidance in my relationships so I may positively influence and show love and kindness to those around me. I pray for your wisdom in my work, that I may use my skills and talents for your glory, and that I may be a good steward of the opportunities and resources you have given me.

I pray for your wisdom in my finances, that I may be a good steward of the resources you have given me, and that I may use them to further your kingdom. I ask for your wisdom in my health so I can care for my body and mind.

I pray for the courage and strength to walk in your ways and to stand firm in my faith, even in the face of opposition. I trust in you and know that you are always with me, guiding me every step of the way. I ask for your continued blessings and guidance in my life. Amen.

Declaration

I declare that I seek wisdom from the Lord for my daily living, and I will trust in His guidance in understanding His word and wisdom. I declare I will apply His word and wisdom in my life. I will make choices that align with His will and way for my life to honor Him in all I do.

I declare that I will consciously seek His guidance in every decision, whether big or small. I will ask for His guidance in my relationships, work, finances, and health. I will seek His wisdom in spending my time and using the resources He has given me.
I will strive to understand His word and apply it to my life. I will seek to live a life that is pleasing to Him and that brings Him glory. I will try to put His teachings into practice in my everyday life.

I declare that I will trust in the Lord's plan for my life and that I will have faith that He is always with me, guiding me every step of the way. I will seek His wisdom in the face of difficult situations and challenges, knowing He is always faithful and will never leave me.

Ivon Valerie

Wisdom for Decision Making

Wisdom for decision-making refers to seeking God's guidance and wisdom in making important life decisions. It's about seeking His will and understanding His plan for our lives before making any choices.

Scripture References

Proverbs 3:5-6 - "Trust in the Lord with all your heart and lean not on your own understanding; in all your ways submit to him, and he will make your paths straight."

Isaiah 30:21 - "Whether you turn to the right or to the left, your ears will hear a voice behind you, saying, "This is the way; walk in it."

James 1:5 - "If any of you lacks wisdom, you should ask God, who gives generously to all without finding fault, and it will be given to you."

Inspirational/Motivational Quotes

"Wise men speak because they have something to say; fools because they have to say something." - Plato

"The man who trusts men will make fewer mistakes than he who distrusts them." - Camillo di Cavour

Prayer Lifestyle

"The best way to predict the future is to create it." - Abraham Lincoln

Prayer

Dear Lord,
I come before you today with a humble heart, seeking your wisdom in making important decisions. I want to seek your guidance and understand your plan for my life before making any choices. Without your wisdom, I may make mistakes and stray from your path, so I ask for your wisdom and discernment in understanding your will for my life.

I pray for the strength to trust in your guidance, even when the path ahead may be uncertain or difficult. I ask for your guidance in understanding your word and for your wisdom in applying it to my life. I pray for the courage to follow your lead and to make choices that align with your will, even when it may be uncomfortable or inconvenient.

I pray for the wisdom to seek counsel from others who have a strong faith and understanding of your word and for the discernment to know whom to trust for guidance. I pray for the humility to admit I am wrong and seek forgiveness when necessary.

I pray for the strength to trust in your plan for my life, knowing that it is perfect and that you have my best interests at heart. I trust that you will guide me every step of the way and that your wisdom will lead me to the path of righteousness. Amen.

Declaration

I declare that I will actively seek wisdom from the Lord for decision-making. Before making any choices, I will trust in His guidance and understanding of His plan for my life. I will take the time to pray, meditate on His word, and seek His wisdom and discernment in understanding His will for my life.

I declare that I will be open to His guidance, even if it may not align with my desires or plans. I will believe that He has a greater plan for my life and that His wisdom will lead me to righteousness. I declare that I will trust in the Lord's guidance in making important decisions, whether it's regarding my relationships, my career, my finances, or any other aspect of my life. I will seek His wisdom in every decision, big or small, and trust in His guidance to lead me to the path He has ordained.

I declare that I will have the courage to follow His lead, even when it may be uncomfortable or inconvenient. I will trust that His guidance will lead me to where I am meant to be and that His wisdom will guide me to make the right choices. I will seek wisdom from the Lord in every decision and trust His guidance to lead me to righteousness.

Prayer Lifestyle

Discernment for Relationships

Discernment for relationships refers to recognizing and understanding a relationship's true nature and making wise decisions about our involvement. It's about understanding whom to trust and keep a distance from, and it's also about recognizing when a relationship is not healthy or when it's time to let it go.

Scripture References

Proverbs 14:7 - "Stay away from a foolish man, for you will not find knowledge on their lips."

1 Corinthians 15:33 - "Do not be misled: 'Bad company corrupts good character'."

Proverbs 13:20 - "Walk with the wise and become wise, for a companion of fools suffers harm."

Inspirational/Motivational Quotes

"Life is a series of natural and spontaneous changes. Don't resist them - that only creates sorrow. Let reality be reality. Let things flow naturally forward in whatever way they like." - Lao Tzu

"The most dangerous people in the world are those who have nothing to lose." - Jo Nesbo

"Discernment is the ability to see the truth in people, situations, and things." - Unknown

Prayer

Dear Lord,

I come before you today seeking your discernment in my relationships. I pray that you will help me to recognize and understand the true nature of the relationships in my life and to make wise decisions about my involvement in them. I know that not all relationships are healthy or beneficial for me, and I pray for the wisdom to know whom to trust and whom to keep a distance from.

I pray for the discernment to recognize when a relationship is not healthy or when it's time to let it go, even if it may be difficult or painful. I pray for the courage to make the necessary changes in my relationships to align them with your will for my life. I ask for the wisdom to build healthy relationships that honor you and bring glory to your name. For the discernment to recognize the red flags in relationships and to have the courage to address them.

I pray for the strength to set boundaries in my relationships and to be assertive when necessary. I pray for the ability to forgive and to extend grace to those who have hurt me, as you have forgiven and extended grace to me.

Prayer Lifestyle

I pray for the discernment to recognize and build healthy relationships and the wisdom and strength to let go of those not beneficial to me. I trust in your guidance and wisdom for my relationships. Amen.

Declaration

I declare that I will continually seek discernment from the Lord for my relationships. I trust in His guidance to recognize and understand the true nature of my relationships and make wise decisions about my involvement in them. I will take the time to pray, meditate on His word, and seek His wisdom to know whom to trust and keep a distance from.

I declare that I will have the strength to recognize when a relationship is unhealthy or when it's time to let it go, even if it may be difficult or painful. I will have the courage to make the necessary changes in my relationships to align them with the Lord's will for my life. I declare that I will build healthy relationships that honor the Lord and bring glory to His name.

I declare that I will be aware of the red flags in relationships and address them proactively. I will set boundaries in my relationships and be assertive when necessary. I will extend forgiveness and grace to those who have hurt me, as the Lord has forgiven and extended grace to me.

My relationships will express my love and devotion to the Lord. I will seek discernment and wisdom in my relationships and trust the Lord's guidance to lead me to righteousness.

Ivon Valerie

Discernment for Opportunities

Discernment for opportunities refers to recognizing and understanding a particular opportunity's potential and making wise decisions about pursuing it. It's about distinguishing between good and bad opportunities and trusting God's guidance when making choices.

Scripture References

Proverbs 22:3 - "The prudent see danger and take refuge, but the simple keep going and pay the penalty."

Psalms 25:12 - "Who, then, is the man that fears the Lord? He will instruct him in the way chosen for him."

James 1:5 - "If any of you lacks wisdom, you should ask God, who gives generously to all without finding fault, and it will be given to you."

Inspirational/Motivational Quotes

"Opportunities are usually disguised as hard work, so most people don't recognize them." - Ann Landers

"The more you are grateful for what you have, the more you will have to be grateful for." - Zig Ziglar

Prayer Lifestyle

"The greatest opportunity for improvement is at the margin." - John C. Bogle

Prayer

Dear Lord,

I come before you today, asking for your discernment in the opportunities that come my way. I pray you will help me recognize and understand these opportunities' potential and make wise decisions about pursuing them. I know that not all opportunities are good or aligned with your will for my life, and I pray for the wisdom to distinguish between good and bad opportunities.

I pray for the discernment to recognize when an opportunity is not in line with your plan for my life, even if it may be tempting or seems like a great opportunity. I pray for the courage to say no to opportunities that do not align with your will for my life.

I pray for the wisdom to discern the opportunities that align with your will for my life and to have the courage to pursue them, even if they may be difficult or uncertain. I pray for the discernment to recognize the opportunities that align with your will for my life and to have the wisdom to know when to act and when to wait.

I pray for the strength to trust in your guidance when making choices and the courage to follow through with the opportunities that align with your will for my life. I trust in your guidance and wisdom for the opportunities that come my way. Amen.

Declaration

I declare that I seek discernment from the Lord for the opportunities that come my way. I trust in His guidance to recognize and understand the potential of these opportunities and make wise decisions about pursuing them. I will use the wisdom that the Lord provides to distinguish between good and bad opportunities, recognizing that not all opportunities align with His will for my life.

I declare that I will have the courage to say no to opportunities that do not align with His will for my life, even if they may be tempting or seem like a great opportunity. I will trust in His guidance and wisdom to discern the opportunities that align with His will for my life and dare to pursue them, even if they may be difficult or uncertain.

I declare that I will trust in His guidance and wisdom to know when to act and wait for opportunities that align with His will for my life. I trust in His guidance to make choices that align with His will for my life and have the strength to follow through with the opportunities that align with His will.

I declare that I will trust in the Lord's guidance and wisdom for the opportunities that come my way and make choices that align with His will for my life.

Prayer Lifestyle

Ivon Valerie

Government and Authority

Government and authority have a monumental impact on our lives. They are responsible for orderliness, securing the public's welfare, and guaranteeing justice for all. This chapter offers prayers and declarations to help readers appreciate and pray for those in esteemed positions of power while challenging. It also provides declarations that will cause us to do more for our leaders to help them in the struggle toward achieving peace worldwide.

Leaders and Government Officials

Praying for leaders and government officials means asking God to guide and protect them and give them wisdom in making decisions that affect the lives of the citizens. It's about asking for God's blessings and protection for those in positions of authority.

Scripture References

1 Timothy 2:1-2 - "First of all, then, I urge that supplications, prayers, intercessions, and thanksgivings be made for all people, for kings and all who are in high positions, that we may lead a peaceful and quiet life, godly and dignified in every way."

Proverbs 21:1 - "The king's heart is a stream of water in the hand of the Lord; he turns it wherever he will."

Romans 13:1 - "Let every person be subject to the governing authorities. For there is no authority except from God, and those that exist have been instituted by God."

Inspirational/Motivational Quotes

"The best leaders... almost without exception and at every level, are master users of stories and symbols." - Warren Bennis

"A good leader takes a little more than his share of the blame, a little less than his share of the credit." - Arnold H. Glasow

"A true leader has the confidence to stand alone, the courage to make tough decisions, and the compassion to listen to the needs of others." - Douglas MacArthur

Prayer

Dear Lord,
I come before you today to lift our leaders and government officials in prayer. I ask that you would guide them and give them the wisdom and discernment they need to lead our nation with integrity, compassion, and fairness.

I pray they will use their power and influence to bring peace and justice to our land and to all those under their leadership. I ask that they be vigilant in protecting the rights and freedoms of all citizens, regardless of their background or beliefs. I pray that their hearts will be aligned with your heart and that they will seek to serve your will in all that they do. I ask that you give them the courage to stand up for what is right, even in the face of opposition, and that they always put the people's needs first.

I pray that your love and grace will guide them and that they will always seek to do your will. I ask that wise counsel surround them and that your spirit guide their decision-making. I pray that they will be shining examples of servant leadership and that they will be a reflection of your light to all those around them. Amen.

Declaration

I declare that I will consistently lift our leaders and government officials in prayer, asking for God's guidance and protection over them and their loved ones. I declare that they seek God's wisdom and discernment as they make decisions that affect the lives of the citizens they serve. I declare blessings and protection for those in positions of authority and that they will be guided by God's hand in all they do.

I declare that they lead with integrity, compassion, fairness, peace, justice, and the protection of rights and freedom for all citizens. I declare that our leaders be guided by God's love and grace in their leadership and that they will be shining examples of servant leadership to those around them.

I declare unity and cooperation among our leaders, and they will work together to improve our nation and its people. I also declare an end to corruption and greed in government and that the highest moral standards will guide our leaders.

I declare God's protection over our nation and its people and for His hand to be evident in the decisions made by our leaders. I declare a spirit of humility and willingness to listen to the voices of the people among those in positions of authority. I trust in the power of God to bring about positive change in our leaders and government.

National and International Issues

Praying for national and international issues means asking God to intervene and bring healing and resolution to the problems that affect our nation and the world. It's about asking for God's guidance and protection in the face of political, economic, and social issues, natural disasters, and other crises.

Scripture References

Isaiah 62:6-7 - "On your walls, O Jerusalem, I have appointed watchmen; all day and all night they will never keep silent. You who remind the Lord, take no rest for yourselves; and give Him no rest until He establishes and makes Jerusalem a praise in the earth."

1 Timothy 2:1-2 - "First of all, then, I urge that supplications, prayers, intercessions, and thanksgivings be made for all people, for kings and all who are in high positions, that we may lead a peaceful and quiet life, godly and dignified in every way."

James 5:16 - "Therefore confess your sins to each other and pray for each other so that you may be healed. The prayer of a righteous person is powerful and effective."

Inspirational/Motivational Quotes

"Prayer is not asking. It is a longing of the soul. It is daily admission of one's weakness. It is better in prayer to have a heart without words than words without a heart." - Mahatma Gandhi

"Prayer is not a 'spare wheel' that you pull out when in trouble, but it is a 'steering wheel' that directs the right path throughout." - Unknown

Prayer

Dear Lord,
I come before you today with heavy hearts, lifting our nation and the world in prayer. I ask that you intervene and bring about healing and resolution to the problems that affect us. I pray for the end of conflicts, the healing of illnesses and diseases, and providing for those struggling.

I ask for your guidance and protection in the face of political, economic, and social issues, natural disasters, and other crises. I pray for leaders and government officials to have wisdom and guidance in making decisions that affect the lives of the citizens. I pray they will lead with integrity, compassion, and fairness and use their power and influence to bring peace and justice.

I pray for the protection of rights and freedom for all, especially those marginalized and oppressed. I pray for an end to discrimination and inequality and justice for those who have been wronged.

I ask for your mercy and grace to be poured out on our world and for your love to be evident in our suffering. I pray for your presence to be felt in the hearts of all people and for your kingdom to come on earth as it is in heaven. I trust in your power and sovereignty. Amen.

Declaration

I declare that God's intervention brings about healing and resolution to the problems that affect our nation and the world. I declare God's guidance and protection in the face of political, economic, and social issues, natural disasters, and other crises. I declare that our leaders and government officials will have wisdom and guidance in making decisions that affect the lives of the citizens and that they will lead with integrity, compassion, and fairness.

I declare peace, justice, and the protection of rights and freedom for all, especially those marginalized and oppressed. I declare an end to discrimination, inequality, and justice for those who have been wronged. Let there be an immediate end to conflicts. I declare the healing of illnesses and diseases and provision for those struggling in our nation and the world. I declare the protection of our environment and sustainable solutions for the issues we face.

I declare God's mercy and grace to be poured out on our world. Let His presence be felt in the hearts of all people, and His kingdom come on earth as it is in heaven. I declare unity and love among all the world's people. I declare that we will bring about positive change in our nation and the world through prayer.

Peace and Justice

Praying for peace and justice means asking God to end conflict and establish a fair society. It's about asking for God's guidance and intervention in the face of war, terrorism, and social injustice.

Scripture References

Psalm 72:3 - "Let the mountains bring peace to the people, and the hills, justice."

Isaiah 9:6-7 - "For to us a child is born, to us a son is given, and the government will be on his shoulders. And he will be called Wonderful Counselor, Mighty God, Everlasting Father, Prince of Peace. Of the increase of his government and peace there will be no end."

Isaiah 42:1-4 - "Here is my servant, whom I uphold, my chosen one in whom I delight; I will put my Spirit on him, and he will bring justice to the nations. He will not shout or cry out, or raise his voice in the streets. A bruised reed he will not break, and a smoldering wick he will not snuff out. In faithfulness he will bring forth justice; he will not falter or be discouraged till he establishes justice on earth. In his teaching the islands will put their hope."

Inspirational/Motivational Quotes

"If you want to make peace with your enemy, you have to work with your enemy. Then he becomes your partner." - Nelson Mandela

"Peace is not the absence of conflict but the ability to cope with it." - Unknown

"Justice will not be served until those who are unaffected are as outraged as those who are." - Benjamin Franklin

Prayer

Dear Lord,
I come before you today with a heavy heart as I lift our world in prayer for peace and justice. I ask that you bring about an end to all big and small conflicts and establish a fair society. I pray for your guidance and intervention in the face of war, terrorism, and social injustice. I beg for your wisdom for leaders and government officials so that they may make decisions that bring peace and justice to all.

I pray for the families affected by war and terrorism that they may find comfort and healing. I pray for the victims of social injustice that they may see justice served and their voices heard. I pray that those in power positions may use their power for good and not for personal gain.

I also ask for the strength and courage of each of us to do our part in creating a more peaceful and just world. Whether it's standing up against injustice, volunteering in our communities, or simply spreading love and kindness, I pray that we may all play a role in bringing about the peace and justice that our world so desperately needs.

I pray for a world where everyone has enough, with no more hunger, poverty, and homelessness. A world where everyone has the right to education, health care, and a safe place to live. I pray for a world where everyone has the right to express themselves freely and is treated with respect and dignity. I pray for a world where love, kindness, and compassion reign. Where people put the needs of others before their own. I pray for a world that reflects your love, mercy, and grace. I pray for a world that reflects your kingdom here on earth. Amen.

Declaration

I declare peace and justice are rising in the world. God's guidance and intervention end conflict and establish a fair society. Let there be wisdom for leaders and government officials so that they may make decisions that prioritize peace and justice for all.

I recognize the devastating impact of war, terrorism, and social injustice on individuals and communities. So I declare that I am committed to doing my part to bring change and stand up against these injustices. Let courage and strength manifest through volunteering, supporting organizations, and even speaking out against injustice.

Ivon Valerie

I also declare my belief in the power of love, kindness, and compassion to bring about change. I declare that God's love will facilitate a world where people put the needs of others before their own and where we learn to respect and appreciate the diversity of our fellow human beings.

I declare we will experience a world where everyone has enough, with no more hunger, poverty, and homelessness. A world where everyone has the right to education, health care, and a safe place to live. A world where everyone has the right to express themselves and treat everyone with respect and dignity freely. Let our world be one where love, kindness, and compassion reign. Where people put the needs of others before their own. Where we learn to respect and appreciate the diversity of our fellow human beings.

I declare that I will not give up on this mission and will keep lifting this world in prayer for peace and justice. I trust that we can bring about a world that reflects His love, mercy, and grace with God's guidance and our collective efforts. A world that is a reflection of His kingdom here on earth.

Prayer Lifestyle

Protection of Religious Freedom

Praying for the protection of religious freedom means asking God to ensure that individuals have the right to practice their faith without fear of persecution or discrimination. It's about asking for God's protection and guidance for those facing religious oppression and for the freedom of all to worship as they choose.

Scripture References

Romans 12:14 - "Bless those who persecute you; bless and do not curse."

2 Corinthians 3:17 - "Now the Lord is the Spirit, and where the Spirit of the Lord is, there is freedom."

Hebrews 13:6 - "So we say with confidence, 'The Lord is my helper; I will not be afraid. What can mere mortals do to me?'"

Inspirational/Motivational Quotes

"Freedom of religion is a principle that is central to our Nation's Declaration of Independence." - George W. Bush

"Religious liberty is the first freedom in our Constitution. And whether the cause is justice for the persecuted, compassion for the needy and the sick, or mercy for the unborn, there is no greater force for good in the nation than Christian conscience in action." - Mitt Romney

"Religious freedom is the first freedom. It is a natural right that is shared by all human beings and it is the foundation of all other rights." - Mike Pence

Prayer

Dear Lord,
I come before you today with a heavy heart as I lift those facing religious oppression in prayer. I ask for your protection and guidance for those who cannot practice their faith freely without fear of persecution or discrimination. I pray for your protection for those facing religious oppression, their families safety, and their communities' protection.

I pray for wisdom for leaders and government officials so they may make decisions that safeguard religious freedom for all. I pray for the courage of those who speak against religious oppression and for the safety of those who provide aid and support to those affected.

I also pray for the hearts of those who persecute and discriminate against others because of their religion. I pray that they may see the error of their ways and understand the importance of religious freedom for all.
I declare that I will do my part in fostering a society where religious freedom is protected and respected. Whether it's through volunteering, supporting organizations, or speaking out

against oppression, I pray for the strength and courage to take action.

I pray for a world where love, kindness, and compassion reign. Where people put the needs of others before their own. Where we learn to respect and appreciate the diversity of our fellow human beings, including their religious beliefs.

I pray for a world where individuals can practice their faith without fear of persecution or discrimination and where religious freedom is protected and respected. A world that reflects your love, mercy, and grace. I pray for a world that reflects your kingdom here on earth. Amen.

Declaration

I declare that those facing religious oppression will be protected, and there will be an immediate stop to religious oppression and discrimination. I declare religious freedom for all and will not rest until this is a reality. I understand the devastating impact of religious oppression on individuals, families, and communities, and I declare that I will do everything possible to bring about change. I will speak out against oppression, support organizations that aid those affected, and use my influence to push for policy changes that safeguard religious freedom.

I declare God's protection and guidance for those facing religious oppression, for their safety and the safety of their families and communities. I declare strength and courage for those who work to bring about change and for the wisdom of leaders and government officials to make decisions that protect religious freedom for all. I envision a world where love, kindness, and compassion reign. Where people put the needs of others before their own. Where we learn to respect and appreciate the diversity of our fellow human beings, including their religious beliefs.

I declare a world where everyone is free to worship as they choose and has the right to express themselves freely. I declare that I will not give up on this mission and will keep fighting for religious freedom. I declare that together we will end religious oppression and discrimination and create a just and fair society where all individuals can practice their religion peacefully. I trust in the power of prayer and in the power of our collective efforts to bring about this change. Amen.

Protection of Human Rights

Praying for the protection of human rights means asking God to ensure that all individuals have the right to live in safety and dignity, free from oppression, discrimination, and violence. It's asking for God's guidance and intervention in the face of human rights abuses and for the freedom and equality of all people.

Scripture References

Isaiah 1:17 - "Learn to do right; seek justice. Defend the oppressed. Take up the cause of the fatherless; plead the case of the widow."

James 2:12 - "Speak and act as those who are going to be judged by the law that gives freedom."

Micah 6:8 - "He has shown you, O mortal, what is good. And what does the Lord require of you? To act justly and to love mercy and to walk humbly with your God."

Inspirational/Motivational Quotes

"Human rights are not only violated by terrorism, repression or assassination, but also by unfair economic structures that create huge inequalities." - Nelson Mandela

"Human rights are not a privilege granted by government. They are every human being's entitlement by virtue of his humanity." - Steve Biko

"Human rights is the soul of our foreign policy, because human rights is the very soul of our sense of nationhood." - Jimmy Carter

Prayer

Dear Lord,
I come before you today with a heavy heart as I pray for those facing human rights abuses. I ask for your guidance and intervention in the face of oppression, discrimination, and violence. I pray for your protection for those who are suffering, for the safety of their families, and for the protection of their communities.

I pray for wisdom for leaders and government officials so they may make decisions that safeguard human rights for all. I pray for the courage of those who speak out against human rights abuses and for the safety of those who provide aid and support to those affected. I also pray for the hearts of those who perpetrate human rights abuses. I pray that they may see the error of their ways and understand the importance of human rights for all people.

All individuals have the right to live safely and with dignity, free from oppression, discrimination, and violence. I pray I will do my part in fostering a society where human rights are protected and respected. Whether it's through volunteering, supporting organizations, or speaking out against abuses, I pray for the strength and courage to take action.

I pray for a world where love, kindness, and compassion reign. Where people put the needs of others before their own. Where we learn to respect and appreciate the diversity of our fellow human beings, including their human rights.

Lord, I pray for a world where individuals have the right to live safely and with dignity, free from oppression, discrimination, and violence. A world that reflects your love, mercy, and grace. I pray for a world that reflects your kingdom here on earth. Amen.

Declaration

I declare that those facing human rights abuses will be protected and that there will be an immediate stop to all forms of oppression, discrimination, and violence. I believe that all individuals have the right to live safely and with dignity, free from abuse, so I declare that human rights should be respected and protected for all people.

I declare that the devastating impact of human rights abuses on individuals, families, and communities will not be experienced by those around me because I will do everything I can to bring about change. I will speak out against human rights abuses, support organizations that aid those affected, and use my influence to push for policy changes that safeguard human rights for all.

Ivon Valerie

I call upon God's guidance and intervention in the face of human rights abuses, for the safety and protection of those suffering and for the safety of their families and communities. I declare God's strength and courage for those who work to bring about change and for the wisdom of leaders and government officials to make decisions that protect human rights for all.

I declare that I will not give up on this mission and will keep fighting for human rights for all. We can bring about a world that reflects His love, mercy, and grace with God's guidance and our collective efforts. A world that is a reflection of His kingdom here on earth. Amen.

Prayer Lifestyle

Ivon Valerie

Community and Outreach

Community and outreach are of tremendous importance in our lives as they grant us a sense of connection, assistance, and friendship. This chapter will emphasize the significance of community and outreach by presenting prayers intended to fortify existing bonds, create new connections, and help those who require it most. It further features supplications for cultivating community spirit, sympathy, and service to others.

Local Communities

Praying for local communities means asking God to bring about positive change and bless the people in your area. It's about asking for God's guidance and intervention in the face of local issues and for the community's well-being.

Scripture References

Isaiah 58:12 - "Your people will rebuild the ancient ruins and will raise up the age-old foundations; you will be called Repairer of Broken Walls, Restorer of Streets with Dwellings."

Matthew 25:35-40 - "For I was hungry and you gave me something to eat, I was thirsty and you gave me something to drink, I was a stranger and you invited me in, I needed clothes and you clothed me, I was sick and you looked after me, I was in prison and you came to visit me...whatever you did for one of the least of these brothers and sisters of mine, you did for me."

James 2:14-17 - "What good is it, my brothers and sisters, if someone claims to have faith but has no deeds? Can such faith save them? Suppose a brother or a sister is without clothes and daily food. If one of you says to them, "Go in peace; keep warm and well fed," but does nothing about their physical needs, what good is it? In the same way, faith by itself, if it is not accompanied by action, is dead."

Inspirational/Motivational Quotes

"The community which has neither poverty nor riches will always have the noblest principles." - Plato

"Community is not just about being geographically close to someone or part of the same social web network. It's about feeling connected and responsible for what happens." - Margaret J. Wheatley

"The best way to not feel hopeless is to get up and do something. Don't wait for good things to happen to you. If you go out and make some good things happen, you will fill the world with hope, you will fill yourself with hope." - Barack Obama

Prayer

Dear Lord,
I come before you today to lift my local community in prayer. I ask for your guidance and intervention as we work towards positive change in our area. I pray for your blessings upon the people in my community and their well-being.

I recognize the importance of community and its impact on the individuals there. My local community reflects your kingdom, and I want to make it a better place for all. I pray for wisdom for local leaders and government officials so that they may make decisions that benefit the community and its residents. I pray for the safety and well-being of our community's most vulnerable members, including the poor and marginalized. I pray for the strength and courage of those who work to bring about positive change in our community and for the support of those who share in this mission.

I also pray for the ability to reach out and show love and compassion to all those in need within my community, regardless of their background or circumstances. I pray I can positively influence my community by volunteering, supporting local organizations, and being a good neighbor, friend, and citizen.

I pray for a community where love, kindness, and compassion reign. Where people put the needs of others before their own. Where we learn to respect and appreciate the diversity of our fellow residents, including their cultural backgrounds and circumstances.

I declare that I will do my part in fostering a community that reflects your love, mercy, and grace. I trust that with your guidance and our collective efforts, we can bring about positive change in our local communities and make it a reflection of your kingdom here on earth. Amen.

Declaration

I declare that I will actively work towards bringing positive change to my local community through prayer and actions. I will strive to be an instrument of God's love and compassion, reaching out to those in need and working towards a better future for all. I commit to positively influencing my community and being a voice for marginalized and overlooked people.

Ivon Valerie

I declare God's guidance and wisdom in all my actions and that I will reflect his love and grace in the world. I declare that through my actions, my community will be blessed and prosper and that the love and light of God will shine through every aspect of our lives.

Prayer Lifestyle

Poor and Marginalized

Praying for the poor and marginalized means asking God to provide for the needs of those struggling economically, socially, or politically. It's about asking for God's compassion and provision for those most vulnerable and for justice to be served on their behalf.

Scripture References

Proverbs 14:31 - "He who oppresses the poor shows contempt for their Maker, but whoever is kind to the needy honors God."

Isaiah 58:6-7 - "Is not this the kind of fasting I have chosen: to loose the chains of injustice and untie the cords of the yoke, to set the oppressed free and break every yoke? Is it not to share your food with the hungry and to provide the poor wanderer with shelter—when you see the naked, to clothe them, and not to turn away from your own flesh and blood?"

Luke 14:13 - "But when you give a banquet, invite the poor, the crippled, the lame, the blind, and you will be blessed."

Inspirational/Motivational Quotes

"The poor need us badly — the rich do not. We must help the poor, therefore, if we want to be happy." - Mother Teresa

"The measure of a country's greatness is its ability to retain compassion in time of crisis." - Thurgood Marshall

"The greatest wealth is to live content with little." - Plato

Prayer

Dear Lord,
I come before you today with a heavy heart for the poor and marginalized in our society. I lift them in prayer, asking for your divine provision and for them to feel your compassion and love. I pray for your justice to be served on their behalf, for them to be treated with dignity and respect, and for their basic needs to be met.

I ask for your guidance and wisdom as I strive to be a voice for the poor and marginalized, to take action on their behalf, and to be a beacon of hope in their lives. I pray for the courage and strength to speak out against injustice and to actively work toward a society where everyone has an equal opportunity to thrive. I ask for your protection and provision for homeless people, those struggling to make ends meet, and those facing discrimination and oppression.

I pray for your healing for those who have been hurt and for your peace for those in turmoil. I pray for your guidance for leaders and government officials to make decisions that prioritize the well-being of the poor and marginalized and for them to have the courage to enact policies that lift people out of poverty and promote equality. Through your grace and love, the poor and marginalized may be lifted, and their cries for justice be heard. Amen.

Declaration

I declare that I will actively advocate for the rights and well-being of the poor and marginalized. I understand that these communities' issues are complex and multifaceted, and I pledge to educate myself on these issues to make informed decisions and take effective action.

I recognize that the poor and marginalized are often invisible and neglected, and I pledge to raise awareness and bring attention to their plight. I will use my voice and platform to speak out against injustice and to call for positive change.

I commit to being a force for good in my community, reaching out to those in need and working to improve their lives through direct action and service. I will not be content with simply offering words of encouragement or sympathy but will take tangible steps to make a real difference in the lives of the poor and marginalized.

I understand that achieving true justice and equality for all is a long-term and ongoing process, and I am prepared to commit to this cause. I trust in God's wisdom and guidance and believe that with His help, we all can positively impact the world.

Ivon Valerie

Sick and Suffering

Praying for the sick and suffering means asking God to provide healing and comfort to those who are going through physical or emotional pain. It's about asking for God's grace and mercy for those struggling and for them to be surrounded by love and support.

Scripture References

Psalm 41:3 - "The Lord sustains them on their sickbed and restores them from their bed of illness."

James 5:14-15 - "Is anyone among you sick? Let them call the elders of the church to pray over them and anoint them with oil in the name of the Lord. And the prayer offered in faith will make the sick person well; the Lord will raise them up. If they have sinned, they will be forgiven."

Isaiah 53:4-5 - "Surely he took up our pain and bore our suffering, yet we considered him punished by God, stricken by him, and afflicted. But he was pierced for our transgressions, he was crushed for our iniquities; the punishment that brought us peace was on him, and by his wounds we are healed."

Inspirational/Motivational Quotes

"The greatest gift of healing is the ability to heal others." - Dr. Robin L. Smith

"Healing may not be so much about getting better, as about letting go of everything that isn't you - all of the expectations, all of the beliefs - and becoming who you are." - Rachel Naomi Remen

"A flower does not think of competing with the flower next to it. It just blooms." - Zen Shin

Prayer

Dear Lord,
I come before you today with heavy hearts, lifting all those suffering and needing healing. I ask that you provide comfort and peace to those struggling with physical or emotional pain. I ask for your grace and mercy to envelope them and for them to be surrounded by love and support from family and friends.

I ask for your strength to sustain them during their trials and restore hope in their hearts. I pray for your healing touch to bring physical and emotional healing to those in need and for them to find peace in your presence. I know that you are a great physician and that nothing is impossible for you, so I trust in your power to heal, and I ask that you would use your healing power in the lives of those suffering.

I ask that you would give them the strength to endure and the hope to persevere. I pray for your guidance for the doctors and nurses caring for the sick and for wisdom for the researchers working to find cures. I ask that you bring healing to our world. Amen.

Declaration

I declare that I continue to lift the sick and suffering in prayer, asking God to provide healing and comfort to those who are going through physical or emotional pain. I declare that I will do my best to stand in faith for their healing and that they are surrounded by love and support. I ask for God's grace and mercy to be upon them during their trials and for them to find peace in His presence. I commit to being a support for them, to offer encouragement, and to assist in any way that I can.

I declare that I will trust in God's sovereignty and in His perfect plan for their healing. I declare that I will pray for their strength and endurance as they go through this difficult time and that they will be able to find hope and joy in the midst of their suffering. I call upon God's wisdom and guidance in this journey and trust His provision and grace. I declare I will not rest until they are fully restored to health and strength. I declare that the power of God will manifest in their bodies, and they will be healed.

Prayer Lifestyle

Missions and Outreach

Praying for missions and outreach means asking God to guide and bless the efforts of those sharing the gospel's good news with others. It's about asking for God's wisdom and provision for mission trips and outreach programs and for people's hearts to be open to the message of salvation.

Scripture References:

Matthew 28:19-20 - "Therefore go and make disciples of all nations, baptizing them in the name of the Father and of the Son and of the Holy Spirit, and teaching them to obey everything I have commanded you. And surely I am with you always, to the very end of the age."

Acts 1:8 - "But you will receive power when the Holy Spirit comes on you; and you will be my witnesses in Jerusalem, and in all Judea and Samaria, and to the ends of the earth."

Isaiah 6:8 - "Then I heard the voice of the Lord saying, "Whom shall I send? And who will go for us?" And I said, "Here am I. Send me!"

Inspirational/Motivational Quotes

"Missions is not the ultimate task of the church. Worship is. Missions exists because worship doesn't." - John Piper

Ivon Valerie

"The task of the church is to make disciples, not converts." - Rick Warren

Prayer

Dear Lord,

I come with a heart full of gratitude for the opportunity to be a part of your mission to bring salvation to the world. I pray for guidance and wisdom for those sharing the gospel's good news with others, that their efforts would be blessed and that many hearts would be open to the message of salvation. I ask for your provision for mission trips and outreach programs so that they may be successful in spreading your love and truth to all nations.

I pray that those on mission trips will be protected and kept safe as they share your message. I pray they would have the courage and boldness to speak the truth in love and be filled with your Spirit as they proclaim the good news. I ask that you raise more laborers for the harvest, those willing to go out into the world and share the gospel. I pray that you will give them the boldness, strength, resources, and support they need to succeed in their efforts.

I also pray for the people who will hear the message of salvation and that their hearts will be open and receptive to the truth. I ask that you remove any obstacles or barriers preventing them from understanding and accepting the gospel. I pray for the church that it would be united in its mission to reach the lost and that it would be a powerful force for spreading the good news of salvation. I pray the church will shine in the darkness, drawing people to you.

I thank you, Lord, for the privilege of being a part of your mission to bring salvation to the world. I trust in your power and love to reach the lost and to bring many into your kingdom. Amen.

Declaration

I commit to spreading the gospel's good news through actively supporting and participating in missions and outreach efforts. I pledge to pray for the success of these endeavors and for the hearts of those we are reaching out to to be open and receptive to the message of salvation. I will strive to educate myself and others about the importance of missions and outreach and their impact on the world.

I acknowledge that this is not an easy task and may come with challenges and obstacles, but I trust in the power of God and His provision to guide and sustain us in this mission. I declare that I will not rest until the love and truth of God reach every corner of the earth and all people have the opportunity to know and follow Him as their Lord and Savior. I call upon God's wisdom and guidance in this journey and trust His provision and grace.

Ivon Valerie

Unity and Harmony Among Different Groups

Praying for unity and harmony among different groups means asking God to bring peace and understanding among people from different backgrounds, cultures, and beliefs. It's about asking for God's love and grace to be evident among different groups and for people to learn to respect and appreciate each other's differences.

Scripture References

John 17:20-23 - "My prayer is not for them alone. I pray also for those who will believe in me through their message, that all of them may be one, Father, just as you are in me and I am in you. May they also be in us so that the world may believe that you have sent me. I have given them the glory that you gave me, that they may be one as we are one: I in them and you in me. May they be brought to complete unity to let the world know that you sent me and have loved them even as you have loved me."

Ephesians 4:3 - "Make every effort to keep the unity of the Spirit through the bond of peace."

Romans 12:18 - "If it is possible, as far as it depends on you, live at peace with everyone."

Prayer Lifestyle

Inspirational/Motivational Quotes

"Unity is strength... when there is teamwork and collaboration, wonderful things can be achieved." - Mattie Stepanek

"The world will never have lasting peace so long as men reserve for war the finest human qualities. Peace, no less than war, requires idealism and self-sacrifice and a righteous and dynamic faith." - John Foster Dulles

Prayer

Dear Lord,
As I lift unity and harmony among different groups in prayer, I ask for your guidance and blessings to bring peace and understanding among people from different backgrounds, cultures, and beliefs. I believe that your love and grace will be evident among different groups and that people will learn to respect and appreciate each other's differences.

I pray that your people will be united in love and that the world will see the love of Christ through our unity. I commit to being an instrument of your peace and spreading love and understanding among all people.

As I lift missions and outreach in prayer, I ask for your guidance and blessings for the efforts of those sharing the gospel's good news with others. I ask for your wisdom and provision for mission trips and outreach programs and for people's hearts to be open to the message of salvation. I believe that your love and truth will be made known to all nations and that many will come to know you as their Lord and Savior. I commit to being an ambassador of your love and spreading the message of salvation to all people. I pray for the boldness, strength, courage, and resources to fulfill this mission and to be a faithful servant in your kingdom. Amen.

Declaration

I declare that I will strive to be an agent of love, compassion, and understanding, promoting unity and harmony among all people. I commit to actively listening, learning, and engaging with those with different perspectives and beliefs to foster a deeper understanding and respect for one another. I pledge to speak up against hate and discrimination and actively work toward justice and equality.

I declare God's wisdom and guidance in this journey and trust His provision and grace. I ask for the strength and courage to be a light in the darkness and reflect the love and unity that can only come from Him. I declare that I will not rest until we are all united in the love and grace of God and that the world may see the love of Christ through our unity.

Prayer Lifestyle

Ivon Valerie

Healing and Deliverance

Healing and deliverance are critical elements of our overall physical, mental, and spiritual health. In this chapter, we will explore the power of healing and deliverance and provide prayers and declarations that can help readers free themselves from oppressive influences in their lives while finding true peace through restoration. We hope to guide readers on a journey towards freedom - both mentally and spiritually - so they may finally experience real joy through healing and deliverance.

Physical Healing

Praying for physical healing means asking God to intervene in a person's physical health and bring healing and restoration. It's about asking for God's wisdom and provision in medical treatments and for the healing power of God to be at work in the person's body.

Scripture References

Isaiah 53:5 - "But he was pierced for our transgressions; he was crushed for our iniquities; upon him was the chastisement that brought us peace, and with his wounds we are healed."

James 5:14-15 - "Is anyone among you sick? Let them call the elders of the church to pray over them and anoint them with oil in the name of the Lord. And the prayer offered in faith will make the sick person well; the Lord will raise them up. If they have sinned, they will be forgiven."

Psalm 103:3 - "He forgives all your sins and heals all your diseases."

Inspirational/Motivational Quotes

"Healing is a matter of time, but it is sometimes also a matter of opportunity." - Hippocrates

"The greatest healing therapy is friendship and love." - Hubert H. Humphrey

Prayer

Dear Lord,
I come to you asking that you heal those who need physical healing. I ask that you intervene in their health and bring healing and restoration to their bodies. I pray for your wisdom and provision in the medical treatments they receive and for the healing power of your love to be at work in their lives. I ask that you would give them strength and hope during their trials and that they may find peace and comfort in your presence.

I trust in your promise to heal and restore, and I ask that you use me as a vessel to bring your healing touch to those in need. I pray for your grace and mercy to be upon them and for them to be surrounded by love and support. I pray for those who care for them, the doctors, nurses, and caregivers, that they would have the wisdom and compassion to provide the best care possible.

I pray for the healing of their mind, body, and soul. I pray to eradicate any disease or illness affecting them and strengthen their immune system. I pray that their pain is alleviated and that they feel your loving embrace. I pray for their emotional well-being and for them to find peace and contentment in your presence, even in the midst of their suffering.

I pray that their financial needs be met, and that they have the resources they need to receive the best possible care. I pray for your wisdom for their doctors and medical professionals and for them to have the knowledge and skill to diagnose and treat their conditions effectively. I pray for a complete and lasting recovery, for them to live a full and healthy life, free from pain and suffering. I pray for them to be able to return to their normal activities, to be able to work, play and enjoy the life that you have blessed them with.

I pray for them to be a testimony of your goodness and faithfulness to all those around them. I trust in your promise to heal and restore; nothing is impossible for you. Thank you for your loving kindness and for always being faithful to those who call on your name. Amen.

Declaration

I declare healing for all those who need physical healing. I call upon the power of God to intervene in their health and bring about complete healing and restoration. I believe God's wisdom and provision will guide medical treatments, and His healing touch will work in their bodies. I declare they will be healed, restored to total health and strength, and made whole again.

I trust in the power of prayer and the healing touch of God. I know He is a loving and compassionate God who is always ready to heal and restore those suffering. I believe that through prayer, I can tap into that healing power and request a miraculous change in the lives of those who are hurting. I know that healing is not always instant and that sometimes the journey to recovery can be long and difficult. But I trust that God is with me every step of the way and that His healing power will sustain and strengthen me through the trials and tribulations.

Ivon Valerie

I declare that I will not lose hope but will continue to pray with faith and confidence, knowing that God can do more than I can ask or imagine. I declare that the healing power of God will be at work in the bodies of those who are sick and suffering. I declare that God will bring about complete and total healing, restoring them to health and strength. I trust in the power of prayer and God's healing touch, and I declare they will be healed and made whole.

Emotional and Mental Healing

Praying for emotional and mental healing means asking God to bring peace and healing to a person's mind, emotions, and inner self. It's about asking for God's wisdom, provision, and guidance in therapy, treatment, and counseling and for the healing power of God to be at work in the person's emotional and mental well-being.

Scripture References

Psalm 147:3 - "He heals the brokenhearted and binds up their wounds."

Isaiah 61:1 - "The Spirit of the Sovereign Lord is on me, because the Lord has anointed me to proclaim good news to the poor. He has sent me to bind up the brokenhearted, to proclaim freedom for the captives and release from darkness for the prisoners."

Matthew 11:28 - "Come to me, all you who are weary and burdened, and I will give you rest."

Inspirational/Motivational Quotes

"The greatest healing therapy is the human touch. The need for love lies at the very foundation of human existence." - Dalai Lama

"Emotional healing is not so much about getting over something, as it is about growing through something." - Iyanla Vanzant

Prayer

Dear Lord,
I come before you today with a heart full of faith and trust in your healing power. I lift those who need emotional and mental healing and ask that you powerfully intervene in their lives. I ask that you bring peace and healing to their minds, emotions, and inner selves and guide them through their challenges.

I know that emotional and mental healing is not always easy and that it can take time and effort to overcome the struggles that they may be facing. But I trust that you are with them every step of the way and that your healing power will sustain and strengthen them. I ask that you give them the wisdom, provision, and guidance they need to navigate therapy, treatment, and counseling and that your healing touch will work in their emotional and mental well-being.

I pray that you will give them the strength and courage to face their struggles head-on and that they may find comfort and hope in your presence. I trust in your love and compassion and know that you can do more than we can ask or imagine. Through prayer, we can tap into your healing power and bring about a miraculous change in the lives of those who are hurting. I lift those who need emotional and mental healing and ask that you bring peace, healing, and restoration to their hearts and minds. I trust your healing power and declare they will be made whole again. Amen.

Declaration

I declare that I will always strive to lift those who need emotional and mental healing in prayer, asking God to bring peace and healing to their minds, emotions, and inner selves. I believe God's healing power can heal the deepest wounds and bring true transformation in the hearts and minds of those hurting. I declare that I stand in faith for God's wisdom, provision, and guidance in therapy, treatment, and counseling and for the healing power of God to be at work in their emotional and mental well-being.

I declare that the power of prayer and God's healing touch will work in the lives of those suffering. I know that healing is not always instant and that the journey to recovery can be long and difficult. But I trust that God is with us every step of the way and that His healing power will sustain and strengthen us through trials and tribulations.

I declare that we will not lose hope but will continue to pray with faith and confidence, knowing that God can do more than we can ask or imagine. I further declare that God will bring complete and total healing in the minds, emotions, and inner selves of those suffering. I ask that He will give them the strength and courage to face their struggles and that they may find comfort and hope in His presence. I declare that they will be able to see the light at the end of the tunnel and will be able to find healing and restoration in their emotional and mental well-being.

I declare that those who are sick and hurting will find peace and healing in their minds, emotions, and inner selves, and they will be able to face their struggles with strength and courage. I trust in the power of prayer and God's healing touch and declare that they will be healed and made whole.

Prayer Lifestyle

Spiritual Healing

Praying for spiritual healing means asking God to restore and renew a person's relationship with Him. It's about asking God to heal the person's heart, mind, and spirit and to bring them closer to Him. It's also about asking for God's wisdom and guidance in the person's spiritual journey and for the Holy Spirit to work in their lives.

Scripture References

Psalm 51:10 - "Create in me a pure heart, O God, and renew a steadfast spirit within me."

Isaiah 57:15 - "For this is what the high and lofty One says— he who lives forever, whose name is holy: "I live in a high and holy place, but also with the one who is contrite and lowly in spirit, to revive the spirit of the lowly and to revive the heart of the contrite."

Matthew 4:17 - "From that time on Jesus began to preach, "Repent, for the kingdom of heaven has come near."

Inspirational/Motivational Quotes

"Spiritual healing is not about fixing something that is broken, it's about awakening to who you truly are." - Eckhart Tolle

"True healing is not the repair of the past, but the re-creation of the present" - Deepak Chopra

Prayer

Dear Lord,
I come before you today to lift those who need spiritual healing in my prayers. I ask that you restore and renew their relationship with you, heal their hearts, minds, and spirits, and bring them closer to you. I ask for your wisdom and guidance in their spiritual journey and for the Holy Spirit to work in their lives.

I ask that they find comfort and hope in your presence and that they may be able to see the beauty of your love and grace. I pray that you would give them the strength and courage to face any struggles they may be facing in their spiritual journey and that they would have the faith and trust in you to persevere.

I pray they will understand your love and grace and be filled with peace and joy. I pray that they will be surrounded by a loving and supportive community that will encourage and uplift them on their journey. I pray they will have the courage to take the necessary steps to grow in their relationship with you and be open to the guidance of the Holy Spirit.

I pray that they will be renewed and refreshed in their spirits and that they will experience the fullness of your love and grace. I pray that they will know that you are with them every step of the way and that you are working all things together for their good and your glory. Amen.

Declaration

I declare that God is restoring and renewing His relationships with those who require spiritual healing. I declare that I stand in faith, believing in God for healing their hearts, minds, and spirits and bringing them closer to Himself.

I declare that they will find comfort and hope in God's presence and that they will be able to see the beauty of His love and grace. I know that God will give them the strength and courage to face any struggles they may face in their spiritual journey and that they will have the faith and trust in God to persevere.

I declare they will understand God's love and grace and be filled with His peace and joy. I trust in the power of prayer and the healing touch of God, and I declare that they will be healed and made whole in their spiritual journey as they deepen their relationship with God and align their hearts, minds, and spirits with His will. I declare that the healing power of God is at work in their lives, bringing about the complete and total restoration of their spiritual well-being.

I know that spiritual healing is not always instant and that sometimes the journey to recovery can be long and difficult, so I declare that God is with them every step and that His healing power will sustain and strengthen them through trials and tribulations. I declare they will not lose hope but will continue to pray with faith and confidence, knowing that God can do more than they can ask or imagine.

Ivon Valerie

Deliverance From Addiction and Negative Patterns

Praying for deliverance from addiction and negative patterns means asking God to help a person break free from harmful habits, behaviors, and dependencies. It's about asking God for the strength, wisdom, and guidance to overcome these struggles and to find healing and freedom in Him.

Scripture References

Psalm 34:18 - "The Lord is close to the brokenhearted and saves those who are crushed in spirit."

Isaiah 43:18-19 - "Forget the former things; do not dwell on the past. See, I am doing a new thing! Now it springs up; do you not perceive it? I am making a way in the wilderness and streams in the wasteland."

1 Corinthians 10:13 - "No temptation has overtaken you that is not common to man. God is faithful, and he will not let you be tempted beyond your ability, but with the temptation he will also provide the way of escape, that you may be able to endure it."

Inspirational/Motivational Quotes

"The only way out of the labyrinth of suffering is to forgive." - John Green

"Addiction is not a choice. Recovery is." - Unknown

Prayer

Dear Lord,

I come before you with a heavy heart, lifting those struggling with addiction and negative patterns. I ask that you help them break free from these harmful habits and dependencies and give them the strength, wisdom, and guidance they need to overcome these struggles.

I pray that they would find healing and freedom in you and that you would surround them with support and love so that they may find hope and peace in your presence. I pray they will learn the truth of your love and grace and find the courage and determination to take the necessary steps to overcome these struggles.

I pray that you would give them the wisdom and understanding to make healthy choices and that they would find the support and encouragement they need to take those steps. I pray that they will find the strength and courage to face their struggles head-on and that they will find hope and peace in the knowledge that you are with them every step of the way. Amen.

Declaration

I declare that I am standing in faith, believing God will help those struggling with addiction and negative patterns break free from these harmful habits and dependencies. I ask God's wisdom and guidance to lead them toward healing and freedom. I trust in God's strength to empower them to overcome their struggles and find hope and peace in His presence.

I declare they will be surrounded by a loving and supportive community that will encourage them on their journey toward a better life. Through prayer and God's healing touch, they will overcome their addiction and negative patterns and find true freedom in Him. I declare I will continue to lift them in prayer and stand in faith for their healing and restoration.

Protection Against Spiritual Attacks

Praying for protection against spiritual attacks means asking God to protect a person from the schemes and strategies of the enemy. It's about asking God to cover and shield a person from the devil's plans and give them the strength and wisdom to stand strong in their faith.

Scripture References

Ephesians 6:10-18 - "Finally, be strong in the Lord and in his mighty power. Put on the full armor of God, so that you can take your stand against the devil's schemes. For our struggle is not against flesh and blood, but against the rulers, against the authorities, against the powers of this dark world and against the spiritual forces of evil in the heavenly realms. Therefore put on the full armor of God, so that when the day of evil comes, you may be able to stand your ground, and after you have done everything, to stand. Stand firm then, with the belt of truth buckled around your waist, with the breastplate of righteousness in place, and with your feet fitted with the readiness that comes from the gospel of peace. In addition to all this, take up the shield of faith, with which you can extinguish all the flaming arrows of the evil one. Take the helmet of salvation and the sword of the Spirit, which is the word of God."

2 Corinthians 10:3-5 - "For though we live in the world, we do not wage war as the world does. The weapons we fight with are not the weapons of the world. On the contrary, they have divine power to demolish strongholds. We demolish arguments and every pretension that sets itself up against the knowledge of God, and we take captive every thought to make it obedient to Christ."

Inspirational/Motivational Quotes

"The devil fears us when we pray." - Unknown

"We have to pray with our eyes on God, not on the difficulties." - Oswald Chambers

Prayer

Dear Lord,
I come before you today with a heavy heart for those facing spiritual attacks. I ask that you would protect them from the schemes and strategies of the enemy. I pray that you cover and shield them from the devil's plans and give them the strength and wisdom to stand strong in their faith. I pray they will be filled with your spirit and have the discernment to recognize the enemy's tactics and the courage to resist them.

I ask that you would surround them with your love and grace and that they may find peace and security in your presence. Lord, I pray that they will be empowered by your word and have the faith to overcome any obstacle that comes their way. I ask that you would give them the wisdom to make the right choices and the strength to overcome temptations. I pray they will find refuge in you and be victorious in their spiritual battles.

Declaration

I declare that heaven is responding as I am interceding on behalf of those under spiritual attack, asking God to surround them with His armor and give them the strength and wisdom to stand firm in their faith. I declare that they will be protected from the schemes and strategies of the enemy and will be covered and shielded by the blood of Jesus.

I also declare they will find peace and security in God's presence, and His love and grace will surround them and give them the courage to face these challenges head-on. I trust in the power of prayer and the protection of God, and I stand in faith that He will keep them safe and secure in these difficult times. I pray that they will have the strength and courage to overcome any obstacles that come their way and that they will find comfort in the knowledge that God is with them every step of the way.

Ivon Valerie

Prayer Lifestyle

Ivon Valerie

Success and Prosperity

Achieving success and prosperity is critical to our quality of life. They enable us to provide for ourselves and those we love while contributing heavily to our well-being. This chapter dives into the importance of achieving success and wealth with powerful prayers and declarations that will assist readers in attaining their objectives, boosting their income levels, embracing true abundance, and ultimately experiencing a prosperous lifestyle.

Prayer Lifestyle

Success in Business and Career

Praying for success in business and career means asking God to bless and guide people in their work and professional endeavors. It's about asking God for wisdom, guidance, and favor in pursuing success and providing the resources needed to achieve it.

Scripture References

Psalm 90:17 - "May the favor of the Lord our God rest on us; establish the work of our hands for us— yes, establish the work of our hands."

Proverbs 16:3 - "Commit to the Lord whatever you do, and he will establish your plans."

Joshua 1:8 - "Keep this Book of the Law always on your lips; meditate on it day and night, so that you may be careful to do everything written in it. Then you will be prosperous and successful."

Inspirational/Motivational Quotes

"The road to success is always under construction." - Lily Tomlin
"Success is not the key to happiness. Happiness is the key to success. If you love what you are doing, you will be successful." - Albert Schweitzer

Prayer

Dear Lord,
I come before you today with gratitude and faith, lifting my business and career aspirations. I ask for your blessings and guidance in my work and professional endeavors. I seek your wisdom and guidance in making important decisions and navigating the challenges of building a successful business and career.

I ask for your favor and provision as I pursue my goals and aspirations. I pray you open doors of opportunity and establish my work. I pray that you bless my efforts and guide me toward success, using my gifts and talents for your glory. I also lift my colleagues, partners, and employees in prayer, asking for your protection and guidance in their work. I ask that you bless their efforts and guide them towards success, help us to work together in harmony, and to provide for our needs.

I pray for the strength and determination to work hard and persevere through the challenges of building a successful business or career. I trust in your faithfulness and love, knowing that you will provide for my needs and guide me toward success. I thank you, Lord, for your provision and blessings in my life, and I look forward to seeing your hand of favor at work in my business and career. Amen.

Declaration

I declare that I am hardworking and diligent, and I trust that God equips me with the necessary skills and talents to excel in my business and career. I believe God has a purpose and plan for my life, and I am confident he will guide me to fulfill that purpose.

I declare God's blessings on my endeavors and that He will protect me from any negative influences or obstacles that may arise. I declare that I will be persistent and consistent in my efforts and will not be discouraged by any challenges coming my way. I trust in God's provision and am confident that he will provide me with all the necessary resources to succeed. I will use my success to glorify God and bless others. I am grateful for God's faithfulness and the abundance he has already placed in my life, and I trust that he will continue to pour out his blessings on my business and career.

Ivon Valerie

Academic Success

Praying for academic success means asking God to bless and guide a person in their studies and educational pursuits. It's about asking God for wisdom, understanding, the ability to retain knowledge, and the provision of the resources needed to succeed academically.

Scripture References

Proverbs 2:1-6 - "My son, if you accept my words and store up my commands within you, turning your ear to wisdom and applying your heart to understanding, and if you call out for insight and cry aloud for understanding, and if you look for it as for silver and search for it as for hidden treasure, then you will understand the fear of the Lord and find the knowledge of God."

Psalm 119:98-105 - "Your commands are always with me and make me wiser than my enemies. I have more insight than all my teachers, for I meditate on your statutes. I have more understanding than the elders, for I obey your precepts. I have kept my feet from every evil path so that I might obey your word. I have not turned away from your laws, for you yourself have taught me. How sweet are your words to my taste, sweeter than honey to my mouth!"

Inspirational/Motivational Quotes

"Education is not the filling of a pail, but the lighting of a fire." - William Butler Yeats

"Success is not the key to happiness. Happiness is the key to success. If you love what you are doing, you will be successful." - Albert Schweitzer

Prayer

Dear Lord,
I come before you today to ask for your blessings and guidance in my academic pursuits. I ask for your wisdom and understanding to guide me in my studies and for the ability to retain knowledge and apply it in my work. I ask you to provide the resources I need to succeed academically, including financial aid, scholarships, and access to necessary materials and technology.

I pray for your guidance in my relationships with my teachers and classmates and for your grace in handling any challenges or difficulties that may arise. I ask that you open doors of opportunity for me and establish my work, giving me the strength and determination to succeed. I trust in your faithfulness to provide for my needs as I strive for academic excellence, and I give you all the glory for any success I may achieve. Amen.

Ivon Valerie

Declaration

As I strive for academic success, I will seek the Lord's guidance in all my studies and educational pursuits. I will trust in God's wisdom and understanding and seek to retain the knowledge I am learning. I will not be limited by my abilities but will trust God for the provision of the resources that I need to succeed.

I declare that the Lord is opening doors of opportunities for me and establishing my hands' works. I will give thanks for the Lord's blessings, and I will trust in the guidance of God for my academic success. I will also seek to share my knowledge and blessings with others who may be in need.

I will be grateful for every success, big or small, and will always give back to the Lord for all the blessings He has given me. I will strive to be an exemplary student and always do my best to serve and glorify the Lord in all my academic pursuits.

Financial Prosperity

Praying for financial prosperity means asking God for provision, abundance, and blessings in one's financial life. It's about asking God for wisdom in managing finances, opportunities to increase income, and protection against financial struggles.

Scripture References

Philippians 4:19 - "And my God will meet all your needs according to the riches of his glory in Christ Jesus."

Proverbs 13:22 - "A good man leaves an inheritance to his children's children, but a sinner's wealth is stored up for the righteous."

Malachi 3:10 - "Bring the whole tithe into the storehouse, that there may be food in my house. Test me in this," says the Lord Almighty, "and see if I will not throw open the floodgates of heaven and pour out so much blessing that there will not be room enough to store it."

Inspirational/Motivational Quotes

"Money is only a tool. It will take you wherever you wish, but it will not replace you as the driver." - Ayn Rand

"The habit of saving is itself an education; it fosters every virtue, teaches self-denial, cultivates the sense of order, trains to forethought, and so broadens the mind." - T.T. Munger

Prayer

Dear Lord,
As I come before you today, I lift my heart and the hearts of all those seeking financial prosperity. I ask that you bless us with abundant provision and blessings in our financial lives. I pray that you would give us wisdom in managing our finances and open doors of opportunity for us to increase our income.

I also pray that you protect us from financial struggles and bless the works of our hands. I ask that you guide us in making wise financial decisions and that we trust in your provision for our every need. Lord, please bless our businesses and careers, and cause us to find success and fulfillment in our work.

I pray that we will be generous with the blessings you have given us and use our resources to help others in need. I ask that you would provide for our families and that we would have enough to meet all our needs. I pray that you will give us peace and joy in our financial lives and that we will glorify you with the blessings you have given us. Amen.

Declaration

I declare I am a child of God and blessed with abundance and provision. I know God has a plan for my financial life, and I trust

Prayer Lifestyle

His wisdom to guide me in managing my finances. I declare that I stand in faith for opportunities to increase my income and for protection against financial struggles. I believe God is the source of all provision and will open doors of opportunity for me and establish the work of my hands. I trust in the power of prayer and the guidance of God for my financial prosperity.

I also declare that my loved ones, friends, and all those around me will be blessed with financial prosperity. I believe that as I stand in faith for my financial prosperity, I also stand in faith for the financial prosperity of those around me. I declare that God's abundance and provision will flow into the lives of those I love and care for. I trust that God will open doors of opportunity and establish the work of their hands as well. I pray for their wisdom and guidance as they manage their finances and protection against financial struggles. I declare that they, too, will experience the blessings of God's provision and abundance in their financial lives.

Abundance and Blessings

Praying for abundance and blessings means asking God for blessings and provision in every area of life. It's about asking God for abundant spiritual, emotional, physical, and financial blessings.

Scripture References

Psalm 23:5 - "You prepare a table before me in the presence of my enemies. You anoint my head with oil; my cup overflows."

Deuteronomy 28:11 - "The Lord will grant you abundant prosperity—in the fruit of your womb, the young of your livestock and the crops of your ground—in the land he swore to your ancestors to give you."

Ephesians 3:20 - "Now to him who is able to do immeasurably more than all we ask or imagine, according to his power that is at work within us"

Inspirational/Motivational Quotes

"Blessed are those who can give without remembering and take without forgetting." - Elizabeth Bibesco

"The more you praise and celebrate your life, the more there is in life to celebrate." - Oprah Winfrey

Prayer

Dear Lord,
I come before you today in humility and gratitude, lifting myself who is seeking abundance and blessings in my life. Please pour out your blessings and provision in every area of my life, including spiritual, emotional, physical, and financial blessings.

Please bless the works of my hands and open doors of opportunity for me. I pray that I have the wisdom to recognize and seize the opportunities you provide for me and that I can walk in the fullness of your provision and blessings.

I pray for your protection over my finances and for the abundance of resources to flow into my life. May I meet all my needs and have more than enough to bless others. Please grant me the ability to manage my resources well and to use them to further your kingdom.

I ask that you grant me emotional and spiritual healing, as I trust in you. May I experience your love and peace that surpasses all understanding and be filled with hope and joy in all circumstances?

Thank you for your goodness, faithfulness, and trust in your ability to provide for me. I ask all these things in the name of Jesus. Amen.

Declaration

I declare that abundance and blessings are manifested in my life, and I have the necessary provision. I stand in faith for God's power to do immeasurably more than I can ask or imagine and for abundant spiritual, emotional, physical, and financial blessings.

I declare that God will open doors of opportunity for me and that I will have the wisdom to recognize and seize the opportunities that He provides for me. I pray that I can walk in the fullness of God's provision and blessings, experiencing His faithfulness in every area of my life.

I declare God's protection over my finances and His abundant resources to flow into my life. I declare I will have more than enough to meet my needs and bless others. I further declare that I can manage my resources well and use them to further God's kingdom.

I declare that I will be filled with hope and joy in all circumstances, knowing God is with me and for me. I declare that He can do immeasurably more than I can ask or imagine, and I trust His power to bring abundance and blessings into my life. Amen.

Favor and Promotion

Praying for favor and promotion means asking God to open doors of opportunity and to establish the work of one's hands. It's about asking God for favor in one's business and career, in relationships, and in every area of life.

Scripture References

Psalm 5:12 - "For surely, O Lord, you bless the righteous; you surround them with your favor as with a shield."

Proverbs 3:4 - "Then you will win favor and a good name in the sight of God and man."

Colossians 1:10 - "And we pray this in order that you may live a life worthy of the Lord and may please him in every way: bearing fruit in every good work, growing in the knowledge of God,"

Inspirational/Motivational Quotes

"Favor ain't fair, but it's necessary." - Unknown

"Favor is the oil that takes the friction out of life." - Joel Osteen

Prayer

Dear Lord,

I come seeking your favor and promotion in my life. I ask that you open doors of opportunity and bless the work of my hands. I pray for your favor in my business, career, relationships, and life.

I trust in your ability to bring forth favor and promotion, and I know that you can do more than I can ask or imagine. I pray that you will guide me in the path you have for me and give me the wisdom and discernment to recognize the opportunities you've provided me. I pray that I will have the courage to walk through the doors you open and that I will be able to use the gifts and talents you have given me to further your kingdom.

I pray for favor in my business, that it will be successful and prosperous, and that I can use it to bless others. I pray for favor in my career, that I will be able to excel in my field, and that I will be able to make a positive impact in the lives of those around me. I pray for favor in my relationships, that they will be healthy and fulfilling, and that I can build meaningful connections with others.

I pray for favor in every area of my life, knowing that you can do immeasurably more than I think. I trust in your ability to bring forth favor and promotion in my life, and I thank you for your goodness and faithfulness. Amen.

Declaration

I declare that I am experiencing promotion in my life and will stand in faith, depending on God's ability to open doors of opportunity and continually bless the work of my hands. I believe God will bring favor in my business, career, relationships, and every area of my life. I declare that I will be a vessel of God's favor and walk in the fullness of His blessings. I know God's favor is not based on my merit or worth but His grace and love for me.

I declare that I will be blessed in the city and country and that I will be blessed by coming in and going out. I declare that God's favor will surround me like a shield and that I will be like a tree planted by the rivers of water that brings forth fruit in its season.
I declare that I will have favor in my business, that it will be successful and prosperous, and that I will be able to use it to bless others.

I declare that I will have favor in my career, that I will be able to excel in my field, and that I will be able to make a positive impact on the lives of those around me. I declare that I will have favor in my relationships, that they will be healthy and fulfilling, and that I will be able to build meaningful connections with others.

I declare that I will be a person of influence and that my presence will bless people. I declare that I will be a light in the darkness and that I will be a shining example of God's love and grace to those around me. I trust God to bring forth favor and promotion in my life, and I thank Him for His goodness and faithfulness.

Ivon Valerie

Prayer Lifestyle

Ivon Valerie

Protection and Guidance

The essentiality of protection and guidance in our life cannot be overstated. They bring us a sense of safety and tranquility while providing prayers to shield ourselves from harm and seek divine direction when making decisions. This chapter is devoted to these two concepts, with special attention paid to the power behind prayerful declarations that help readers find courage during difficult times, allowing them peace of mind knowing they are safeguarded by divine intervention.

Prayer Lifestyle

Protection Against Physical Harm

Praying for protection against physical harm means asking God to keep one safe from accidents, injuries, and other forms of physical harm. It's about asking God for protection in one's daily life while traveling and in the workplace.

Scripture References

Psalm 91:1-2 - "He who dwells in the secret place of the Most High shall abide under the shadow of the Almighty. I will say of the Lord, 'He is my refuge and my fortress; my God, in Him I will trust.'"

Isaiah 54:17 - "No weapon formed against you shall prosper, and every tongue which rises against you in judgment You shall condemn."

John 10:28 - "And I give them eternal life, and they shall never perish; neither shall anyone snatch them out of My hand."

Inspirational/Motivational Quotes

"I pray that the Lord will protect you from all harm and danger, from all trouble and pain, from all sickness and disease, from all fear and worry, from all enemies and evil, from all sin and temptation, and from all doubts and worries." - Unknown

"God's protection is like a fortress around us, a defense against the enemy's attacks." - Unknown

Prayer

Dear Lord,
I come before you today with a humble and contrite heart, seeking your protection and guidance. I ask that you surround me with your loving embrace and keep me safe from all physical harm.

I ask for your protection in my daily life as I go about my tasks and responsibilities. Please guide me and keep me safe from accidents and injuries, and protect me from any harm that may come my way. I also ask for your protection as I travel, whether near or far. Please watch over me, guide me safely to my destination, and protect me from any dangers that may arise on my journey.

I further ask for your protection as I do my duties and responsibilities. Please give me the strength and wisdom to do my job to the best of my ability and protect me from any harm or danger that may come my way.

Lord. I know you are always with me and will never leave or forsake me. I give you all the praise and glory, for you are my savior and protector. Amen.

Declaration

I declare that I am committed to lifting myself in prayer and seeking the protection of God against physical harm. I firmly stand in my faith, knowing God is always with me and will protect me in all aspects of my life. I have complete trust in His power to keep me safe, not just in my daily routine but also while traveling and working. God will shield me from accidents, injuries, and physical harm.

I that I am continually receiving the protection I need. I refuse to be afraid because I know God is my protector, shield, and defense. I declare that I will not be shaken by fear or anxiety because I trust the Lord to keep me safe. I am aware that He is always with me and that nothing can harm me as long as I remain in His will.

I further declare that God's love and grace protect me at all times and that nothing can overcome me as long as I keep my faith in Him. I am confident in my ability to overcome any obstacles that may come my way and rise above any challenges that I may face. I trust in the Lord to guide me, protect me, and keep me safe, always.

Ivon Valerie

Protection Against Negative Influences

Praying for protection against negative influences means asking God to keep one safe from negative people, situations, and thoughts. It's about asking God for protection from anything that can harm one's spirit and soul.

Scripture References

Proverbs 4:23 - "Above all else, guard your heart, for everything you do flows from it."

2 Corinthians 10:5 - "We demolish arguments and every pretension that sets itself up against the knowledge of God, and we take captive every thought to make it obedient to Christ."

Ephesians 6:11-12 - "Put on the full armor of God, so that you can take your stand against the devil's schemes. For our struggle is not against flesh and blood, but against the rulers, against the authorities, against the powers of this dark world and against the spiritual forces of evil in the heavenly realms."

Inspirational/Motivational Quotes

"God is my protection, I shall not fear. What can man do to me?"
- Unknown

Prayer Lifestyle

"God will protect you from the evil one." - Unknown

Prayer

Dear Lord,
I come before you today with a heavy heart, seeking your protection and guidance. I ask that you surround me with your loving embrace and keep me safe from negative influences.

I ask for your protection from negative people, those who seek to harm me, those who spread negativity and hate, and those who seek to bring me down. Please guide me to surround myself with positive and uplifting individuals who will encourage and support me.

I also ask for your protection from negative situations, whether it be in my personal or professional life. Please give me the wisdom and guidance to navigate challenging circumstances and to see the good and positive in all things.

I also ask for your protection from negative thoughts and emotions, such as fear, doubt, and anxiety. Please give me the strength to overcome these thoughts and focus on your truth and love. I ask for your protection for my spirit and soul, that I may be grounded in your love and grace, and that I may always remain true to my authentic self.

I trust in your ability to protect and keep me safe, Lord. I know you are always with me and will never leave or forsake me. I give you all the praise and glory, for you are my savior and protector. Amen.

Declaration

I declare that I am committed to lifting myself in prayer and seeking protection from negative influences that can harm my spirit and soul. I firmly believe God is always with me and will protect me from negative people, situations, and thoughts. I trust in His power to keep me safe from anything that may try to harm my spiritual and emotional well-being.

I am aware that there are forces in this world that can try to bring me down, but I choose to rise above them. I refuse to be affected by negative energies; instead, I surround myself with positivity and light. I declare that God's love and grace protect me and that nothing can overcome me as long as I keep my faith in Him.

When I pray, I invite God's presence and protection into every aspect of my being. I am confident that He will guide me and keep me safe from any negative influences that may try to harm my spirit and soul. I declare that I am strong, protected, and a child of God, and I will not be moved by any negative influences that may come my way. I am grounded in my faith and trust in the Lord to guide and protect me.

Prayer Lifestyle

Guidance in Decision Making

Praying for guidance in decision-making means asking God for wisdom and direction when making important decisions. It's about asking God for discernment and clarity when faced with difficult choices.

Scripture References

James 1:5 - "If any of you lacks wisdom, you should ask God, who gives generously to all without finding fault, and it will be given to you."

Proverbs 3:5-6 - "Trust in the Lord with all your heart and lean not on your own understanding; in all your ways submit to him, and he will make your paths straight."

Psalm 32:8 - "I will instruct you and teach you in the way you should go; I will counsel you with my loving eye on you."

Inspirational/Motivational Quotes

"God's guidance is like a light in the darkness, leading us to the path of righteousness." - Unknown

"God's wisdom is the best guidance we can ever receive." - Unknown

Prayer

Dear Lord,

I come before you today seeking your guidance and direction in my decisions. I ask that you grant me wisdom, discernment, and clarity as I navigate the important choices ahead of me. I ask for your guidance as I make decisions that will impact my personal life, such as relationships, education, and career choices. Please give me the wisdom to weigh the pros and cons and make the best decision for myself and those around me.

I also ask for your guidance as I make decisions that will impact my professional life, such as business ventures, investments, and partnerships. Please give me the discernment to see the opportunities and potential risks and to make choices that will bring about success and prosperity.

I further ask for your guidance when faced with difficult choices and moral dilemmas. Please give me the clarity to understand your will and act according to your principles and values. I trust in your ability to guide and direct my path, Lord. You have a plan for my life and will never lead me astray. I give you all the praise and glory. Amen.

Declaration

I declare that I will keep praying and seeking God's guidance in my decision-making. I believe God is always with me and will give me wisdom and direction when facing important choices. I trust His power to discern and clarify any difficult decision-making process.

Prayer Lifestyle

I understand that making important decisions can be challenging, but I trust the Lord and His guidance. I declare that I am not alone in this process and that God is always with me, providing me with the wisdom and understanding I need to make the best choices for my life.

I am confident that God will guide me and give me the discernment and clarity I need to make the right choices. I declare that I am strong, guided, and a child of God, and I will make decisions with confidence and certainty, knowing that the Lord is always with me, providing me with the wisdom and understanding I need to navigate this life.

Ivon Valerie

Guidance in Relationships

Praying for guidance in relationships means asking God for wisdom and direction in all relationships, including family, friends, and romantic relationships. It's about asking God for insight and discernment in building and maintaining healthy relationships.

Scripture References

Proverbs 17:17 - "A friend loves at all times, and a brother is born for adversity."

Colossians 3:12-14 - "Therefore, as God's chosen people, holy and dearly loved, clothe yourselves with compassion, kindness, humility, gentleness and patience. Bear with each other and forgive one another if any of you has a grievance against someone. Forgive as the Lord forgave you. And over all these virtues put on love, which binds them all together in perfect unity."

Ephesians 4:2 - "Be completely humble and gentle; be patient, bearing with one another in love."

Inspirational/Motivational Quotes

"God's guidance is like a compass in our relationships, leading us to love and respect." - Unknown

"God's wisdom is the key to building and maintaining healthy relationships." - Unknown

Prayer

Dear Lord,
I come before you today asking for your guidance and direction in my relationships. I ask that you grant me wisdom, insight, and discernment as I navigate the complexities of my relationships with my family, friends, and romantic partners.

I ask for your guidance in my relationships with my family so that I may be a loving and supportive son/daughter, brother/sister, and grandson/granddaughter. Please give me the wisdom to reconcile conflicts and strengthen the bonds of love and loyalty.

I also ask for your guidance in my relationships with my friends so that I may be a true and loyal friend who listens and supports others and is always there in times of need. Please give me the discernment to surround myself with friends who will lift me and bring out the best in me.

I also ask for your guidance in my romantic relationships so that I may be a loving and caring partner, faithful and committed. Please give me the insight to understand my partner's needs and build a healthy relationship. I trust in your ability to guide and direct my relationships, Lord. I know you have a plan for my life and will bring the right people into my life at the right time. I give you all the praise and glory. Amen.

Declaration

I declare that I am fully committed to lifting myself in prayer and seeking guidance from God in all of my relationships. I believe God is always with me and will give me wisdom and direction when building and maintaining healthy relationships. I trust His power to give me insight and discernment in all my interactions with family, friends, and romantic partners.

I understand that building and maintaining relationships can be challenging, but I choose to trust in the Lord and His guidance. I declare that I am not alone in this process, and God is always with me, providing me with the wisdom and understanding I need to navigate the complexities of human interactions.

I trust God to guide my relationships and to bring me the direction and clarity I need in all my interactions. I invite God's presence and wisdom into my thoughts and actions. I am confident that He will guide me and give me the insight and discernment I need to build and maintain healthy relationships.

I declare that I am strong, I am guided, and I am a child of God. I will navigate all my relationships with confidence and certainty, knowing that the Lord is always with me, providing me with the wisdom and understanding I need to interact with others positively and healthily.

Prayer Lifestyle

Guidance in Personal Growth and Development

Praying for guidance in personal growth and development means asking God for wisdom and direction in all aspects of one's personal growth and development. It's about asking God for insight and discernment in becoming the best version of oneself.

Scripture References

Proverbs 4:7 - "Wisdom is supreme; therefore get wisdom. Though it cost all you have, get understanding."

Philippians 4:13 - "I can do all things through Christ who strengthens me."

Inspirational/Motivational Quotes

"God's guidance is the compass that leads us on the path to personal growth and development." - Unknown

"God's wisdom is the key to unlocking our full potential." - Unknown

Prayer

Dear Lord,

I come before you today with a willing and open heart, seeking your guidance and direction in my personal growth and development. I ask that you grant me wisdom, insight, and discernment as I strive to become the best version of myself.

As I work towards self-improvement, I ask for your guidance so that I may be a kinder, more patient, and more compassionate person. Please give me the wisdom to understand my strengths and weaknesses and the determination to work on areas that need improvement.

I also ask for your guidance as I set goals and work towards achieving them to become more ambitious, self-motivated, and productive. Please give me the insight to set realistic and achievable goals and the discernment to understand when it's time to adjust or change them.

I also ask for your guidance as I build my self-esteem to be more confident and self-assured. I trust your ability to guide and direct my personal growth and development, Lord. I know you have a plan for my life and will bring the right experiences, people, and opportunities to help me become the best version of myself. I give you all the praise and glory. Amen.

Declaration

I declare that I am fully committed to lifting myself in prayer and seeking guidance from God in all aspects of my personal growth and development. I stand in faith, knowing that God is always with me and will provide me with wisdom and direction as I strive to become the best version of myself. I trust in His power to give me insight and discernment as I navigate the journey of self-improvement.

I understand that personal growth and development can be challenging, but I trust the Lord and His guidance. I declare that I am not alone in this process and that God is always with me, providing me with the wisdom and understanding I need to navigate the complexities of personal growth. I am confident that He will guide me and give me the insight and discernment I need to improve and grow.

I declare that I am strong, I am guided, and I am a child of God. I will navigate my personal growth and development with confidence and certainty, knowing that the Lord is always with me, providing me with the wisdom and understanding I need to become the best version of myself.

Ivon Valerie

Prayer Lifestyle

Ivon Valerie

Strength and Courage

Strength and courage are invaluable traits that can assist us in confronting our struggles head-on. This chapter will provide practical guidance on finding inner strength and bravery, defeating fear, and conquering obstacles confidently. We have provided prayers and declarations to help motivate you throughout this journey of self-discovery!

Prayer Lifestyle

Inner Strength

Praying for inner strength means asking God for the resilience and determination to face challenges and difficult situations with grace and perseverance. It's about asking God for the strength to overcome inner turmoil and negative emotions.

Scripture References

Isaiah 40:29-31 - "He gives strength to the weary and increases the power of the weak. Even youths grow tired and weary, and young men stumble and fall; but those who hope in the Lord will renew their strength. They will soar on wings like eagles; they will run and not grow weary, they will walk and not be faint."

2 Corinthians 12:9-10 - "But he said to me, 'My grace is sufficient for you, for my power is made perfect in weakness.' Therefore I will boast all the more gladly about my weaknesses, so that Christ's power may rest on me. That is why, for Christ's sake, I delight in weaknesses, in insults, in hardships, in persecutions, in difficulties. For when I am weak, then I am strong."

Philippians 4:13 - "I can do all things through Christ who strengthens me."

Inspirational/Motivational Quotes

"God's strength is the source of our inner strength." - Unknown

"Inner strength comes from trusting in God during difficult times." - Unknown

Prayer

Dear Lord,
I come before you today with a heavy heart, seeking your guidance and strength as I face the challenges and difficult situations that come my way. I ask that you grant me resilience and determination to face these struggles with grace and perseverance and to always trust in your plan for my life.

I ask for your strength as I confront my inner turmoil and negative emotions to overcome them and find peace. I ask for the courage to confront my fears and insecurities and let go of the things holding me back. I also ask for your strength as I navigate through difficult times and situations to find the silver lining in every cloud and never lose hope. I ask for the wisdom to understand that everything happens for a reason and that you are always with me, guiding me through the darkest times.

I ask for your strength as I strive to become a better person, overcome my flaws, and become a kinder, more compassionate, and more understanding individual. I trust in your ability to give me inner strength. I know that you are always with me, even in my darkest moments, and that you will never leave or forsake me. Amen.

Declaration

I declare that I am lifting those who need inner strength in prayer, including myself. I stand firmly in my faith, believing God will grant us the resilience and determination to face challenges and difficult situations with grace and perseverance. I trust in God's power to give us the strength to overcome any inner turmoil and negative emotions we may face and help us rise above any obstacles we encounter. I understand that life can be difficult and sometimes feel like we are fighting a losing battle. But I declare that we will come out victorious with God on our side. I trust in God's plan for our lives and know we are equipped with the strength to succeed.

I declare we will live a life full of strength, courage, and resilience. I am confident that we will be able to face whatever comes our way, knowing God is with us every step. I declare that we can overcome any obstacle, no matter how big or small, with the help of God's strength. I trust that we will face our fears and overcome them with God's guidance and protection.

I declare that we will be able to find peace and tranquility in chaos, knowing that God is with us. I trust that we will be able to find the strength we need to move forward, even in the darkest of times. I also declare that we can find the courage to keep going, even when things seem impossible. I trust we will find the resilience to keep fighting, even when the odds are against us.

I further declare that we will be able to find the inner strength we need to live a fulfilling and meaningful life. I trust that we will find the courage to chase our dreams and the resilience to make them a reality.

Ivon Valerie

I declare that with God's strength, we will be able to overcome any obstacle, face any challenge, and live a life full of strength, courage, and resilience.

Emotional Strength

Praying for emotional strength means asking God for the ability to cope with difficult emotions and maintain emotional stability. It's about asking God for the strength to overcome emotional turmoil and negative emotions.

Scripture References

Psalm 34:18 - "The Lord is close to the brokenhearted and saves those who are crushed in spirit."

John 14:27 - "Peace I leave with you; my peace I give you. I do not give to you as the world gives. Do not let your hearts be troubled and do not be afraid."

Philippians 4:6-7 - "Do not be anxious about anything, but in every situation, by prayer and petition, with thanksgiving, present your requests to God. And the peace of God, which transcends all understanding, will guard your hearts and your minds in Christ Jesus."

Inspirational/Motivational Quotes

"God's strength is the source of our emotional strength." - Unknown

"Emotional strength comes from trusting in God during difficult times." - Unknown

Prayer

Dear Lord,
I come before you today with a heavy heart, seeking your guidance and strength as I face the emotional turmoil and difficulties that come my way. I ask that you grant me the ability to cope with difficult emotions and maintain emotional stability, even in adversity.

I ask for your strength as I confront my inner turmoil and negative emotions to overcome them and find peace. I ask for the wisdom to understand my emotions and to process them healthily. I ask for the courage to confront my fears and insecurities and let go of the things holding me back emotionally. I pray for your strength as I navigate through difficult times and situations to find the silver lining in every cloud and never lose hope. I ask for the wisdom to understand that everything happens for a reason and that you are always with me, guiding me through the darkest times.

I pray for your strength as I strive to become more emotionally stable, overcome my emotional flaws, and become a kinder, more compassionate, and more understanding person. I trust in your ability to give me emotional strength, Lord. Amen.

Declaration

I declare that I seek emotional strength from God and align my thoughts and actions with His will. I declare that I am open to receiving guidance and support from God in overcoming emotional turmoil and negative emotions. I declare that I trust in God's love and care for me, and I have faith in His ability to provide me with the emotional strength I need to face any challenge that may come my way.

I declare that I will not let fear, doubt, or insecurity control my thoughts and emotions, but instead, I will choose to trust in God's promises and let His peace reign in my heart. I declare that I will speak positively and meditate on God's word to strengthen my faith and emotional well-being.

I am grateful for the emotional strength God is providing me, and I will use it to influence the lives of those around me positively. I declare that my emotional strength is rooted in my faith in God, and I am grateful for the blessings that come with it.

Physical Strength

Praying for physical strength means asking God for the ability to overcome physical limitations and maintain physical health. It's about asking God for the strength to overcome physical obstacles and to heal from illnesses or injuries.

Scripture References

Psalm 103:3 - "Praise the Lord, my soul; all my inmost being, praise his holy name."

Isaiah 40:31 - "But those who hope in the Lord will renew their strength. They will soar on wings like eagles; they will run and not grow weary, they will walk and not be faint."

1 Peter 5:10 - "And the God of all grace, who called you to his eternal glory in Christ, after you have suffered a little while, will himself restore you and make you strong, firm and steadfast."

Inspirational/Motivational Quotes

"God's strength is the source of our physical strength." - Unknown

"Physical strength comes from trusting in God during difficult times." - Unknown

Prayer

Dear Lord,

As I come before you today, I lift my heart in humility and gratitude for all you have done for me. I ask for your strength and guidance in my physical well-being, as I know that without you, I am nothing. I ask for your protection and guidance in maintaining my physical health, overcoming any illnesses or injuries, and facing any physical limitations or obstacles that may come my way. I trust in your healing power and your ability to give me the strength to overcome any challenges.

I pray for the wisdom to make wise decisions regarding my physical health and well-being. I ask for your guidance in seeking the best medical treatment and care when needed and for the strength to follow through on any necessary changes or treatments. I pray for the courage to face any difficult diagnoses or prognoses with grace and faith, knowing that you are with me every step.

I ask for your blessings on my body so that it may be strong and healthy to carry out your will for my life. I pray for strength in my mind and emotions to handle daily stress and demands with peace and joy. I ask for the wisdom to make wise choices in my diet, exercise, and overall lifestyle, so that I may be able to care for my body in the way you would have me do.

Most of all, Lord, I ask for your presence and guidance. I pray that you will be with me always, that I may feel your loving embrace and know your peace in every moment. I trust in your ability to guide and direct my path, and I pray that you will give me the strength and courage to follow your will for my life, no matter where it may lead.

Thank you for your love and your faithfulness, Lord. I pray that you will continue to guide and protect me in all aspects of my physical well-being and that I may always give you the glory and praise for the blessings you have given me. Amen.

Declaration

I declare that I am now receiving physical strength from the Lord. I declare that I will continue to stand in faith, trusting God's ability to help me overcome physical limitations and maintain good health. I believe that God will give me the strength to overcome any physical obstacles that come my way and to heal from any illnesses or injuries. I trust in the power of prayer to bring physical strength to my body.

I declare that I will listen to my body and take care of it, knowing it is a temple of the Lord. I will nourish it with nutritious food, exercise regularly, and get enough rest. I will also surround myself with positive influences and avoid anything that may harm my physical health. I declare that I am strong in the Lord and in the power of His might.

I am confident I can do all things through Christ who strengthens me. I am blessed with good health and strength, and I will thank the Lord for it every day. I declare that my body is healed and made whole.

Courage To Face Difficult Situations

Asking for courage in prayer is about seeking the strength and confidence to face difficult situations, whether it be personal or professional. It's about asking God for the courage to face challenges and overcome obstacles.

Scripture References

Joshua 1:9 - "Be strong and courageous. Do not be afraid; do not be discouraged, for the Lord your God will be with you wherever you go."

Psalm 27:14 - "Wait for the Lord; be strong and take heart and wait for the Lord."

2 Timothy 1:7 - "For the Spirit God gave us does not make us timid, but gives us power, love and self-discipline."

Inspirational/Motivational Quotes

"Courage is not the absence of fear, but the triumph over it." - Nelson Mandela

"Courage doesn't always roar. Sometimes courage is the quiet voice at the end of the day saying, 'I will try again tomorrow'." - Mary Anne Radmacher

Prayer

Dear Lord,
I come before you today with a humble heart, seeking your guidance and protection in difficult situations. I ask that you give me the courage to face any challenges that may come my way and have the strength and confidence to overcome them. I pray for the wisdom to make the right choices and the determination to see them through.

I pray for your guidance as I navigate life's ups and downs and for the inner strength to persevere through difficult times. I pray for the ability to face challenging situations with hope and determination, knowing I can overcome any obstacle with your guidance and support.

I ask for the courage to take risks and step out of my comfort zone, knowing I can accomplish anything with you. I pray for the strength to face my fears and overcome any limitations that may hold me back. I trust your loving and sovereign hand to guide, protect, and give me the courage and strength to navigate life's difficulties. I know that with you, I can face anything. Amen.

Declaration

I declare that I am empowered with the courage to face difficult situations. I declare that I will stand firm in my faith, believing in God's ability to provide me with the strength and confidence I need to overcome any obstacles that come my way. I am determined to face challenges with hope and determination, knowing that with God's guidance, I can overcome anything that comes my way.

I trust in the power of God to give me the courage to face difficult situations head-on and come out victorious. I am claiming this courage for myself, knowing that with God's help, I can do all things. I will not be held back by fear or doubt but will press forward with strength and courage, knowing that God is guiding me every step.

Courage To Take Action

Praying for courage to take action is about asking God for the determination and willpower to take action toward something. It's about asking God for the courage to pursue our goals and dreams, overcome procrastination, and make difficult decisions.

Scripture References

Ecclesiastes 3:1 - "There is a time for everything, and a season for every activity under the heavens."

James 2:17 - "In the same way, faith by itself, if it is not accompanied by action, is dead."

Philippians 4:13 - "I can do all things through Christ who strengthens me."

Inspirational/Motivational Quotes

"Action is the foundational key to all success." - Pablo Picasso

"Courage is not having the strength to go on; it is going on when you don't have the strength." - Theodore Roosevelt

Prayer

Dear Lord,
I come before you today, humbly seeking your guidance and strength. I ask that you give me the courage to face the difficult situations that come my way. I pray for the strength and confidence to overcome obstacles and challenges. I ask for the courage to face difficult situations with hope and determination, knowing that you always lead me.

I pray I will possess the determination and willpower to pursue and accomplish my goals and dreams. I pray for the courage to overcome procrastination and make difficult decisions that will lead me closer to achieving my aspirations. I trust your ability to give me the courage to take action and make positive changes in my life.

I pray for your guidance and protection as I journey through life. I thank you for the blessings you have bestowed upon me and for your continued presence in my life. I trust in your love and grace, and I am grateful for the courage you give me to face the unknown. Amen.

Declaration

I declare that I am taking control of my courage and determination. I trust in God's ability to help me find the courage and willpower to pursue my goals and dreams, overcome procrastination and make difficult decisions. I declare that through prayer and my faith in God, I will be given the courage to take action toward my aspirations and aspirations. I trust in

Ivon Valerie

the power of God to bring forth the courage to take action and move toward my purpose. I will no longer be held back by fear or doubt; I am confident in my abilities and trust in God's plan. I will take action toward my goals with determination and courage, knowing that God is guiding me every step of the way.

Prayer Lifestyle

Ivon Valerie

Purity and Holiness

Achieving purity and holiness are essential components of our spiritual growth. Purity is defined by a clean conscience and the absence of impure thoughts, while holiness refers to being devoted to God's will. This chapter explores how one can be purer in life choices and cultivate greater dedication to Him through prayers, declarations, meditations, and other practices. Our goal should be cultivating an unblemished heart that sets us apart from others as we grow in His grace.

Purity of Heart

Praying for purity of heart is asking God to cleanse our hearts from impurities, such as sin and selfishness. It's about asking God to help us have a pure and undivided heart focused on loving and serving Him.

Scripture References

Psalm 51:10 - "Create in me a pure heart, O God, and renew a steadfast spirit within me."

Matthew 5:8 - "Blessed are the pure in heart, for they will see God."

1 John 3:3 - "Everyone who has this hope in him purifies himself, just as he is pure."

Inspirational/Motivational Quotes

"Purity and simplicity are the two wings with which man soars above the earth and all temporary nature." - Thomas a Kempis

"The greater the purity, the greater the power." - Mahatma Gandhi

Prayer

Dear Lord,

I come before you today humbly seeking Your guidance and direction in purifying my heart. I ask for Your forgiveness for the sins I have committed, and for the moments I have allowed selfishness to take hold of me. I ask that You cleanse my heart and renew my mind, filling me with Your love and grace.

I pray for the strength and determination to resist temptations and to turn away from actions and thoughts that do not align with Your will. I ask for Your guidance in learning to love and serve You with a pure, undivided heart.

I trust in Your power to transform me and to make me into a better person, one with a pure heart that reflects Your image. I pray that through this process of purification, I will become more like You and be able to bring glory to Your name. Amen.

Declaration

I declare that all those who seek purity of heart, including myself, will receive it now. I believe in the power and grace of God to cleanse our hearts of impurities, such as sin and selfishness. I trust in His ability to give us a pure, undivided heart focused on loving and serving Him.

I acknowledge that our hearts can be clouded by the distractions and temptations of this world, but I declare that we can be transformed and renewed through prayer and obedience to God's word. I declare that as we surrender ourselves fully to

Prayer Lifestyle

Him, He will work in us and through us to bring forth the purity of heart that we so desire.

I declare that this purity of heart is not just a one-time event but an ongoing process of conforming to the image of Jesus Christ. I trust in the power of the Holy Spirit to guide and lead us in this journey of sanctification.

I also declare that as we receive this purity of heart, we will become beacons of light in a dark world, shining the love and truth of Jesus Christ to those around us. I declare that through our pure hearts, many will be drawn to the saving knowledge of Jesus Christ.

Ivon Valerie

Purity of Mind

Praying for purity of mind is asking God to help us have a mind free from impurities, such as negative thoughts, worries, and fears. It's about asking God to help us have a mind focused on Him, His will, and His ways.

Scripture References

Philippians 4:8 - "Finally, brothers and sisters, whatever is true, whatever is noble, whatever is right, whatever is pure, whatever is lovely, whatever is admirable—if anything is excellent or praiseworthy—think about such things."

2 Corinthians 10:5 - "We demolish arguments and every pretension that sets itself up against the knowledge of God, and we take captive every thought to make it obedient to Christ."

Isaiah 26:3 - "You will keep in perfect peace those whose minds are steadfast, because they trust in you."

Inspirational/Motivational Quotes

"A pure mind is a pure life." - Mahatma Gandhi

"The mind is everything; what you think, you become." - Buddha

Prayer

Dear Lord,
I come before you today with a humble heart, seeking your guidance and strength in my journey toward purity of mind and heart. I ask that you would cleanse my mind of impurities such as negative thoughts, worries, and fears that cloud my thoughts and distract me from your will. I ask for the wisdom, discernment to recognize and reject these impurities and the strength to focus my mind on you, your will, and your ways.

I ask that you would give me a pure, undivided heart focused on loving and serving you. I know that I am not perfect and that I have strayed from your path in the past. I ask for your forgiveness and grace as I strive to become a better person who is more like you.

I trust your ability to give me the strength and guidance I need to overcome the impurities in my mind and heart. With your help, I can achieve purity of mind and heart and become the person you created me to be. Thank you, Lord, for your guidance and love. Amen.

Declaration

I declare in faith that I am lifting those who need purity of mind in prayer. I stand in faith in God's ability to help them have a mind free from impurities, such as negative thoughts, worries, and fears. I declare that God will give them a mind focused on Him, His will, and His ways. I trust in the power of prayer to bring forth purity of mind.

Ivon Valerie

I recognize that our minds can be cluttered with the distractions and pressures of this world. Still, I declare that through renewing our minds with God's word and focusing on what is true, noble, right, pure, lovely, admirable, excellent, and praiseworthy, we can have a clear and pure mind.

I declare that renewing our minds is a daily process, and I commit to making it a priority. I trust in the power of the Holy Spirit to guide and lead me in this journey of sanctification. I also declare that as we receive purity of mind, we can hear God's voice more clearly and discern His will for our lives. I declare that through our pure minds, we can walk in the fullness of God's plan and purpose for our lives.

Prayer Lifestyle

Purity of Body

Praying for purity of body is about asking God to help us take care of our physical bodies, which are His temple. It's about asking God to help us free our bodies from impurities, such as unhealthy habits, addictions, and temptations.

Scripture References

1 Corinthians 6:19-20 - "Do you not know that your bodies are temples of the Holy Spirit, who is in you, whom you have received from God? You are not your own; you were bought at a price. Therefore honor God with your bodies."

1 Thessalonians 4:3-4 - "It is God's will that you should be sanctified: that you should avoid sexual immorality; that each of you should learn to control your own body in a way that is holy and honorable."

Proverbs 4:23 - "Above all else, guard your heart, for everything you do flows from it."

Inspirational/Motivational Quotes

"The greatest wealth is to live content with little." - Plato

"The body is a sacred garment. It's your first and last garment; it is what you enter life in and what you depart life with, and it should be treated with honor." - Martha Graham

Prayer

Dear Lord,
I come before you today humbly seeking your guidance and strength in my journey toward purity. I ask that you cleanse my heart from impurities such as sin and selfishness and give me a pure, undivided heart focused on loving and serving you. I ask for your help purifying my mind of negative thoughts, worries, and fears. I ask for your help in purifying my body, taking care of it as your temple, and keeping it free from impurities such as unhealthy habits, addictions, and temptations.

I confess my weaknesses and shortcomings and ask for your forgiveness and grace. I trust in your ability to give me the strength and willpower to overcome these impurities and to live a life that is pleasing to you. I thank you, Lord, for the gift of salvation and the power of the Holy Spirit that dwells within me. I pray that you will use me as a vessel to be a shining light of purity in this world. Amen.

Declaration

I, [Your Name], declare with conviction and faith that I am lifting in prayer those who need purity of body. I stand in faith in God's ability to help them take care of their physical bodies, which are His temple. I declare that God will help them free their bodies from impurities, such as unhealthy habits, addictions, and temptations. I trust in the power of prayer to bring forth purity of body.

I acknowledge that our bodies can be tempted by the desires and pleasures of this world, but I declare that through honoring God with our bodies by caring for them and keeping them free from impurities, we can have a pure and healthy body.

I declare that taking care of our bodies is a daily responsibility, and I commit to prioritizing it. I trust in the power of the Holy Spirit to guide and lead me in this journey of sanctification.

I also declare that as we receive purity of body, we will be able to serve God and others more effectively. I declare that through our pure body, we can glorify God and be a living testimony of His goodness and faithfulness.
In Jesus's name, I make this declaration for myself and all those seeking purity of body. Amen.

Ivon Valerie

Holiness in Daily Living

Praying for holiness in daily living is about asking God to help us live a life that is set apart for Him and His ways. It's about asking God to help us make choices that align with His will and obey His commands.

Scripture References

1 Peter 1:15-16 - "But just as he who called you is holy, so be holy in all you do; for it is written: "Be holy, because I am holy.""

Romans 12:1-2 - "Therefore, I urge you, brothers and sisters, in view of God's mercy, to offer your bodies as a living sacrifice, holy and pleasing to God—this is your true and proper worship. Do not conform to the pattern of this world, but be transformed by the renewing of your mind. Then you will be able to test and approve what God's will is—his good, pleasing and perfect will."

Colossians 3:12-14 - "Therefore, as God's chosen people, holy and dearly loved, clothe yourselves with compassion, kindness, humility, gentleness and patience. Bear with each other and forgive one another if any of you has a grievance against someone. Forgive as the Lord forgave you. And over all these virtues put on love, which binds them all together in perfect unity."

Inspirational/Motivational Quote

"Holiness is not the way to God, it is God." - J.I. Packer

Prayer

Dear Lord,
I come before you today humbly seeking your guidance and strength. I ask that you grant me the grace to lead a holy and set-apart life devoted to your will and ways. Please help me to rid myself of impurities in my thoughts, actions, and habits that do not align with your teachings. Please give me the courage and determination to resist temptations and overcome obstacles that stand in the way of my walk with you.

I pray for the strength to love and serve others selflessly and to act with integrity and honesty in all that I do. I ask that you give me the wisdom to make choices that honor you and the humility to admit when I fall short.

I trust in your ability to sanctify me, to make me holy, and to mold me into the person you have called me to be. I pray for your continued guidance, protection, and blessings as I strive to live a life that is pleasing to you. Amen.

Declaration

I declare that I am praying for those who need holiness in daily living. I stand in faith in God's ability to help them live a life set apart for Him and His ways. I declare that God will help them make choices that align with His will and obey His commands. I trust in the power of prayer to bring forth holiness in daily living.

I recognize that it can be challenging to live a life that is holy and pleasing to God in all aspects of our lives. Still, I declare that we can live holiness through the power of the Holy Spirit and by striving to obey God's commands and make choices that align with His will.

I declare that living a holy life is not just about avoiding sin but also about living a life of love, joy, peace, patience, kindness, goodness, faithfulness, gentleness, and self-control. I commit to making these fruits of the Spirit a priority.

I also declare that as we receive holiness in daily living, we will be able to witness and share the love of Christ more effectively with those around us. I declare that through our holy living, we can glorify God and be a living testimony of His grace and love.

Personal Sanctification

Praying for personal sanctification is asking God to help us become more like Him in our thoughts, words, and actions. It's about asking God to help us become holy and set apart for Him and His ways.

Scripture References

2 Corinthians 3:18 - "And we all, who with unveiled faces contemplate the Lord's glory, are being transformed into his image with ever-increasing glory, which comes from the Lord, who is the Spirit."

Hebrews 12:14 - "Make every effort to live in peace with everyone and to be holy; without holiness no one will see the Lord."

1 John 3:2-3 - "Dear friends, now we are children of God, and what we will be has not yet been made known. But we know that when Christ appears, we shall be like him, for we shall see him as he is. Everyone who has this hope in him purifies himself, just as he is pure."

Inspirational/Motivational Quotes

"The ultimate end of all spiritual striving is not to get a new experience but to become a new kind of person." - A.W. Tozer

"Sanctification is the process of becoming holy, and holiness is becoming like Jesus." - R.C. Sproul

Prayer

Dear Lord,
I come before you today to lift myself and ask for your help in becoming more like you. I ask for your guidance and strength as I strive for personal sanctification in my thoughts, words, and actions. I recognize that without your help, I cannot truly become holy and set apart for you and your ways.

I ask that you renew my mind and give me a greater understanding of your will and ways. Please help me crucify my flesh and its desires and put it on your mind and your ways.
I ask that you empower me to resist temptations and overcome sin. Please help me to be obedient to your commands and to walk in your ways.

I ask that you would empower me to love you with all my heart, soul, mind, and strength and to love my neighbors as myself.
I trust in your grace, your power, and your ability to transform me into the image of your son, Jesus Christ. With your help, I can become the person you created me to be and live the life you have planned for me. Amen.

Declaration

I declare with conviction and faith that I am lifting those who seek personal sanctification in prayer. I stand in faith in God's ability to help them become more like Him in their thoughts, words, and actions. I declare God will help them become holy and set apart for Him and His ways. I trust in the power of prayer to bring forth personal sanctification.

I understand that personal sanctification is a lifelong process, and it is not something we can achieve on our own. Only through the power of the Holy Spirit and by submitting to God's will can we become more like Jesus in our thoughts, words, and actions.

I declare that as we seek personal sanctification, we will be transformed by renewing our minds. We can discern God's will for our lives and make choices that align with His will. We will be able to resist the temptations of the world and the devil and walk in the power of the Holy Spirit.

I also declare that as we become more like Jesus in our thoughts, words, and actions, we will be able to love God and others more deeply. We will be able to bear much fruit for God's kingdom and be a shining light in this dark world.

Ivon Valerie

Prayer Lifestyle

Ivon Valerie

Grace and Mercy

God's grace and mercy are integral elements of His character. Grace is God's unmerited favor, while mercy represents His kindness and understanding toward us. This chapter plays a significant role in teaching readers about the importance of grace and mercy in their lives by providing prayers and declarations that explain how we can experience God's grace and mercy. Love for yourself, forgiving others, and extending compassion to those around you are just a few of the strategies that readers will learn.

Prayer Lifestyle

Grace in Times of Need

In times of need, we often feel overwhelmed and unsure of how to move forward. We may feel like we are failing or that we have exhausted all of our resources. In these moments, it is important to turn to God and ask for His grace. Grace is unmerited favor; it is something that we do not deserve but that God freely gives to us. When we ask for grace, we acknowledge our need for God's help and submit ourselves to His will.

Scripture References

Ephesians 2:8-9 - "For it is by grace you have been saved, through faith—and this is not from yourselves, it is the gift of God—not by works, so that no one can boast."

Hebrews 4:16 - "Let us then approach God's throne of grace with confidence, so that we may receive mercy and find grace to help us in our time of need."

James 4:6 - "But he gives more grace. Therefore it says, "God opposes the proud, but shows favor to the humble.""

Inspirational/Motivational Quotes

"Grace is the beauty of form under the influence of freedom." - Friedrich Schiller

"Grace is the free and unmerited favor of God, as manifested in the salvation of sinners and the bestowal of blessings." - Charles Haddon Spurgeon

"Grace is the enabling gift of God not to sin. Grace is power, not just pardon." - John MacArthur

Prayer

Dear God,
I come before you today in need of your grace. I am feeling overwhelmed and unsure of how to move forward. I struggle with doubt and fear and desperately need your guidance and support.

I know you are always with me and see every part of my life. You know the depths of my pain and the struggles that I am facing. And I trust that you are working together for my good, even when I cannot see how.

I pray that you will give me the strength and wisdom I need to navigate my circumstances. I pray that you will give me the courage to face my fears and the determination to keep moving forward. I pray that you will give me peace, even in the storm.
I pray you will give me your grace, unending love, and mercy. I pray that you will forgive me for all the times I failed and fell short. I pray that you will give me your healing for all of the wounds that I carry.

I pray you will be my rock, stronghold, and shelter in the storm. I pray that you will be my guide, light, and hope. I pray that you will be my everything, my all in all.

I trust in your love and ability to work together for my good. Amen.

Declaration

I declare with conviction and faith that I receive God's grace. I understand that God's grace is a gift, unearned and undeserved, that He freely gives to all who believe in Him. I declare that in my times of need, I will turn to God and ask for His grace. I believe God's grace is sufficient for me, and His power is perfect in my weakness. I trust that God will work all things together for my good and that even in my struggles, He will bring about a greater good for His glory.

I declare that I will be a reflection of God's grace to those around me. I understand that as a recipient of God's grace, I must share it with others. I will be a vessel of God's grace, showing love, kindness, and forgiveness to all around me, just as God has shown them to me.

I also declare that I will be a student of God's grace, continually seeking to deepen my understanding of it and how it applies to my life. I will meditate on God's word, which is full of grace, and ask for the Holy Spirit's guidance in understanding and applying it to my life.

Ivon Valerie

Mercy in Times of Failure

Failure is an inevitable part of life, and it can be difficult to move on from mistakes and disappointments. In these moments, it is important to turn to God and ask for His mercy. Mercy is not getting what we deserve; it demonstrates God's love and compassion toward us, even when we have fallen short. When we ask for mercy, we acknowledge our faults and ask for God's forgiveness and grace to help us overcome our failures.

Scripture References

Psalm 51:1-2 "Have mercy on me, O God, according to your unfailing love; according to your great compassion blot out my transgressions. Wash away all my iniquity and cleanse me from my sin."

Isaiah 55:7 "Let the wicked forsake his way and the evil man his thoughts. Let him turn to the Lord, and he will have mercy on him, and to our God, for he will freely pardon."

Micah 7:18 "Who is a God like you, who pardons sin and forgives the transgression of the remnant of his inheritance? You do not stay angry forever but delight to show mercy."

Inspirational/Motivational Quotes

"Mercy is the noblest attribute of God." - St. Thomas Aquinas

"Mercy is the love that we extend to those who have no claim on us." - J.D. Greear

"Mercy is the face that love wears when it meets imperfection." - Fulton J. Sheen

Prayer

Dear Lord,
I come before you today with a heavy heart, filled with regret and disappointment. I have failed to live up to your expectations and am deeply remorseful for my actions. I have made mistakes and poor choices that have hurt others and myself, and I am in need of your mercy and forgiveness.

I humbly ask for your grace to help me overcome my failures and to become the person you created me to be. I know I can't change the past, but with your help, I can change my future. I ask for your guidance and wisdom as I strive to make things right and to walk in your way.

I trust in your love and ability to turn my mistakes into something good, and I pray that you will give me the strength and courage to face the consequences of my actions with humility and repentance. I pray for the healing of those whom I have hurt and for the restoration of any relationships that have been damaged. I am fully aware that I am not worthy of your forgiveness, but I ask for it in the name of Jesus, knowing that his sacrifice on the cross has made it possible for me to receive it. I pray you will cleanse me of all unrighteousness and renew my mind and heart so I may walk in your ways.

I pray that you will give me your mercy in my time of need and that you will continue to be my rock and my salvation. I pray that you will be my guide and my light as I strive to follow you and live a life that is pleasing to you. I thank you for your love and grace. Amen.

Declaration

I declare that I am fully reliant on God's mercy. I understand that I am a sinner and that without His mercy, I would be doomed to eternal separation. But I declare that I trust in the truth that God's mercy is new every morning and that His love endures forever.

I will seek His forgiveness daily and strive to live a life that reflects His mercy. I declare that I will extend grace and forgiveness to others, just as God has shown grace and forgiveness to me.

I understand that my ability to show mercy to others directly results from the mercy I have received from God. I will prioritize extending that same mercy to those around me, reflecting the mercy of our Lord and Savior, Jesus Christ.

Prayer Lifestyle

Grace and Mercy for Others

We all need God's grace and mercy, and it is important to lift our loved ones and those around us in prayer, asking God to extend His grace and mercy to them. This can be a powerful way to support others during difficult times and to help them find the strength and forgiveness they need to overcome their challenges.

Scripture References

James 5:16: "Therefore confess your sins to each other and pray for each other so that you may be healed. The prayer of a righteous person is powerful and effective."

1 Timothy 2:1-2: "I urge, then, first of all, that petitions, prayers, intercession and thanksgiving be made for all people—for kings and all those in authority, that we may live peaceful and quiet lives in all godliness and holiness. This is good, and pleases God our Savior."

Ephesians 6:18: "And pray in the Spirit on all occasions with all kinds of prayers and requests. With this in mind, be alert and always keep on praying for all the Lord's people."

Inspirational/Motivational Quotes

"Grace is not simply leniency when we have failed, but the enabling gift of God not to fail." - John Piper

"Mercy is the rain that falls on the parched earth, providing new life and growth. Grace is the sunshine that warms the soil, encouraging the seed to sprout and flourish." - Unknown

Prayer

Dear Lord,
I lift my loved ones and those around me in prayer today. I ask that you extend your grace and mercy to them as they face difficult times and challenges. I know that they are going through a hard time, and I pray that you will be with them every step of the way. I pray that you will give them comfort and peace in their troubles and guide them in the path you have for them.

I ask that you give them the strength and forgiveness they need to overcome their struggles. I pray that you will give them the wisdom to make the right decisions and the courage to face their fears. I pray that you will give them the peace that only you can, even when they feel like they can't go on.

I pray you will protect them from harm and anything that seeks to harm them. I pray you will give them the favor and blessings they need to succeed. I pray that you will bring them into a deeper relationship with you and that they will come to know you more intimately.

Prayer Lifestyle

I trust in your love and your ability to work all things for good. I know that you are sovereign and have a plan for their lives. I pray that they will see your hand at work in their lives and that they will come to trust you more deeply. Amen.

Declaration

I declare that I will lift my loved ones and those around me in prayer daily, asking for God's grace and mercy to be upon them. I declare that I will have faith in the power of prayer and believe that God's grace and mercy will be extended to them through it. I declare that I trust in God's ability to work all things for good and that He will guide and protect my loved ones through difficult times.

I trust that God will give them strength and peace during hard times. I declare that I will continue to pray for others and to be a vessel of grace and mercy to those around me, showing them love and kindness, just as God has shown me. I will reflect God's grace and mercy in my actions and words, being a light in the darkness for those who need it. And I will trust in God's timing and plan for their lives and mine.

Ivon Valerie

Grace and Mercy for the World

Praying for grace and mercy for the world is an important aspect of our faith as believers. We are called to love and care for our neighbors, including those suffering in other parts of the world.

Scripture References:

Isaiah 42:3 "A bruised reed he will not break, and a smoldering wick he will not snuff out. In faithfulness he will bring forth justice."

Matthew 5:7 "Blessed are the merciful, for they shall obtain mercy."

Romans 2:4 "Or do you show contempt for the riches of his kindness, forbearance and patience, not realizing that God's kindness is intended to lead you to repentance?"

Inspirational/Motivational Quotes:

"Mercy is the child of grace, and grace is the child of love." - Saint Augustine

"Mercy is the noblest attribute of God." - Thomas Watson

"Mercy is the love that sees a person in the midst of their sin and still loves them." - Rick Warren

Prayer

Dear Lord,

I come before you today, lifting those who need your grace and mercy in prayer. I know that your love and compassion are not limited to just a few but are available to all people. I pray that those hurting and in pain may experience your healing touch and find comfort in your loving arms.

I pray that those struggling and in poverty may know they are not alone and that you are their provider and sustainer. I pray that you would give them the resources they need to meet their basic needs and that you would give them hope for a better future.

I pray that marginalized and oppressed people know you see them and care for them. I pray that you would give them the strength and courage to stand up for themselves and that you would bring justice and righteousness to their situation.

I also pray that I may be a vessel of your grace and mercy to those around me. I pray that I will have eyes to see the needs of others and a heart to respond with compassion. I pray that I will step out of my comfort zone and be a light in the darkness.

Your grace and mercy are not limited and available to all. I pray that those who need your grace and mercy will tangibly experience it and that they will know that you are the one who truly cares for them. Amen.

Ivon Valerie

Declaration

I declare that the world is receiving God's mercy and grace. I declare that the broken and the lost are being lifted and healed by the love and compassion of our Lord. I declare that God's grace and mercy bring justice and righteousness to the lives of the poor, the hurting, the marginalized, and the oppressed.

I declare that through the power of prayer and the work of the Holy Spirit, the world will see the goodness and love of God and be drawn to Him. I declare that I will actively work to be a vessel of God's grace and mercy in the world through my words, actions, and deeds, and I will continue to pray for the world to experience the love and compassion of our Lord. I trust that God's grace and mercy will bring about a world filled with love, peace, and righteousness.

Prayer Lifestyle

Increase of Grace and Mercy in the Church

Praying for increased grace and mercy in the Church means asking God to fill His Church with His unmerited favor and compassionate forgiveness. It means asking for a deeper understanding and application of the principles of grace and mercy in believers' lives and the Church.

Scripture References:

Ephesians 4:29 "Let no corrupting talk come out of your mouths, but only such as is good for building up, as fits the occasion, that it may give grace to those who hear."

Colossians 4:5-6 "Walk in wisdom toward outsiders, making the best use of the time. Let your speech always be gracious, seasoned with salt, so that you may know how you ought to answer each person."

James 3:17 "But the wisdom from above is first pure, then peaceable, gentle, open to reason, full of mercy and good fruits, impartial and sincere."

Inspirational/Motivational Quotes

"Grace is the beauty of form under the influence of freedom." - Friedrich Nietzsche

"The Church is not a museum for saints but a hospital for sinners." - Augustine of Hippo

"The Church is not a human society; it is a divine society, the Body of Christ." - J. I. Packer

Prayer

Dear Lord,
I come before you today, praying to the Church and the body of Christ. I know the Church is your Bride, and I pray that it reflects your love and grace to the world.

I ask that you increase the grace and mercy within the Church, that it would be a place of refuge for those who are hurting and in need. I pray that the Church would be a place where people can experience your love and compassion and that they would find healing and restoration for their brokenness and loss.

I pray that the Church would be a place where people can find forgiveness and salvation through Jesus Christ and that it would be a beacon of hope and light in an often dark and lost world. I pray that the Church would be a place where people can find community and support and that they would be encouraged and uplifted by the love of others.

I also pray for myself that I would be a reflection of your grace and mercy within the Church. I pray that I would be a vessel of your love and compassion to others and that I would be a source of hope and encouragement to those around me. I pray that I will be willing to be a part of the Church and to serve in the body of Christ.

Your grace and mercy are not limited and available to all. I pray that the Church would reflect that grace and mercy to the world and that through it, many would come to know Jesus Christ as their savior. Amen.

Declaration

I declare that I believe in God's grace and mercy. I declare that I will seek God's grace and mercy in my times of need and extend it to those around me. I declare that I trust in God's grace and mercy to bring healing and restoration to my life and those around me.

I declare that I will strive to live a pleasing life to God and be an example of His grace and mercy to others. I declare that I will be a light in the darkness, shining forth God's love and compassion to all I encounter. I will be an instrument of God's grace and mercy, allowing Him to work through me to bring about His will and kingdom on earth.

I declare that the Church will be a beacon of God's grace and mercy, a sanctuary for the hurting and the lost, and a place of hope and salvation for all who enter. I declare that the world will see the love and mercy of God in the Church and that many will be drawn to His love and redemption.

Ivon Valerie

Prayer Lifestyle

Ivon Valerie

Mental Health and Emotional Well-being

Mental and emotional health are vital parts of our lives. This chapter gives useful information on the importance of taking care of your mental and emotional well-being, such as prayers to help you find stability within yourself, faith-filled declarations that can help reduce stress levels, and other techniques to cultivate more positive emotions in life.

Relief From Anxiety

Anxiety is a normal human emotion that can become overwhelming and debilitating when it becomes chronic. When we are anxious, we can feel stuck in a cycle of worry and fear that can prevent us from living our lives to the fullest. It is important to pray for relief from anxiety, asking God to give us the peace and calm we need to overcome our struggles.

Scripture References

Isaiah 41:10: "So do not fear, for I am with you; do not be dismayed, for I am your God. I will strengthen you and help you; I will uphold you with my righteous right hand."

Psalm 94:19: "When anxiety was great within me, your consolation brought me joy."

Matthew 6:27: "Can any one of you by worrying add a single hour to your life?"

Inspirational/Motivational Quotes

"Anxiety is the dizziness of freedom." - Søren Kierkegaard

"Anxiety is a thin stream of fear trickling through the mind. If encouraged, it cuts a channel into which all other thoughts are drained." - Arthur Somers Roche

"Anxiety is a natural and normally positive emotion. It is your body's way of preparing to face an important challenge or 'fight or flight' response." - Dr. Phil McGraw

Prayer

Dear Lord,
I am filled with anxiety and fear today, seeking peace and comfort. I know that I can easily become overwhelmed by worry, and I ask for your calm presence to surround me and give me the strength I need to face my struggles.

I pray for the courage to trust your guidance and protection, even in uncertainty. Help me to remember that you are always with me and that your love is more powerful than any fear. I ask for your wisdom and discernment as I navigate through difficult situations, and I trust in your ability to work all things for good. Please give me the grace to trust in your plan, even when it is unclear to me.

Lord, I know that anxiety can be a heavy burden, but I trust your promise of peace and restoration. Help me rest in your presence and let go of my worries, knowing that you are always in control. May your love and grace fill me with peace and hope, and I find the courage to face each day confidently. Amen.

Declaration

I declare that I am surrendering my anxiety to God. I acknowledge that it has been a source of discomfort and uncertainty in my life, and I choose to trust in God's sovereignty and love. I declare that I will not allow anxiety to dictate my thoughts and actions but instead trust God's promise to give me peace and calm.

I declare that I seek God's wisdom and discernment in difficult situations. I trust in His ability to work all things for good, and I will not lose hope in His plans for my life. I know that with God on my side, I am never alone and equipped to handle any obstacle that comes my way.

I declare that I trust in God's love and provision, even in the midst of uncertainty. I trust God for the courage to face my fears and the peace that surpasses all understanding to guard my heart and mind. I declare I have a clear and steady mind to hear God's voice guiding me and see His hand at work.

I declare that I will not allow anxiety to take control of my life. Instead, I choose to focus on God's goodness and His faithfulness. I will meditate on His word and remind myself of His promises. I will seek refuge in Him and trust in His protection.

I am grateful for God's love and the peace that He offers. I declare that I will trust in Him, no matter what. I know He is always with me, and I am confident in His ability to heal and restore my soul. I give all my worries to God and trust in His ability to bring comfort and calm to my life.

Ivon Valerie

Relief From Depression

Depression is a serious mental health condition that can cause sadness, hopelessness, and worthlessness. Finding the motivation and energy to go through daily life can be difficult, and it can be hard to find joy in things that once brought happiness. It is important to pray for relief from depression, asking God for healing and strength to overcome these feelings.

Scripture References

Psalm 34:17-18: "The righteous cry out, and the Lord hears them; he delivers them from all their troubles. The Lord is close to the brokenhearted and saves those who are crushed in spirit."

Isaiah 61:1-3: "The Spirit of the Sovereign Lord is on me, because the Lord has anointed me to proclaim good news to the poor. He has sent me to bind up the brokenhearted, to proclaim freedom for the captives and release from darkness for the prisoners, to proclaim the year of the Lord's favor and the day of vengeance of our God, to comfort all who mourn, and provide for those who grieve in Zion— to bestow on them a crown of beauty instead of ashes, the oil of joy instead of mourning, and a garment of praise instead of a spirit of despair. They will be called oaks of righteousness, a planting of the Lord for the display of his splendor."

Jeremiah 31:13: "Then young women will dance and be glad, young men and old as well. I will turn their mourning into gladness; I will give them comfort and joy instead of sorrow."

Inspirational/Motivational Quotes

"You yourself, as much as anybody in the entire universe, deserve your love and affection." - Buddha

"Depression is the inability to construct a future." - Rollo May

"The best way out of a difficult situation is through it." - Walt Disney

Prayer

Dear Lord,
I come before you today, seeking your comfort and healing for my broken heart. I have been feeling overwhelmed by depression, feeling sad, hopeless, and worthless. I ask for your strength to overcome these feelings and bring me peace and happiness again.

I pray for the motivation and energy to face each day and the ability to find joy in the things that once brought me happiness. Lord, this is a difficult journey, but I trust your love and grace to guide me through it.

I ask for your wisdom and discernment as I navigate this dark path, and I trust in your ability to work all things for good. Please help me to see the light in the darkness and to trust in your promise of hope and restoration. Lord, I know that I am not alone in this struggle and that you are always with me.

Please give me the courage to reach out for help and support, and help me to find comfort in your loving arms. May your peace fill my heart and comfort me in my darkest moments. I pray for your healing hand to touch my heart and restore me to the person I was created to be. I desire to find joy in your presence and for my heart to be filled with hope again. Amen.

Declaration

I declare that I am turning to God, seeking His healing and relief of my depression. I acknowledge that these feelings have weighed heavy on my heart and mind, and I trust God's power to heal and restore me. I declare that I will not allow depression to define me or dictate my thoughts and actions, but instead trust in God's promise to give me strength and hope.

I seek God's wisdom and discernment in navigating this difficult time. I trust in His ability to work all things for good, and I will not lose hope in His plans for my life. I know that with God by my side, I am never alone, and I am equipped to overcome any challenge that comes my way.

I trust God's love and provision, even in my struggles. I pray for the strength to face my fears and for the peace that surpasses all understanding to guard my heart and mind. I pray for a clear and steadfast spirit to hear God's voice guiding me and see His hand at work.

Prayer Lifestyle

I declare that I will not allow depression to control me. Instead, I choose to focus on God's goodness and His faithfulness. I will meditate on His word and remind myself of His promises. I will seek refuge in Him and trust in His protection. I will surround myself with positive and uplifting influences and care for my physical and mental health.

I am grateful for God's love and the hope that He offers. I declare that I will trust in Him, no matter what. I know He is always with me, and I am confident in His ability to heal and renew my mind. I give depression to God and trust in His ability to bring healing and comfort to my life. Amen.

Ivon Valerie

Emotional Stability

Emotional stability is the ability to manage our emotions and reactions healthily. It is important to pray for emotional stability, asking God for wisdom and self-control to navigate difficult situations and emotions.

Scripture References

Proverbs 16:32: "Better a patient person than a warrior, one with self-control than one who takes a city."

Galatians 5:22-23: "But the fruit of the Spirit is love, joy, peace, forbearance, kindness, goodness, faithfulness, gentleness and self-control. Against such things there is no law."

James 1:19: "My dear brothers and sisters, take note of this: Everyone should be quick to listen, slow to speak and slow to become angry, because human anger does not produce the righteousness that God desires."

Inspirational/Motivational Quotes

"Emotional stability is the capacity to feel emotions, to be aware of them, to be able to express them, and to be able to use them in an adaptive way." - Daniel Goleman

"The greatest discovery of my generation is that a human being can alter his life by altering his attitudes." - William James

"Your emotional stability is your capacity to stay in control of your emotions, regardless of the circumstances." - Dr. Marshall Goldsmith

Prayer

Dear Lord,
I come to you today seeking stability and control over my emotions. I know that I can struggle with healthily managing my reactions and emotions, and I ask for your wisdom and self-control to guide me through difficult situations.

I pray for the grace and patience to be quick to listen, slow to speak, and slow to become angry. I desire to embody your love and compassion in all I do and strive for righteousness in my thoughts and actions.

I ask for your guidance and protection as I navigate the ups and downs of life, and I trust in your ability to bring peace and stability to my heart. May I be grounded in your truth, and may my emotions be guided by your love.

Lord, I know I cannot do this alone, and I ask for your strength and guidance as I strive for emotional stability. May I find comfort in your presence, and may your love be a source of peace in my life. Amen.

Ivon Valerie

Declaration

I declare that I am turning to God for emotional stability. I have struggled to maintain control over my emotions and need His wisdom and self-control to help me navigate life's challenges. I declare that I will not let my emotions control me but instead trust God's power to give me peace and stability.

I declare that I will strive to embody God's righteousness in all that I do. I will seek to honor Him in my thoughts, words, and actions, and I will be quick to listen, slow to speak, and slow to become angry. I understand this is a journey, but with God's help, I am confident I can grow in maturity and self-control.

I declare that God's wisdom guides me. God's peace keeps me calm and centered, even in difficult situations and emotions. I am thankful for the strength to resist temptation and the courage to make wise decisions. I declare I have a heart that is quick to listen and slow to anger to reflect God's love and grace on those around me.

I declare that I will not be defined by my emotions but by God's love and His plan for my life. I will focus on His goodness and faithfulness and surround myself with positive and uplifting influences. I will seek out opportunities to serve others and to be a positive influence in their lives. I will take care of my physical and emotional health and make time for self-care and rest.

I am grateful for God's wisdom, self-control, and the peace and stability He offers. I declare that I will trust in Him, no matter what. I know He is always with me, and I am confident in His ability to help me navigate life's challenges. I give my emotions to God and trust in His ability to bring peace and self-control to my life.

Ivon Valerie

Self-Care and Self-Compassion

Self-care and self-compassion are essential for maintaining physical, emotional, and spiritual well-being. It is important to pray for the ability to take care of ourselves and to be kind and compassionate toward ourselves.

Scripture References

Psalm 139:14: "I praise you because I am fearfully and wonderfully made; your works are wonderful, I know that full well."

Proverbs 31:17: "She sets about her work vigorously; her arms are strong for her tasks."

1 Corinthians 6:19-20: "Do you not know that your bodies are temples of the Holy Spirit, who is in you, whom you have received from God? You are not your own; you were bought at a price. Therefore honor God with your bodies."

Inspirational/Motivational Quotes

"Self-care is never a selfish act—it is simply good stewardship of the only gift I have, the gift I was put on earth to offer to others." - Parker Palmer

Prayer Lifestyle

"Self-compassion is simply giving the same kindness to ourselves that we would give to others." - Christopher Germer

"Self-care is not selfish. You cannot serve from an empty vessel." - Eleanor Brown

Prayer

Dear Lord,
I come to you today asking you to give me the ability to take care of myself and to have self-compassion. I know that self-care and self-compassion are essential for maintaining physical, emotional, and spiritual well-being, and I ask for your guidance and wisdom as I strive to care for my body, mind, and soul.

Please help me to remember that my body is a temple of the Holy Spirit and that I am fearfully and wonderfully made. May I treat my body with respect and dignity and nourish it with healthy food, exercise, and rest.

Lord, I ask for the wisdom to care for my mind and soul, to be mindful of my thoughts and emotions, and to engage in activities that bring peace and joy. May I be compassionate towards myself and not judge or condemn myself for my mistakes or weaknesses.

I pray that I may be kind and gentle with myself and have the courage to forgive and let go of past failures and regrets. Please give me the strength to face my struggles and to trust in your guidance and protection. Amen.

Declaration:

I declare that I am coming to God for self-compassion. I trust in His divine wisdom to show me how to properly care for my physical, mental, and emotional well-being. I vow to treat my body with respect and dignity, knowing it is a sacred temple where the Holy Spirit dwells. I declare that I am fearfully and wonderfully made and will embrace my imperfections and flaws with self-compassion.

I declare I possess the strength to prioritize self-care and the courage to be gentle and kind to myself. I am thankful for guidance on nourishing my body with nutritious food, engaging in physical activity that benefits my health, and managing my stress levels effectively. I will continue to trust God for wisdom in making choices that promote my overall well-being and to recognize when I need rest and rejuvenation.

I am determined to cultivate a mindset of self-love and compassion, recognizing that I am a child of God and deserving of love and kindness. I will practice gratitude and focus on the positive aspects of my life while embracing my mistakes and failures as opportunities for growth and learning. I will continuously pray for the courage to seek help and support when I need it and to be open to receiving love and encouragement from others.

I am confident that God will equip me with everything I need to live a healthy, fulfilling life, and I will continue to rely on Him for support and encouragement as I strive to take care of myself in every aspect of my life.

Inner Peace and Calm

Inner peace and calm is a state of being that allow us to live in a peaceful and serene state of mind. It is important to pray for inner peace and calm, asking God to give us the strength and wisdom to manage our thoughts and emotions in a way that leads to peace and serenity.

Scripture References

Isaiah 26:3: "You will keep in perfect peace those whose minds are steadfast, because they trust in you."

Psalm 29:11: "The Lord gives strength to his people; the Lord blesses his people with peace."

John 14:27: "Peace I leave with you; my peace I give you. I do not give to you as the world gives. Do not let your hearts be troubled and do not be afraid."

Inspirational/Motivational Quotes

"Peace is the beauty of life. It is sunshine. It is the smile of a child, the love of a mother, the joy of a father, the togetherness of a family. It is the advancement of man, the victory of a just cause, the triumph of truth." - Menachem Begin

"Peace is not something you wish for; it's something you make, something you do, something you are, and something you give away." - Robert Fulghum

"Peace is not the absence of conflict, it is the ability to handle conflict by peaceful means." - Ronald Reagan

Prayer

Dear Lord,
I come to you today, humbly asking for your peace and calm to surround me. I know I can easily become overwhelmed by the chaos and turmoil of life, and I ask for your wisdom and guidance to help me navigate these challenges.

I ask for your grace to give me the strength and courage to face my fears and to trust in your plan and protection. I pray that your love and compassion would fill my heart and mind and that I would know the peace that passes all understanding.

I pray for your help to quiet my mind and let go of any worries and anxieties weighing me down. I pray that I will find refuge in you and that your peace will be my stronghold in times of trouble. I ask for your guidance to be a peacemaker in my relationships and to radiate your love and compassion to those around me. I pray that I will be a reflection of your peace and light in a world that is often filled with darkness. I pray for inner peace and calm, and I trust in your ability to work all things for good. Amen.

Declaration

I declare that I am surrendering to God for inner peace and calm. I trust in His divine wisdom and strength to keep my mind steadfast and to give me comfort and security in times of uncertainty. I am confident that God will guide and protect me as I face life's challenges and that I will be able to endure any difficulty with His grace and peace.

I acknowledge that God is the source of all peace and will provide me with the stability and calmness I seek. I declare that I will put my faith in Him and trust His plan for my life. I declare that I will not let the worries and fears of this world control me but that I will find my strength in Him.

I declare my trust in God's grace to allow me to love and accept myself, have compassion for my weaknesses and flaws, and treat myself with gentleness on my journey toward inner peace and calm. I declare that I will cultivate a peaceful spirit and radiate the peace of God to those around me. I also declare my dependence on God for inner peace and calm and confidently rely on His goodness, mercy, and grace to sustain me, knowing that He will never leave or forsake me.

Ivon Valerie

Prayer Lifestyle

Ivon Valerie

Financial Freedom

Financial freedom is integral to our lives, and this chapter emphasizes why it's so crucial. It consists of prayers and statements to help readers combat financial obstacles, attain economic stability, and ultimately reach true financial liberty.

Debt Elimination

Debt can be a heavy burden that can cause stress and negatively impact one's financial stability. It is important to pray for debt elimination, asking God for wisdom and guidance on managing and eliminating debt.

Scripture References

Proverbs 22:7: "The rich rule over the poor, and the borrower is slave to the lender."

Psalm 37:21: "The wicked borrow and do not repay, but the righteous give generously."

Matthew 6:12: "And forgive us our debts, as we also have forgiven our debtors."

Inspirational/Motivational Quotes

"Debt is not the worst thing in the world. The worst thing in the world is to not be able to pay your debt." - John C. Maxwell

"The most powerful weapon on earth is the human soul on fire." - Ferdinando Galiani

"Debt is like any other trap, easy enough to get into, but hard enough to get out of." - Josh Billings

Prayer

Dear Lord,
I come to you today seeking your help with my financial struggles. I know that debt can be a burden that causes stress and negatively impacts my life, and I need your wisdom and guidance in managing and eliminating it.

I pray for the strength and determination to make wise financial decisions and the courage to seek help when needed. I know that with your help, I can overcome this debt and become financially stable. I trust in your provision and abundance and know I can live a debt-free life with your guidance.

I ask that you give me the wisdom to budget my finances and make smart decisions about how I spend my money. Please help me prioritize my debts and focus on paying off the ones causing the most stress. I pray for the grace to resist the temptation to make impulsive purchases and instead focus on paying off my debts.

Lord, I know that debt can also be a source of shame and embarrassment, but I choose to trust your love and forgiveness. I ask that you help me overcome these negative feelings and focus on the positive changes I am making. Please give me the patience and persistence to keep working towards my debt-free goal, even when it feels like it is taking too long.

Prayer Lifestyle

Thank you for the blessings you have already given me, and I ask that you continue to provide for my needs. I pray that you will help me to be a good steward of the resources you have given me and that I will use them wisely. I pray for the wisdom and discernment to make wise financial decisions and the courage to seek help when needed. Amen.

Declaration

I declare I am turning to and depending on God for my debt elimination. I trust God's wisdom and guidance to manage and eliminate my debt, knowing He will lead me to financial freedom. I recognize that managing debt can be a challenge and requires wise financial decisions. I am committed to seeking help and guidance to overcome my debt and become debt-free. I am confident that with God's help, I can make the right choices and take the necessary steps to eliminate my debt.

I declare that God is providing for my needs. I will continue to trust in His guidance and protection, knowing He has a plan for my financial success. I seek God's wisdom and guidance to make wise financial decisions, the courage and determination to seek help, and the strength to trust in God's provision and abundance.

I declare that I will remain steadfast in my faith and trust in God and will not be swayed by the challenges and obstacles that may come my way. With God's help, I can overcome my debt and live a life of financial freedom.

Financial Stability

Financial stability is maintaining a balance between income and expenses and having enough savings to meet unexpected needs. It is important to pray for financial stability, asking God for wisdom and guidance on managing our finances in a way that leads to stability.

Scripture References

Proverbs 21:20: "The wise store up choice food and olive oil, but fools gulp theirs down."

Proverbs 30:8-9: "Give me neither poverty nor riches, but give me only my daily bread. Otherwise, I may have too much and disown you and say, 'Who is the Lord?' Or I may become poor and steal, and so dishonor the name of my God."

Matthew 6:33: "But seek first his kingdom and his righteousness, and all these things will be given to you as well."

Inspirational/Motivational Quotes

"Finance is not the art of passing coins, but the art of passing on risks." - Robert C. Merton

"Wealth is not about having a lot of money; it's about having a lot of options." - Chris Rock

Prayer Lifestyle

"The habit of saving is itself an education; it fosters every virtue, teaches self-denial, cultivates the sense of order, trains to forethought, and so broadens the mind." - T.T. Munger

Prayer

Dear Lord,
I come to you today with a heart full of gratitude, seeking your wisdom and guidance on managing my finances. I know financial stability is essential for a peaceful and fulfilling life, and I need your help.

I pray for the wisdom to make wise financial decisions, save and budget my money, and prioritize your kingdom and righteousness in all I do. Please help me to trust that you will provide for all my needs and to resist the temptation to rely on my resources. I ask for your protection as I strive for financial stability and the grace to overcome any challenges that may arise.

I also pray for the strength and discipline to stick to my budget and to make responsible financial decisions. Please help me resist the urge to make impulsive purchases. I pray that you will give me the insight to identify any bad financial habits I may have and the courage to break them.

Lord, I ask that you help me to be a good steward of the resources you have given me. Please give me the wisdom to understand how to use my finances in a way that honors you and the humility to seek your guidance when I am unsure. I pray that you will help me to grow in generosity and to use my finances to bless others and to further your kingdom.

I trust in your provision and abundance, and I know that with your help, I can achieve financial stability. I thank you for your grace and for your never-ending love and support. I pray that you will continue to bless me and my finances and use me to bring glory to your name. Amen.

Declaration

I declare I am turning to God for financial stability. I am placing my trust in God's wisdom and guidance to manage my finances in a way that leads to stability and security. I recognize that managing finances can be complex and overwhelming. Still, I am determined to prioritize God's kingdom and righteousness in all I do, knowing that this will lead to financial stability. I am committed to making wise financial decisions and trusting God's provision and abundance.

I am aware that financial stability requires effort and discipline, but I am confident that with God's help, I can achieve financial stability and live a life of abundance. I am determined to trust in God's guidance and protection and to rely on His wisdom and grace in all my financial decisions.

I declare financial stability, wisdom, guidance to make wise financial decisions, courage, determination to prioritize God's kingdom and righteousness, and the strength to trust in God's provision and abundance. I declare that I will remain steadfast in my faith and trust in God and will not be swayed by the

Prayer Lifestyle

challenges and obstacles that may come my way. I will continue to rely on God's wisdom and guidance and always trust His provision and abundance. I know that with God's help, I can achieve financial stability and live a life of abundance.

Increase in Income

An increase in income can help to improve one's financial stability and ability to meet their needs and the needs of their loved ones. It is important to pray for an increase in income, asking God for opportunities and blessings that increase income.

Scripture References

Proverbs 10:22: "The blessing of the Lord brings wealth, without painful toil for it."

Psalm 112:3: "Wealth and riches are in their houses, and their righteousness endures forever."

Ephesians 3:20: "Now to him who is able to do immeasurably more than all we ask or imagine, according to his power that is at work within us."

Inspirational/Motivational Quotes

"Income is what you make, wealth is what you keep." - Robert Kiyosaki

"The more you learn, the more you earn." - Frank Clark
"The best investment you can make is in yourself." - Warren Buffett

Prayer

Dear Lord,

I come to you today with a humble heart, seeking your blessings and guidance concerning my income. I know that an increase in income can bring greater financial stability and the ability to meet my needs and the needs of my loved ones.

I pray for the wisdom and discernment to identify the opportunities you have placed before me and the courage to seize them. Please help me be diligent and hardworking in my pursuits and not be afraid to take risks when necessary. I pray that you will bless my efforts and increase my income.

I also pray for the strength to resist the temptation to rely on material wealth and always prioritize your kingdom and righteousness in all I do. Help me to be a good steward of my finances and to use my resources to bless others and to further your kingdom.

Lord, I ask that you open doors of opportunity and bless me with the skills and talents necessary to succeed. I pray that you will use me to bring glory to your name and grant me the grace to bless those around me.

I trust in your power to do more than I could ask or imagine, and I ask for your guidance and protection as I strive for financial stability. I pray that you will bless me with peace and contentment, regardless of my income, and that you will help me to trust in your provision and abundance. Amen.

Ivon Valerie

Declaration

I declare that God is increasing my income. I believe in God's blessings and opportunities and trust that He will lead me to an increase in income. I am aware of the power of prayer and the impact that it can have on my life, and I am committed to seeking God's guidance and protection as I strive for financial stability. I know God's power is more than I could ask or imagine, and I trust His ability to bring abundance into my life.

I also declare that God is increasing my wisdom and guidance in financial decisions. I believe in God for opportunities to grow my income and the courage and determination to trust in his blessings. I am determined to trust in God's power to do more than I could ask or imagine, and I will not be swayed by the challenges and obstacles that may come my way.

I will continue to rely on God's guidance and protection and to trust in His wisdom and grace as I journey toward financial stability and an increase in income. I know that with God's help, I can achieve financial stability and live a life of abundance. I am committed to relying on Him for guidance and protection as I strive for financial stability.

Prayer Lifestyle

Wise Financial Management

Wise financial management is making sound decisions about using financial resources. It is important to pray for wise financial management, asking God for wisdom and guidance on managing our finances in a way that leads to stability and success.

Scripture References

Proverbs 21:5: "The plans of the diligent lead to profit as surely as haste leads to poverty."

Proverbs 16:9: "In their hearts humans plan their course, but the Lord establishes their steps."

1 Timothy 6:17-19: "Command those who are rich in this present world not to be arrogant nor to put their hope in wealth, which is so uncertain, but to put their hope in God, who richly provides us with everything for our enjoyment. Command them to do good, to be rich in good deeds, and to be generous and willing to share. In this way they will lay up treasure for themselves as a firm foundation for the coming age, so that they may take hold of the life that is truly life."

Inspirational/Motivational Quotes

"The art of living lies less in eliminating our troubles than in growing with them." - Bernard M. Baruch

"The best way to predict your future is to create it." - Abraham Lincoln

"The best time to start was last year. The second-best time is now." - Mark Twain

Prayer

Dear Lord, I come to you today with a heart full of gratitude and a spirit of dependence on you. I pray for wisdom and guidance about my financial management, for I know this is an area where I need your help.

I ask for the wisdom to make sound decisions about my finances and prioritize your kingdom and righteousness in all I do. Help me to be a good steward of the resources you have given me and to use them wisely to further your kingdom and bless others.

I pray for the discipline to stick to a budget and to save for the future. Please help me to resist the temptation to overspend and make wise investments that will benefit me and my loved ones in the long run.

I ask for your guidance and protection as I navigate the challenges of financial management, and I trust in your provision and abundance. I pray that you will bless me with peace and contentment, regardless of my financial situation, and that you will help me trust your plan for my life.

Lord, I pray that you will give me the strength to resist the temptation to be consumed by material wealth and always prioritize your kingdom and righteousness in all I do. Help me to be a generous giver and to use my resources to bless others and to further your kingdom. Amen.

Declaration

I declare I am coming to God for wise financial management. I am committed to putting my faith in God's wisdom and guidance as I work towards managing my finances in a way that leads to stability and success.

I understand that sound financial management requires making wise decisions about my financial resources, and I am determined to seek God's guidance and protection as I strive for financial stability. I recognize that with God's help, I have the power to make the right decisions and turn my financial struggles into triumphs.

I am grateful for this opportunity to declare my faith in God's wisdom and guidance and for His power to bring stability and success into my life. I will continue to trust in Him and rely on His guidance and protection as I work toward wise financial management.

I am confident that with God's help, I can turn my financial struggles into triumphs and live a life of abundance. I am determined to seek God's wisdom and guidance and to make wise financial decisions that will lead to stability and success. I know that with God's help, I can achieve wise financial management, and I am committed to relying on Him for guidance and protection as I strive for stability and success.

Prayer Lifestyle

Provision and Abundance

Provision and abundance refer to having enough resources, whether material or spiritual, to meet our needs and the needs of others. It is important to pray for provision and abundance, asking God to bless us with the resources we need to live a fulfilling and abundant life.

Scripture References

Psalm 23:1: "The Lord is my shepherd, I lack nothing."

Philippians 4:19: "And my God will meet all your needs according to the riches of his glory in Christ Jesus."

Matthew 6:33: "But seek first his kingdom and his righteousness, and all these things will be given to you as well."

Inspirational/Motivational Quotes

"Abundance is not something we acquire. It is something we create." - John Randolph Price

"Abundance is not about material possessions. It's about having a rich inner life." - Eckhart Tolle

"The more you have, the more you have to give." - Oprah Winfrey

Ivon Valerie

Prayer

Dear Lord,
I come to you today with hope and trust in your goodness. I pray for your blessings, provision, and abundance in all areas of my life. I know that I need your help to meet my needs and the needs of those around me, and I ask for your generosity and kindness.

I trust in your promise to meet all my needs according to the riches of your glory in Christ Jesus, and I pray that you will pour out your blessings upon me and those I love. Help me to be a good steward of the resources you have given me and to use them wisely to further your kingdom and bless others.

I ask for your guidance and protection as I strive for provision and abundance, and I trust your ability and goodness. I pray for the wisdom to prioritize your kingdom and righteousness in all that I do and for the strength to resist the temptation to be consumed by material wealth. Lord, I pray for spiritual abundance so I may grow closer to you daily and be filled with your peace and joy. Amen.

Declaration

I declare my trust and belief in God's provision and abundance. I declare that I will live a life filled with blessings and fulfillment, knowing that God's hand is upon me and His grace is sufficient for all my needs. I am confident that God's goodness and mercy will follow me all the days of my life, and I am fully persuaded that all things work together for my good because I love Him and am called according to His purpose.

I declare I will seek His kingdom and righteousness first, trusting in His promises and relying on His guidance. I understand that my life is not defined by my circumstances but by my faith in Christ and my relationship with Him. I know that my Heavenly Father is a good and loving God who desires to give me the kingdom, and I believe He will provide all my needs according to the riches of His glory in Christ Jesus.

I declare my trust in God's provision and abundance, and I know that with His help, I will live a rich and fulfilling life in every way. I am grateful for His love and grace, and I pray that I may always reflect His goodness and generosity in all I do.

Ivon Valerie

Prayer Lifestyle

Ivon Valerie

Overcoming Obstacles

No matter who we are, our lives will be filled with obstacles and difficulties. But if you arm yourself with the right tools and outlook, these challenges can be conquered! This chapter is devoted to helping readers learn how to face their difficulties without fear or hesitation—through prayerful declarations of strength and courage; this chapter emphasizes how important it is to have a positive mindset for overcoming whatever may come your way.

Overcoming Fear and Doubt

Fear and doubt can hold us back from achieving our goals and living the life God has planned for us. It is important to pray for the strength and courage to overcome fear and doubt and to trust in God's guidance and protection.

Scripture References

Isaiah 41:10: "So do not fear, for I am with you; do not be dismayed, for I am your God. I will strengthen you and help you; I will uphold you with my righteous right hand."

2 Timothy 1:7: "For the Spirit God gave us does not make us timid, but gives us power, love and self-discipline."

1 John 4:18: "There is no fear in love. But perfect love drives out fear, because fear has to do with punishment. The one who fears is not made perfect in love."

Inspirational/Motivational Quotes

"I learned that courage was not the absence of fear, but the triumph over it. The brave man is not he who does not feel afraid, but he who conquers that fear." - Nelson Mandela

"The only thing we have to fear is fear itself." - Franklin D. Roosevelt

"Fear is only as deep as the mind allows." - Japanese Proverb

Prayer

Dear Lord,

Today, I come to you humbly, seeking your strength and courage to overcome the fears and doubts holding me back from living the life you have planned for me. I know that fear and doubt can be powerful, but I am confident that with your guidance, I can conquer them and move forward with faith and confidence.

I ask for your protection as I take the steps necessary to face my fears and doubts head-on. I pray that you will give me the courage to trust in you and believe that you are always with me, even in the toughest times.

I know that I am not alone in my struggles and that you are always there to support and guide me. I ask that you fill me with your grace and peace so that I may have the strength to persevere through the challenges.

Lord, I know that you have a plan for my life, a plan to prosper me and not to harm me, a plan to give me hope and a future. I pray that you will give me the wisdom to understand your plan and the courage to follow it, even when it is difficult.

I ask that you help me to focus on your goodness and love and to let go of the things that cause me fear and doubt. I pray that you will fill me with your strength so that I may overcome any obstacles that come my way.

Thank you for your faithfulness and for always being there for me. I trust your promises and know you will never leave or forsake me. I pray that you would help me to live a life of courage and faith and to be a shining light in this world, reflecting your love and grace to all those around me. Amen.

Declaration

I declare I am coming to God for the strength and courage to overcome the fears and doubts holding me back. I declare that I am putting my trust in God's guidance and protection as I face my fears and doubts head-on, understanding that He is always with me, guiding me and providing me with the necessary strength to succeed.

I declare that I will have the courage to take bold steps forward, even when my fears and doubts threaten to hold me back. I know that with God guiding me, I can conquer anything that comes my way. I declare that I will have the faith to trust in God, even when the path is uncertain, knowing He has a plan for me and will never leave or forsake me.

I declare that I will be a person of courage and faith, inspired by God's love and grace and driven by the desire to live a life that is pleasing to Him. I will not let fear or doubt dictate my thoughts or actions, but I will focus on God's promises and the blessings He has in store for me.

I declare that I am a child of God, loved and accepted just as I am, and that I have been created for a purpose. I declare that I will fulfill my destiny and live a life that glorifies God, regardless of the future. I declare that I will trust in God's plan for my life and live a life of courage and faith, knowing that He is always with me, guiding me and providing me with the strength I need to succeed.

Overcoming Self-Doubt

Self-doubt can lead to inadequacy and a lack of confidence in our abilities. It is important to pray for the strength and assurance to overcome self-doubt and to trust in God's plan for our lives.

Scripture References

Psalm 139:14: "I praise you because I am fearfully and wonderfully made; your works are wonderful, I know that full well."

Ephesians 2:10: "For we are God's handiwork, created in Christ Jesus to do good works, which God prepared in advance for us to do."

Jeremiah 29:11: "For I know the plans I have for you," declares the Lord, "plans to prosper you and not to harm you, plans to give you hope and a future."

Inspirational/Motivational Quotes

"Self-doubt is an enemy to creativity." - Edith Head

"You are capable. You are powerful. You are deserving. Don't let self-doubt hold you back." - Unknown

Ivon Valerie

Prayer

Dear Lord,
I come to you today humbly seeking your strength and guidance to overcome the overwhelming feelings of self-doubt that have taken hold of me. I know these thoughts and feelings are not from you and that I am fearfully and wonderfully made in your image.

But, Lord, it is easy for me to become consumed by my insecurities and question my abilities and worth. I ask for your protection as I overcome these feelings and trust your plan for my life. Please continue to remind me that I am fearfully and wonderfully made and that you have a purpose for me.

Help me to have the confidence to take bold steps forward in life, knowing that you are always with me and that I can trust in your plan. Please give me the courage to face my fears and to believe in my abilities, even when others may doubt me.

I pray that you will give me a deep sense of peace and calm, knowing that you are in control and that your love for me is unending. Please help me be steadfast in my faith and trust in your promises, even when things seem uncertain.

I desire never to forget the truth that I am your child and that you have good things in store for me. Help me live confidently, knowing that you love and value me. Amen.

Declaration

I declare I am coming to God for the strength and assurance to overcome self-doubt. I understand that self-doubt is a common challenge many faces, but I declare that I will not let it hold me back any longer. I am putting my trust in God's plan for my life, knowing that I am fearfully and wonderfully made in His image, with unique talents and abilities that have been given to me for a purpose.

I declare that I will have confidence in my abilities and will not let self-doubt dictate my thoughts or actions. I will take bold steps forward, relying on God's strength and guidance, knowing He has equipped me with everything I need to succeed. I declare that I will trust in God's plan for my life and will not let self-doubt cloud my vision or prevent me from pursuing my dreams.

I declare that I am a child of God, loved and accepted just as I am, and that I have been created for a purpose. I declare that I will fulfill my destiny and live a life that glorifies God with confidence and assurance in who I am and what I am capable of. I declare that I will trust in God's plan for my life and will not let self-doubt hold me back, but I will live a life of courage and confidence, relying on God's strength and guidance at every step.

Ivon Valerie

Overcoming Negative Thoughts

Negative thoughts can lead to feelings of hopelessness and despair. It is important to pray for the strength and positivity to overcome negative thoughts and to trust in God's love and plan for our lives.

Scripture References

Philippians 4:8: "Finally, brothers and sisters, whatever is true, whatever is noble, whatever is right, whatever is pure, whatever is lovely, whatever is admirable—if anything is excellent or praiseworthy—think about such things."

Isaiah 26:3: "You will keep in perfect peace those whose minds are steadfast, because they trust in you."

Proverbs 4:23: "Above all else, guard your heart, for everything you do flows from it."

Inspirational/Motivational Quotes

"Positive thinking will let you do everything better than negative thinking will." - Zig Ziglar

"The only way to do great work is to love what you do." - Steve Jobs

Prayer Lifestyle

"Positive anything is better than negative nothing." - Elbert Hubbard

Prayer

Dear Lord,
I come to you today burdened by the weight of negative thoughts that have taken hold of me. I know these thoughts are not from you and do not reflect your truth and love for me. But, Lord, lately, it's become easy for me to get caught up in these negative thoughts, focus on my fears and worries, and feel hopeless and discouraged. I ask for your protection and guidance as I overcome these thoughts and focus on what is true, noble, right, pure, lovely, admirable, excellent, and praiseworthy.

Help me to guard my heart and mind and to trust in your love and plan for my life. Remind me that you are always with me and that your love for me is never-ending. Please give me the strength to focus on the good things in my life and be grateful for all you have done for me.

I pray that you will help me to see the world through your eyes and to believe that all things are possible with you. Please help me have a positive outlook, be hopeful, and trust in your promises, even when things seem uncertain.

Lord, I desire never to forget that I am your child and that you have good things in store for me. Help me live confidently and positively, knowing that you love and value me. Amen.

Declaration

I declare today that I am fully committed to seeking and relying on God for the strength and positivity to overcome negative thoughts and to live a life filled with joy, peace, and purpose. I acknowledge that the battles in my mind can sometimes be overwhelming, but I know I am not alone in this journey.

I declare that I will focus on what is true, noble, right, pure, lovely, admirable, excellent, and praiseworthy. I will fill my heart with gratitude, love, and grace and push out any negative thoughts that try to take over. I understand this requires effort, and I am determined to succeed with God's help.

I declare that I will guard my heart and trust God's love and plan for my life. I will surrender my fears, worries, and doubts to Him and trust that He is leading me on the right path. I will be mindful of the words I speak and the things I allow into my life, as I know they can shape my thoughts and emotions.

I declare that I will cultivate a positive mindset and approach each day with love and joy. I will find purpose and fulfillment in all I do, knowing that I serve a higher purpose. I will be grateful for all of the blessings in my life and focus on the good, even when things are difficult.

I declare that I will inspire others as I live my life to the fullest and shine God's light into the world. I am grateful for this journey and the opportunities it presents, and I will not let negative thoughts hold me back. I am a child of God, loved, valued, and worthy.

Overcoming Difficult Circumstances

Difficult circumstances can be overwhelming and can test our faith. It is important to pray for the strength and guidance to overcome difficult circumstances and to trust in God's plan and purpose for our lives.

Scripture References

Psalm 46:1: "God is our refuge and strength, an ever-present help in trouble."

2 Corinthians 4:8-9: "We are hard pressed on every side, but not crushed; perplexed, but not in despair; persecuted, but not abandoned; struck down, but not destroyed."

Isaiah 43:2: "When you pass through the waters, I will be with you; and when you pass through the rivers, they will not sweep over you. When you walk through the fire, you will not be burned; the flames will not set you ablaze."

Inspirational/Motivational Quotes

"Difficulties in your life do not come to destroy you, but to help you realize your hidden potential and power." - Unknown

Ivon Valerie

"It is during our darkest moments that we must focus to see the light." - Aristotle

"Adversity causes some men to break; others to break records." - William Arthur Ward

Prayer

Dear Lord,
I come to you today struggling to face the difficult circumstances in my life. I know that these challenges are not from you and that you do not wish me to suffer. Lord God, it's become easy for me to feel overwhelmed and discouraged in the face of adversity. So, I ask for your refuge, strength, and ever-present help in times of trouble. I trust in your plan and purpose for my life and ask for your guidance and protection as I navigate these trying times.

Please help me to have faith in your provision and to believe that you are working all things together for good. Remind me that you are always with me, even in the darkest moments, and that your love for me is never-ending.

I pray that you will give me a deep sense of peace and calm, knowing that you are in control and that your plans for me are good. Please help me be strong and courageous, even in the face of adversity, and trust in your promises, even when things seem uncertain. Please help me to remember that I am your child and that you have good things in store for me. Help me live with confidence and hope, knowing that you are always with me and will never forsake me. Amen.

Declaration

I declare today that I am overcoming difficult circumstances with God's strength and love. I understand that life can be challenging sometimes, but I am not alone in this journey. I am confident that God is with me and will never abandon me.

I declare that I trust in God's plan and purpose for my life and that He is my refuge and strength. No matter what comes my way, I know God has a good plan for me and will work everything out for my good. I will not be crushed, perplexed, persecuted, abandoned, struck down, or destroyed, but I will come out victorious with God's help.

I declare that I will focus on the light during dark times and break records and not break under adversity. My circumstances will not defeat me; instead, I will rise above them and trust God's sovereignty. I will seek His guidance and strength in all things and know He is the source of my peace, hope, and joy.

I declare that I will be a testimony of God's grace, love, and strength to those around me. I will be an ambassador that spreads hope, encouragement, and joy to those in need. I will be grateful for every opportunity to grow and to serve, and I will not let difficult circumstances defeat me.

Ivon Valerie

Overcoming Addiction and Negative Patterns

Addiction and negative patterns can have a fatalistic impact on us, and it is important to pray for the strength and guidance to overcome them and to trust in God's love and plan for our lives.

Scripture References

1 Corinthians 10:13: "No temptation has seized you except what is common to man. And God is faithful; he will not let you be tempted beyond what you can bear. But when you are tempted, he will also provide a way out so that you can endure it."

Isaiah 41:10: "So do not fear, for I am with you; do not be dismayed, for I am your God. I will strengthen you and help you; I will uphold you with my righteous right hand."

Psalm 34:18: "The Lord is close to the brokenhearted and saves those who are crushed in spirit."

Inspirational/Motivational Quotes

"Recovery is something that you have to work on every single day and it's something that doesn't get a day off." - Demi Lovato

Prayer Lifestyle

"The greatest step towards a life of recovery is the next one." - Unknown

"Recovery is not just about stopping the drinking and using, it's about healing the mind, the body, and the spirit." - Unknown

Prayer

Dear Lord,
I come to you today humbly asking for your strength and guidance as I face the struggle of addiction and negative patterns. I know these things have a destructive hold on my life, and I cannot overcome them alone.

My Lord and my God, I ask for your love and help. I know your love is greater than any addiction or negative pattern, and I trust your power to break the chains that bind me. I pray that you will give me the courage and strength to take the necessary steps toward recovery and that you will be with me every step.

Please help me to overcome the temptations and triggers that lead me down the path of destruction and to resist the urge to give in to these negative patterns. I ask for your wisdom and guidance as I navigate the challenges of recovery and for your protection as I face the difficulties that may arise.

I trust in your plan for my life, Lord, and I ask that you help me see the good you have in store for me. I pray that you would help me to live with hope and joy, knowing that I am a new creation in Christ and that your love is transforming me from the inside out.

Please help me remember that I am your child and that you are always with me, even in my darkest moments. Please help me to walk in your light and to live a life that brings glory to your name. Amen.

Declaration

I declare today that I am coming to God for the strength and guidance to overcome addiction and negative patterns. I understand that this journey will take time, effort, and dedication, but I am ready to face it head-on with God by my side.

I declare that I trust in God's love and plan for my life and that He is close to the brokenhearted and saves those who are crushed in spirit. My struggles with addiction and negative patterns do not define me, even though I often feel they do. I declare I am a beloved child of God, created for a purpose and a great plan. I will hold onto this truth and trust God's love and guidance as I recover.

I declare that I will work on my recovery every day and will not give up. I understand that recovery is a process, and there will be ups and downs, but I will not allow setbacks will not discourage me. Instead, I will learn from my mistakes, stay the course, and keep moving forward with God's help.

I declare that I will take the necessary steps toward recovery and healing my mind, body, and spirit. I will seek support and help from those who can encourage and guide me, and I will be intentional about taking care of myself in every aspect. I will do

Prayer Lifestyle

the necessary work and will not be afraid to confront the difficult aspects of my addiction and negative patterns.

I declare that I will be a testimony of God's grace, love, and power to those around me. I will share my story of hope and redemption, and I will encourage others who are struggling with addiction and negative patterns. I will not be ashamed of my past; instead, I will use it to serve and encourage others with God's help.

Ivon Valerie

Prayer Lifestyle

Ivon Valerie

Career and Business

Our career and business endeavors are crucial parts of our lives that profoundly impact our overall well-being. Therefore, it is essential to recognize the importance of success and prosperity in these fields. This chapter will provide you with prayers and declarations geared towards helping you reach your goals, discover rewarding work opportunities, and attain unparalleled levels of success in your professional life and entrepreneurial aspirations.

Prayer Lifestyle

Job Opportunities

Finding a job can be challenging and stressful; it's important to pray for guidance and opportunities in finding a job that aligns with our skills and passions.

Scripture References

Psalm 37:4: "Take delight in the Lord, and he will give you the desires of your heart."

Proverbs 16:3: "Commit to the Lord whatever you do, and he will establish your plans."

Ephesians 2:10: "For we are God's handiwork, created in Christ Jesus to do good works, which God prepared in advance for us to do."

Inspirational/Motivational Quotes

"Your work is going to fill a large part of your life, and the only way to be truly satisfied is to do what you believe is great work. And the only way to do great work is to love what you do." - Steve Jobs

"The only limit to our realization of tomorrow will be our doubts of today." - Franklin D. Roosevelt

"Success is not final, failure is not fatal: it is the courage to continue that counts." - Winston Churchill

Prayer

Dear Lord,
I come to you today seeking guidance and direction in my job search. Finding a job can be challenging and stressful, but I trust that with your help, I will find the perfect job for me.

I am grateful for the skills and passions you have given me, and I ask that you lead me to a job that allows me to use these gifts to their full potential. I pray for the wisdom to understand what opportunities are best for me and the courage to pursue them. I ask that you establish my plans and give me the strength to persevere in my job search. I trust your guidance and know you have already prepared good work for me.

I pray that you bless my interactions with potential employers and that I may communicate my skills and passions in a way that showcases my strengths. I ask that you open and close doors that are not meant for me.

Lord, I pray for peace and clarity in my heart and mind as I navigate this job search. I ask that you help me stay focused on you and your plans for my life, even in uncertainty. I thank you for your continued grace and provision in my life. I know that you are always with me and have a purpose for my life. I trust in your timing and in your plans for my future. Amen.

Declaration

I declare that I am on a journey toward finding my purpose in my career. I seek guidance and direction from the Lord as I navigate this path. I trust He has a plan for my life, including finding a job that aligns with my skills, gifts, and passions. I am confident that He has created me for a purpose and that I have been gifted with unique talents and abilities to fulfill that purpose.

I declare that I am committed to this job search and will not give up until I find the right fit. I know that the Lord has the perfect opportunity for me and that He will lead me to it in His timing. I am open to new possibilities and willing to take risks in pursuing my dreams. I understand that the journey may not be easy, but I am determined to trust in the Lord every step of the way.

I declare that the Lord has made me worthy of success, and I will use my talents and abilities for the good of others. I am committed to loving my work and positively impacting the lives of those around me. I will shine in the workplace and use my gifts to glorify God.

I also declare my faith in the Lord and rely on His strength and guidance during this time. I declare wisdom, clarity, and opportunities to present themselves to me. I know I have God's protection as I make important decisions about my career. I trust in His provision and know He will meet my every need.

I declare that I am created in the image of Christ Jesus and that I have the power to do great things for His kingdom. I am a child of God and have been chosen for a specific purpose. I will not be discouraged or swayed by the opinions of others. I will listen to the voice of the Lord and follow His guidance.

I declare that my career path will be a success, and I will find joy and fulfillment in my work. I trust that the Lord will lead me to the perfect job and that I will love the work that I do. I declare that I am ready for the adventure ahead and am grateful for the opportunities the Lord has in store for me. Amen.

Successful Business Ventures

Starting and running a successful business takes hard work and dedication; praying for wisdom and guidance in making important business decisions and financial stability and success is important.

Scripture References

Proverbs 3:5-6: "Trust in the Lord with all your heart and lean not on your own understanding; in all your ways submit to him, and he will make your paths straight."

Psalm 112:1: "Praise the Lord. Blessed is the man who fears the Lord, who finds great delight in his commands."

Proverbs 22:29: "Do you see a man skilled in his work? He will serve before kings; he will not serve before obscure men."

Inspirational/Motivational Quotes

"Your most unhappy customers are your greatest source of learning." - Bill Gates

"The biggest adventure you can ever take is to live the life of your dreams." - Oprah Winfrey

"Your work is going to fill a large part of your life, and the only way to be truly satisfied is to do what you believe is great work. And the only way to do great work is to love what you do." - Steve Jobs

Prayer

Dear Lord,

Today, I ask for wisdom and guidance in making important decisions for my business venture. Starting and running a business takes hard work and dedication, and I ask for your support and guidance. I pray for financial stability and success for my business. I ask that you bless my efforts and help me to make sound decisions that will lead to growth and prosperity for my venture. I trust in your guidance and ask that you establish my plans.

I pray for the strength and perseverance to overcome any challenges that may come my way. I ask that you grant me wisdom in managing finances, making decisions that affect my employees, and finding new growth opportunities. Lord, I pray that my business will serve you first and foremost and bring glory to your name. I pray that my business will have a positive impact on my community and that it will serve as a blessing to those around me.

I ask that you give me the courage to submit to your will in all my ways, even when it may be difficult. I pray that I will always seek your guidance and trust in your plans for my life and business. I pray that my business will serve before kings and not only before obscure men and that it will bring honor and prestige to your name. I trust in your provision and know that you will always be with me, guiding and supporting me in all my endeavors. Amen.

Declaration

I declare that I seek wisdom and guidance from the Lord as I embark on this new business venture. I understand that this is a significant step in my life and that I cannot do it alone. I rely on the Lord to guide me and provide me with the wisdom and knowledge I need to make important business decisions.

I declare that I trust in God's plan for my business and will submit to His will in all my ways. I know He has a purpose for my life and that my business venture is a part of that plan. I am confident that He will lead me to success and that my business will flourish under His guidance.

I declare that my business will be financially stable and successful. I know the Lord will provide me with the resources I need to grow my business and serve my customers in the best possible way. I believe that my business will serve before kings and not only before obscure men and bring glory to God.

I declare my faith in the Lord and my commitment to running my business with integrity and honor. I rely on His strength and guidance as I navigate the ups and downs of entrepreneurship. I am determined to be a good steward of the resources He has given me and use my business to impact the world positively.

Ivon Valerie

I declare I will seek God for wisdom and guidance in making important business decisions. I declare that I will love my work and find joy and fulfillment in the success of my business. I am grateful for the opportunity to serve the Lord through my work, and I am confident that He will lead me to great things. I trust in His plan and am ready to embrace the adventure ahead. I declare my business venture is successful and glorifies God.

Prayer Lifestyle

Promotions and Advancements

Advancing in our careers is important for professional growth and financial stability. Praying for guidance and opportunities for promotions and career advancements are important.

Scripture References

Psalm 75:6-7: "For promotion cometh neither from the east, nor from the west, nor from the south. But God is the judge: he putteth down one, and setteth up another."

Proverbs 16:9: "In his heart a man plans his course, but the Lord determines his steps."

Colossians 3:23-24: "Whatever you do, work at it with all your heart, as working for the Lord, not for human masters, since you know that you will receive an inheritance from the Lord as a reward. It is the Lord Christ you are serving."

Inspirational/Motivational Quotes

"The only limit to our realization of tomorrow will be our doubts of today." - Franklin D. Roosevelt

"The only place where success comes before work is in the dictionary." - Vidal Sassoon

Ivon Valerie

"The future belongs to those who believe in the beauty of their dreams." - Eleanor Roosevelt

Prayer

Dear Lord,

I come to you today seeking guidance and opportunities for promotions and advancements in my career. Advancing in my career is important for my professional growth and financial stability, and I trust in your plan for my life. I pray for the wisdom to understand the opportunities best for me and the courage to pursue them. I ask for your guidance in developing new skills and for the ability to work with diligence and excellence in all that I do.

I will work on my career with all my heart as if I am working for you, and I trust that you will determine my steps. I pray for the strength and perseverance to overcome any challenges that may come my way and maintain a positive attitude and outlook in the face of adversity.

I ask that you bless my interactions with my colleagues and superiors and that I may communicate my skills and abilities in a way that showcases my strengths. I pray that you will open and close doors that are not meant for me.

Lord, I pray for a deep sense of purpose and fulfillment in my career. I ask that you help me find meaning and satisfaction in my work and that I may positively influence the workplace. I trust in your provision and know that you have a reward for me. I pray that I will receive an inheritance from you as a reward for my hard work and dedication. Amen.

Declaration

I declare that the Lord is guiding and advancing my career in ways that only He can. I understand that my career is a journey and that I cannot do it alone, so I rely on the Lord to lead me to where I am meant to be and provide me with the opportunities I need to grow and succeed.

I declare that I trust in God's plan for my career and will work at it with all my heart as if I am working for the Lord. I know that the Lord has a purpose for my life and that my career is a part of that plan. I am confident that He will lead me to success and that my efforts will not be in vain.

I declare that the Lord will order my steps and that I will receive an inheritance from the Lord as a reward. I believe He has great things in store for me and will reward me for my hard work and dedication. I know I am an heir to the Kingdom of God and have been called to greatness.

I rely on God's strength and guidance as I navigate the ups and downs of my journey. I am determined to be a good steward of the talents and abilities He has given me and use my career to impact the world positively. I declare that I rely completely on God's guidance and opportunities for promotion and advancement in my career.

Ivon Valerie

I declare that I will strive for success and love my work. I am grateful for the opportunity to serve the Lord through my career, and I am confident that He will lead me to great things. I trust in His plan and am ready to embrace the journey ahead.

Wisdom and Guidance in Career Decisions

Making important career decisions can be challenging; praying for wisdom and guidance is important to make the best choices for our future.

Scripture References

James 1:5: "If any of you lacks wisdom, you should ask God, who gives generously to all without finding fault, and it will be given to you."

Proverbs 2:6: "For the Lord gives wisdom; from his mouth come knowledge and understanding."

Isaiah 30:21: "Whether you turn to the right or to the left, your ears will hear a voice behind you, saying, 'This is the way; walk in it'."

Inspirational/Motivational Quotes

"The best way to predict your future is to create it." - Abraham Lincoln

"The future belongs to those who believe in the beauty of their dreams." - Eleanor Roosevelt

"The greatest mistake you can make in life is continually being afraid you will make one." - Elbert Hubbard

Prayer

Dear Lord,

I seek wisdom and guidance in making important career decisions today. I am grateful for the talents and abilities you have given me, and I pray you will use them for your glory. I know that making these choices can be challenging, but I trust in your guidance, and I ask that you give me the wisdom and knowledge I need to make the best decisions for my future. I pray for clarity and direction in my path and the courage to walk in it.

I pray for your guidance in every aspect of my career, from the opportunities that come my way to the relationships I form with my colleagues and superiors. I ask that you help me to make the best use of my time and to work with diligence and excellence in all that I do.

I pray for the ability to be flexible and adaptable in my career and the wisdom to make changes. I ask that you give me the courage to pursue new opportunities and take risks in pursuing my goals.

I pray for a deep sense of purpose and fulfillment in my career and that I may use my gifts and abilities to serve others and positively impact the world. I ask that you help me balance my life and prioritize the things most important to me. Amen.

Declaration

I declare my reliance on the Lord for wisdom and guidance as I navigate the complexities of my career. I trust in the Lord's sovereignty and believe He has a plan for my life to prosper and not harm me, giving me hope and a future. I declare my unwavering faith in God's wisdom and ability to guide me in making the best decisions for my future.

I declare that the Lord will grant me the wisdom to discern His will for my life and the courage to follow it. He will reveal the opportunities that align with my skills and passions and open doors for me to advance in my career. My God has blessed me with a clear mind, sharp insight, and a deep understanding of the complexities of my career.

I declare that I will seek God's wisdom and trust in His guidance. I will listen for His voice and follow His leading, no matter where it takes me. I declare that I will have the courage to take risks and pursue the path the Lord has set for me. I will trust in the Lord's promises and believe He will make my career prosper and succeed. I further declare that the Holy Spirit empowers me to make wise decisions in my career and commit to being a faithful and obedient servant of the Lord.

Ivon Valerie

Financial Stability and Success in Business

Financial stability and success are crucial for the growth and sustainability of a business. Praying for guidance in managing finances and providing abundance in the business is important.

Scripture References

Proverbs 3:9-10: "Honor the Lord with your wealth, with the firstfruits of all your crops; then your barns will be filled to overflowing, and your vats will brim over with new wine."

Psalm 23:1: "The Lord is my shepherd, I shall not want."

Psalm 34:10: "The lions may grow weak and hungry, but those who seek the Lord lack no good thing."

Inspirational/Motivational Quotes

"If you want to be financially free, you need to become a different person than you are today and let go of whatever has held you back in the past." - Robert Kiyosaki

"The most important quality for an entrepreneur is accounting skills. You must know how to read and understand financial statements." - Bill Gates

Prayer Lifestyle

"The only limit to our realization of tomorrow will be our doubts of today." - Franklin D. Roosevelt

Prayer

Dear Lord,
I come to you today asking for your guidance in managing the finances of my business. I am grateful for the blessings and opportunities you have given me, and I pray that you will continue to provide for all my needs.

I ask for wisdom in making decisions that will ensure my business's financial stability and success. I trust in your provision and know that as my Shepherd, I will be led to green pasture. I pray you will bring my barns and vats to brim with new wine.

I commit to honoring you with my wealth and using it for your glory. I pray that I will be a wise steward of the resources you have entrusted to me and use them to bless others and advance your kingdom.

I ask for your protection and guidance in all my business dealings and that you will keep me from making decisions that are not in line with your will. I pray for abundance and prosperity, not just for myself but also those I serve and those who work with me. I ask that you help me to use my resources to bring you glory and to live a life that is pleasing in your sight. Amen.

Declaration

I declare that I am walking with the Lord in all aspects of my business, including financial management. I declare that I trust in God's promise of abundance and that He will provide for all my needs according to His riches in glory. I declare that I will be faithful in tithing and giving and that my storehouses will overflow with blessings. I declare that I will make wise investments and decisions in managing my finances and that my business will bless many.

I declare the Lord's guidance in every decision I make, the wisdom to understand His ways, and the discernment to recognize opportunities for growth and prosperity. I declare that I have a heart of generosity, the courage to be faithful in giving, and the grace to handle wealth responsibly.

I declare that the Lord is continually blessing the work of my hands and causing my business to flourish and bring forth an abundance of good fruit. I declare that my business will bring honor and glory to His name and that I will use the resources He has entrusted to me to bless others and advance His kingdom. I declare success in all business areas and a deep trust in the Lord's provision and guidance.

Prayer Lifestyle

Ivon Valerie

Education and Learning

Education and learning are essential elements of personal and professional growth. This chapter considers the powerful impact that knowledge can have on our lives by providing prayers and declarations to assist readers in reaching their educational objectives, searching for suitable learning opportunities, and nurturing consistent development throughout life.

Academic Success

Academic success is important for personal growth and future opportunities. It's important to pray for wisdom and understanding in studies, as well as the strength and motivation to succeed.

Scripture References

Proverbs 2:1-6: "My son, if you accept my words and store up my commands within you, turning your ear to wisdom and applying your heart to understanding, and if you call out for insight and cry aloud for understanding, and if you look for it as for silver and search for it as for hidden treasure, then you will understand the fear of the Lord and find the knowledge of God."

Psalm 119:99: "I have more insight than all my teachers, for I meditate on your statutes."

Psalm 1:2: "But his delight is in the law of the Lord, and on his law he meditates day and night."

Inspirational/Motivational Quotes

"Education is not the filling of a pail, but the lighting of a fire." - W.B Yeats

"The more that you read, the more things you will know. The more that you learn, the more places you'll go." - Dr. Seuss

"Success is no accident. It is hard work, perseverance, learning, studying, sacrifice and most of all, love of what you are doing or learning to do." - Pelé

Prayer

Dear Lord,
I come to you today with a humble heart, seeking your guidance and wisdom in my studies. I pray for the strength and motivation to succeed academically and to bring honor to your name through my efforts. I know that with your help, I can overcome any obstacles that may come my way.

I am grateful for the opportunities you have given me to learn and grow, and I ask that you would grant me the gift of understanding and insight. I am determined to apply my heart and mind to wisdom and to turn my ear to your commands. I will meditate on your statutes and find the knowledge of God that I may be equipped to fulfill your purpose for my life.

I know that without your help, I can do nothing, but with your guidance and support, I can achieve great things. I pray that you would fill me with your grace and wisdom so that I may be a shining example of your love and truth to all those around me.

Thank you for your faithfulness and for always being there for me, even in my struggles. I trust in your love and know you are working all things out for my good. I will cling to your promises and rest in your care, knowing that you are always with me and that your plans for me are for my good and for your glory. Amen.

Declaration

I declare with all my heart and soul that I am turning to God for guidance and wisdom in my academic pursuits. I am determined to seek out His wisdom and understanding, knowing that it is through Him that I will succeed in my studies.

I declare that I will listen attentively to God's word and store His commands within me, allowing His wisdom to shape and guide my academic journey. I will be diligent in my efforts to gain a deeper understanding of God's teachings and allow His wisdom to direct my thoughts and actions.

I declare that I will meditate on God's statutes, seeking the knowledge and understanding that only He can provide. I will not be swayed by the opinions of others but will instead seek out the truth found in God's word. I will not be afraid to ask for guidance and clarity and strive to find wisdom from God.

I declare that I will not be limited by my current understanding but will seek to expand my knowledge and understanding through my continuous relationship with God. I also declare that I will have the strength and motivation to succeed academically, knowing that it is through God's grace that I can accomplish all things. I will not be discouraged by obstacles or setbacks but will remain steadfast.

Ivon Valerie

I declare I will stand firm in my faith and trust in God, knowing that I can accomplish all things through Him. I will not waiver in my commitment to seek out His wisdom and understanding, for I know that it is only through Him that I will find the success and fulfillment I seek.

Prayer Lifestyle

Wisdom and Understanding

Wisdom and understanding are crucial for making informed decisions and navigating life's challenges. It's important to pray for these gifts to gain a deeper understanding of ourselves, others, and the world around us.

Scripture References

Proverbs 4:7: "Wisdom is supreme; therefore get wisdom. Though it cost all you have, get understanding."

Colossians 1:9-10: "For this reason, since the day we heard about you, we have not stopped praying for you and asking God to fill you with the knowledge of his will through all spiritual wisdom and understanding. And we pray this in order that you may live a life worthy of the Lord and may please him in every way: bearing fruit in every good work, growing in the knowledge of God"

James 1:5: "If any of you lacks wisdom, you should ask God, who gives generously to all without finding fault, and it will be given to you."

Inspirational/Motivational Quotes

"The only true wisdom is in knowing you know nothing." - Socrates

"The more that you read, the more things you will know. The more that you learn, the more places you'll go." - Dr. Seuss

"To acquire knowledge, one must study; but to acquire wisdom, one must observe." - Marilyn vos Savant

Prayer

Dear Lord,

I come before you today, humbly seeking your wisdom and understanding. I know these gifts are essential for navigating life's complexities and making informed decisions that honor you. I pray that you would grant me a deeper understanding of myself, others, and the world around me, so that I may live a life that brings glory to your name.

I ask that you would fill me with the knowledge of your will so that I may live in a way that pleases you in every aspect of my life. I desire spiritual wisdom and understanding from you so I can live a life that reflects your love and grace.

I understand that gaining wisdom and understanding cannot be achieved overnight. It is a journey that requires my commitment and dedication. I am willing to put in the effort and to seek after you with all my heart, mind, and soul.

I pray that you would open my eyes to the truth and that I may understand your ways clearer. I ask that you give me the courage to follow your lead, even when the road ahead is unclear. I trust in your guidance and know that with your help, I will excel beyond my expectations.

I am grateful for your love and the many blessings you have given me. I know that I can rely on your grace to carry me through even the toughest of times. I will continue to trust in your goodness and seek your wisdom and understanding to live a life that brings honor to your name. Amen.

Declaration

I declare that I am turning to God for wisdom and understanding in all aspects of my life. I understand that these gifts are essential in navigating the challenges and complexities of this world and making informed decisions that honor God.

I declare that I will seek a deeper understanding of myself, others, and the world around me through God's wisdom. I will strive to gain insight into the motivations and perspectives of those around me and to respond with compassion, grace, and understanding. I will work to cultivate a heart of wisdom, make choices that align with God's will and bring honor to His name.

I declare I will stand firm in my faith and trust in God. I know that through Him, I can gain wisdom and understanding and live a life that brings honor to His name. I will not waiver in my commitment to seek out His wisdom and understanding, for I know that it is only through Him that I will find the peace, joy, and fulfillment that I seek.

Ivon Valerie

Guidance in Choosing a Career or Field of Study

Choosing a career or field of study can be daunting. It's important to pray for guidance in making these essential decisions to ensure that we are on the path that aligns with our passions, strengths, and God's plan for our lives.

Scripture References

Psalm 32:8: "I will instruct you and teach you in the way you should go; I will counsel you with my loving eye on you."

Proverbs 3:5-6: "Trust in the Lord with all your heart and lean not on your own understanding; in all your ways submit to him, and he will make your paths straight."

Isaiah 30:21: "Whether you turn to the right or to the left, your ears will hear a voice behind you, saying, 'This is the way; walk in it'."

Inspirational/Motivational Quotes

"Your work is going to fill a large part of your life, and the only way to be truly satisfied is to do what you believe is great work. And the only way to do great work is to love what you do." - Steve Jobs

"Choose a job you love, and you will never have to work a day in your life." - Confucius

"The best way to predict your future is to create it." - Abraham Lincoln

Prayer

Dear Lord,
I come before you today seeking guidance and direction in choosing a career or field of study. I know this decision will significantly impact my future, and I want to ensure that I am on the path that aligns with my passions, strengths, and the plan you have for my life.

I am grateful for your loving guidance and ask that you would instruct, teach, and counsel me on the steps I should take. I trust in your wisdom and know that you have a perfect plan for my life, one that is filled with purpose and meaning. I pray you will reveal this plan to me so I can walk confidently and joyfully.

I understand that choosing a career is a complex decision, and I may face many challenges along the way. But I trust in your power and know that with your help, I can overcome any obstacle that may come my way. I pray that you will give me the courage and determination to pursue my dreams and make the best decision for my future.

I ask that you give me clarity of mind so I may see the opportunities in front of me. I pray that you will open doors for me and lead me to the people and resources I need to succeed. I trust in your guidance and know that you will make my path straight, even when the future is uncertain.

I am grateful for your love and the many blessings you have given me. I will continue to trust in your guidance and seek your wisdom and understanding to live a life that brings honor to your name. I submit to you in all my ways and know that you will lead me to where I am meant to be. Amen.

Declaration

I declare that I seek God's guidance in choosing a career or field of study. I understand that this is a crucial decision that will shape the direction of my life, and I am eager to trust in God's wisdom and guidance in making this choice.

I declare that I will submit to God in all my ways, trusting that He will instruct, teach, and counsel me on my path. I will not be swayed by the opinions of others but will instead seek God's voice and guidance in every step. I will be patient as I wait for God's timing and will not be afraid to seek His wisdom even when it leads me in unexpected directions.

I declare that I will choose a career or field of study that aligns with my passions, strengths, and God's plan for my life. I understand that God has unique and specific plans for my life, and I am eager to discover what He has in store for me. I will diligently seek God's guidance and listen to His voice as I weigh different options and make this important decision.

Prayer Lifestyle

I also declare that I will not be deterred by fear or uncertainty. I know God is always with me, guiding me and helping me navigate this life. I am confident in His love and care for me, and I trust that He will bring me to a place of peace and fulfillment as I follow His plan for my life.

Ivon Valerie

Success in Professional Development

Professional development is important for growth and advancement in one's career. Praying for success in this area, the ability to acquire new skills and knowledge, and opportunities to improve and excel are of utmost importance.

Scripture References

Psalm 119:18: "Open my eyes that I may see wonderful things in your law."

Proverbs 22:29: "Do you see a man skilled in his work? He will serve before kings; he will not serve before obscure men."

Colossians 3:23-24: "Whatever you do, work at it with all your heart, as working for the Lord, not for human masters, since you know that you will receive an inheritance from the Lord as a reward. It is the Lord Christ you are serving."

Inspirational/Motivational Quotes

"Learning is the beginning of wealth. Learning is the beginning of health. Learning is the beginning of spirituality. Searching and learning is where the miracle process all begins." - Jim Rohn

Prayer Lifestyle

"Learning is not attained by chance, it must be sought for with ardor and attended to with diligence." - Abigail Adams

"Professional development is the commitment to learn, grow, and better oneself for the betterment of oneself and others." - Lolly Daskal

Prayer

Dear Lord,
Today, I come to you with a heart full of gratitude and a deep desire for success in my professional development. I pray for the ability to acquire new skills, gain knowledge, and seek opportunities to improve and excel in my field. I am so thankful for your grace and blessings, and I ask that you continue guiding me in all I do.

I ask that you open my eyes to the wonderful things in my work and that I may have the opportunity to serve before kings. I understand that my work is not just for the benefit of my employers or for my gain, but it is also a way for me to serve you and to bring glory to your name.

I pray that you will give me the strength and courage to work hard, persevere, and never give up on my goals and aspirations. I ask that you bless my efforts and give me success in all I do. I trust in your goodness and know that you will provide for my needs and meet all my desires as long as they align with your will.

I understand that my professional success is not just about what I can achieve on my own but also about how I can use my skills and talents to serve others and make a positive impact in the world. I pray that you will give me a heart for service and a desire to use my gifts to make a difference in the lives of those around me.

I thank you for the inheritance you promised me, and I trust in your faithfulness to reward me for my hard work and dedication. I know that my ultimate reward is not just financial success or professional recognition but the reward of a well-lived life that brings honor to your name. Amen.

Declaration

I declare that I am turning to God for success in my professional development. I am eager to learn, grow and become more skilled in my field. I understand that this success is for my gain and to bring glory to God's name. I will strive to do my best in everything I do as if I were working for the Lord himself and not just for those above me at work.

I trust the Lord's guidance and direction in my professional journey. I believe He has a plan for me and will lead me to opportunities to flourish and succeed in my work. I declare that I will have the eyes to see wonderful things in my career, have a positive outlook and perspective, and serve with excellence and dedication.

I declare that I will invest my time, energy, and resources into professional development, and I believe that I will receive an inheritance from the Lord as a reward for my hard work and dedication. I will be mindful of my work's impact on others and work to make a positive difference in the lives of those I encounter. I declare success in my professional development and the Lord's continued guidance and wisdom in all my endeavors.

Success in Continuing Education

Continuing education is important for staying current in one's field and for personal growth. It's important to pray for success in this area, the ability to acquire new skills and knowledge, and opportunities to learn and expand one's understanding.

Scripture References

Proverbs 1:5: "Let the wise listen and add to their learning, and let the discerning get guidance."

Isaiah 54:13: "All your children shall be taught by the Lord, and great shall be the peace of your children."

2 Timothy 2:15: "Do your best to present yourself to God as one approved, a worker who has no need to be ashamed, rightly handling the word of truth."

Inspirational/Motivational Quotes

"Education is not the filling of a pail, but the lighting of a fire." - W.B. Yeats

"The more that you read, the more things you will know. The more that you learn, the more places you'll go." - Dr. Seuss

Prayer Lifestyle

"Education is the key to unlock the golden door of freedom." - George Washington Carver

Prayer

Dear Lord,
I come to you today asking for success in continuing my education. I am grateful for the opportunity to further my understanding and knowledge, and I pray for your guidance as I embark on this journey.

Help me have a teachable spirit and an open heart so I may receive all you have. Let me not be discouraged by the challenges and obstacles that may come my way, but let me trust in your plans and purposes for my life.

Grant me wisdom and understanding so that I may apply what I learn to my life and positively impact the world. Please give me the strength and discipline to remain focused and diligent in my studies to accomplish all you have called me to do.

Let my love for learning reflect my love for you, and let me use my knowledge and skills to serve and glorify your name. Amen.

Declaration

I declare that I am seeking God's wisdom and guidance in my pursuit of continued education. I declare that I believe in the power of knowledge and am eager to expand my understanding in a way that honors and glorifies God. I declare that I will diligently apply myself to my studies, seeking to grasp the deeper meanings and implications of what I am learning. I declare that I will be receptive to new ideas and perspectives, always striving to be a lifelong learner and to grow in wisdom and understanding.

I pray that God will open doors of opportunity for me to continue my education through traditional means or unconventional methods. I pray that He will provide me with the resources and support I need to succeed, including financial provision, supportive friends and mentors, and a strong community of believers.

I declare that I will use my knowledge and skills for the good of others and that I will be a faithful steward of the gifts and talents God has given me. I further declare that I will continue to seek God's wisdom and guidance in all aspects of my life, including my education, and that I will be obedient to His will. I pray that my continued education will bring me closer to God, deepen my relationship with Him, and prepare me for the work He has called me to do.

Prayer Lifestyle

Ivon Valerie

Children and Family

Our children and families are fundamental aspects of our lives that give us a sense of belonging, guidance, and comfort. In this chapter, we will emphasize the value of children and family in our lives by providing readers with prayers to strengthen their relationships with those dearest to them— enabling them to build strong connections rooted in love.

Prayer Lifestyle

Children's Well-Being

As parents, grandparents, or caregivers, it is natural to want the best for the children in our lives. Praying for their well-being is a powerful way to support and protect them and help them grow into healthy and happy adults.

Scripture References

Psalm 127:3: "Children are a heritage from the Lord, offspring a reward from him."

Proverbs 22:6: "Start children off on the way they should go, and even when they are old they will not turn from it."

Isaiah 54:13: "All your children shall be taught by the Lord, and great shall be the peace of your children."

Inspirational/Motivational Quotes

"The most important thing a father can do for his children is to love their mother." - Theodore Hesburgh

"Children are the living messages we send to a time we will not see." - John W. Whitehead

"Children are the hands by which we take hold of heaven." - Henry Ward Beecher

Ivon Valerie

Prayer

Dear Lord,
I come to you today with a grateful heart, lifting the precious children in my life. I pray for their health and happiness, asking that you bless them with your grace and protection. I ask that you watch over them, guiding them in all their ways so they may grow in wisdom and spirit.

I pray for their future that they may be a heritage and a reward from you, a blessing to all those around them. I ask that you fill their hearts with love and joy, and they may always know your peace. I pray they may grow in their faith and walk in your ways, seeking your truth and living according to your will.

Lord, I also ask for wisdom and guidance as a parent. Help me to lead by example, showing them your love and grace in all I do. Give me patience in the trials and joy in the blessings, and help me raise them in accordance with your word. I pray that I may reflect your light and love in their lives and that they may come to know you more and more each day.

I pray these children may be a shining testimony of your goodness and a light in this dark world. I ask that you bless them with your presence so they may grow in grace, wisdom, and strength. I pray they may bring you honor and glory in all they do. Amen.

Declaration

I declare that the children in my life are a gift from God, and I am honored to have been chosen as their caregiver and guide. I am lifting them in prayer, asking for God's blessings of good health, happiness, and wisdom to be upon them at all times. I trust in God's guidance for the children, and I know that He has a plan for their lives that is good and perfect.

I declare that the children are a heritage from the Lord, a reward from Him and that they have been entrusted to my care with a purpose and a destiny. I know that the Lord will teach and guide them in all they do and that He will be with them every step. I declare that I have wisdom, guidance, and discernment as I seek to parent and raise children in a way that honors God and reflects His love and grace.

I declare I will lead by example, showing the children the love, compassion, and kindness God has shown me. I will model a life of faith and obedience, teaching them to trust God, even in trials and challenges. I will encourage them to grow in their relationship with God, develop a deep love and knowledge of His Word, and follow His will for their lives.

I declare that I will be there for the children, no matter what life may bring. I will listen to them, support them, and provide comfort and encouragement. I will be patient, kind, and understanding, always seeking to show the love of Christ in all that I do. I will pray for the children, interceding on their behalf and asking God to meet their every physical and spiritual need.

Ivon Valerie

I declare that the children will be a blessing to others, a shining light in a dark and lost world. I will teach them to serve others, show kindness and compassion, and positively influence the lives of those around them. I will encourage them to use their talents and gifts for the glory of God, knowing that He has equipped them with everything they need to fulfill their purpose and destiny.

With the help of God, I declare that I will love, cherish, and pray for the children in my life, always seeking to guide and encourage them on their faith journey. I trust in God's guidance, knowing that He will lead and direct their paths, and I will be faithful in my role as a parent, always seeking to honor Him in all that I do. May the children's peace be great and their future bright as they walk in the light of God's love and grace.

Prayer Lifestyle

Children's Protection

As parents, grandparents, or caregivers, it is natural to want to protect the children in our lives from harm. Praying for their protection is a powerful way to ensure their safety and give them a sense of security.

Scripture References

Psalm 91:11: "For he will command his angels concerning you to guard you in all your ways."

Psalm 121:3: "He will not let your foot slip—he who watches over you will not slumber."

Proverbs 22:3: "A prudent man foresees danger and takes precautions; the simpleton goes blindly on and suffers the consequences."

Inspirational/Motivational Quotes

"The best protection any woman can have... is courage." - Elizabeth Cady Stanton

"The more you know about the past, the better prepared you are for the future." - Theodore Roosevelt

"The only real security that a man can have in this world is a reserve of knowledge, experience, and ability." - Henry Ford

Prayer

Dear Lord,
I come to you today lifting the precious children in my life. I pray for your protection upon them, asking that you command your angels to guard them in all their ways. I ask that you would keep them safe from harm, that you would not let their feet slip, and that you would watch over them and not slumber.

I pray for wisdom for myself and others who care for these children so that we may have the foresight to see danger and take precautions for their safety. I ask that you give us the strength and courage to be their protectors, to stand between them and any harm that may come their way.

I trust your goodness and love and know you will always protect and watch over these children. I pray they may grow up in a safe and loving environment, surrounded by your love and grace. I ask that you would fill their hearts with peace and joy and that they may always know your protection.

Lord, I pray for their future that they may live long and fulfilling lives, walking in your ways and seeking your truth. I ask that you bless them with the gifts of the Spirit and that they may use them for your glory. I pray that they may grow in their faith and become beacons of light in this dark world, shining forth your love and grace to all those around them.

I pray that these children may be a testimony of your goodness and love and that they may grow up to be strong and faithful servants of your kingdom. I trust in your protection and love and ask that you be their guide and shield in all they do. Amen.

Declaration

I declare that the children in my life are precious in the sight of God, and I am lifting them in prayer, asking for His protection and care. I trust in God's protection, knowing He has promised to command His angels to guard them in all their ways, watch over them, and not slumber.

I declare that I will pray for wisdom and discernment for myself and all those who care for them so that we may foresee danger and take all necessary precautions for their safety. I will trust in God's goodness and love, knowing that He is always watching over the children and that His hand of protection is upon them.

I declare that I will teach the children to trust in God and seek His protection in all they do. I will encourage them to lean on Him and to put their faith and confidence in His care. I will help them to understand that God is always with them, no matter where they go or what they do, and that they can always turn to Him for help and guidance.

I declare that the children will be surrounded by God's protection day and night. I declare that the children will grow in their faith and trust in God, and they will understand the depth and breadth of His love and protection. I declare that they will be able to withstand the trials and temptations of this world and that they will be able to stand firm in the face of adversity. I declare that they will be able to find comfort and hope in the knowledge that God is always with them and that He will never leave them or forsake them.

With the help of God, I declare that I will trust in God's protection for the children in my life and will lift them in prayer every day, asking for His care and guidance. I will be vigilant in my role as a parent or caregiver, seeking to ensure their safety and well-being at all times. I will trust in God's goodness and love, knowing that He will always protect and watch over the children and that they will grow in their faith and trust in Him.

Prayer Lifestyle

Children's Spiritual Growth

As parents, grandparents, or caregivers, it is important to pray for the spiritual growth of the children in our lives. This includes their understanding, relationship with God, and moral and ethical development.

Scripture References

Deuteronomy 6:6-7: "These commandments that I give you today are to be on your hearts. Impress them on your children. Talk about them when you sit at home and when you walk along the road, when you lie down and when you get up."

Proverbs 22:6: "Start children off on the way they should go, and even when they are old they will not turn from it."

Ephesians 6:4: "Fathers, do not exasperate your children; instead, bring them up in the training and instruction of the Lord."

Inspirational/Motivational Quotes

"The greatest legacy one can pass on to one's children and grandchildren is not money or other material things accumulated in one's life, but rather a legacy of character and faith." - Billy Graham

Ivon Valerie

"The foundation of every state is the education of its youth." - Diogenes

"Children are a great comfort in your old age, and they help you reach it faster, too." - Lionel Kauffman

Prayer

Dear Lord,
I come before you today, lifting the precious children in my life and asking for your guidance and wisdom in their spiritual growth. I pray they will have a strong understanding and relationship with you and develop strong moral and ethical values. I pray that they will grow in their faith and become rooted in your truth, that they may always turn to you for guidance and comfort.

I pray they may see your love and grace in my actions and words and be inspired to follow in your ways. I ask for your guidance and wisdom in leading them on the way they should go, and I trust in your goodness and love to guide them every step of the way. I pray that they may have the strength and courage to follow your will, even when it is difficult, and that they may have the perseverance to see it through.

I pray they will not turn from your ways, even when they are old, but they will continue to seek your truth and follow your will. I ask that they will always have a love for your word and that they may grow in their knowledge and understanding of your will for their lives. I trust in your love and guidance for these children, and I pray they will always find their way back to you, no matter their challenges. I ask that you would bless them with your presence and your peace and that they may grow to be strong and faithful servants of your kingdom. Amen.

Declaration

I declare that the children in my life are destined for great spiritual growth, and God's guidance and wisdom are leading them on the right path. I declare these children will have a deep and abiding relationship with God and grow in understanding His love, grace, and mercy.

I declare that I have God's wisdom and guidance in leading the children on the path they should go. I declare that the children will be filled with the Holy Spirit and a strong desire to grow in their faith and knowledge of God. I also declare that they will be gifted with discernment and understanding and be able to apply the teachings of God to their lives in meaningful ways. I declare that they will be able to resist the temptations of the world and that they will be able to stand firm in their faith, no matter what challenges they may face.

With the help of God, I declare I will be a diligent and faithful parent or caregiver, lifting the children in my life in prayer for their spiritual growth and well-being. I will be a good example, teaching them the ways of God and leading them on the path they should go. I will trust in God's wisdom and guidance, knowing that He is the only one who can lead the children to the fulfillment of their potential, and I will pray without ceasing for their spiritual growth and success in life. Amen.

Guidance in Parenting

Being a parent can be a challenging and rewarding experience, but it can also be difficult to know the best way to raise and guide our children. Praying for guidance in parenting is a powerful way to seek wisdom and direction in this important role.

Scripture References

Proverbs 22:6: "Start children off on the way they should go, and even when they are old they will not turn from it."

Ephesians 6:4: "Fathers, do not exasperate your children; instead, bring them up in the training and instruction of the Lord."

Colossians 3:21: "Fathers, do not embitter your children, or they will become discouraged."

Inspirational/Motivational Quotes

"It's not what you do for your children, but what you have taught them to do for themselves, that will make them successful human beings." - Ann Landers

"The best thing parents can do for their children is to love each other." - Fred Rogers

"The most important thing a father can do for his children is to love their mother." - Theodore Hesburgh

Prayer

Dear Lord,
I come to you today with a grateful heart, thanking you for entrusting me with the responsibility of raising these precious children, and I ask for your guidance and wisdom as I navigate this journey. I pray that I will raise my children how they should grow and that they will not turn from it even when they are old. I pray that I will not anger or frustrate my children, but instead, I will bring them up in the training and instruction of the Lord. I ask for your grace and mercy as I make mistakes and seek to learn and grow as a parent.

I pray for patience and understanding as I navigate parenting challenges and the strength to lead by example, showing my children your love and grace. I pray that I may be an instrument of your peace, bringing comfort and hope to my children in times of trouble. I pray for wisdom as I teach my children about your ways and the ability to help them grow in their faith and understand your will for their lives. I pray that I may be able to provide for their physical, emotional, and spiritual needs and that I may be a source of encouragement and support for them.

Lord, I trust in your love and guidance for me as a parent and for my children, and I pray that they may grow to be strong and faithful servants of your kingdom. I ask that you bless me with your presence and your peace and that I may have the courage and perseverance to follow your will, no matter what challenges come my way. Amen.

Declaration

I declare that as a parent, I will be a diligent and faithful steward of the children entrusted to me, striving to nurture their physical, emotional, and spiritual well-being. I will teach them about God's love, mercy, and grace and that they will come to know Him personally. I declare that I will model healthy and loving relationships and encourage the children to treat others with kindness and respect. I also declare that I will pray for my children's future, that they will grow to be responsible, faithful, and loving individuals who bring honor and glory to God.

I declare that I will listen to my children, truly hear their concerns and feelings, and help them navigate life's challenges. I will be supportive and understanding, always quick to offer a comforting hug and a listening ear. I declare that I will create a safe, loving, and nurturing environment where the children feel loved, valued, and appreciated. I will encourage their interests and talents and help them develop their gifts and abilities.

I declare that I will have the courage and strength to make difficult decisions, the wisdom to know what is best for my children, and the grace to forgive myself and others when we fall short. I declare that I will pray for my children's protection, safety, and well-being and that they will be surrounded by love and support. I declare that I will always trust in God's plan and purpose for their lives and that I will be confident in His ability to guide them on the path they should take. I declare that I will be

Prayer Lifestyle

a faithful and loving parent and that the children in my life will be blessed and prosperous.

Family Unity and Harmony

Family is a vital part of our lives, and we must pray for unity and harmony within our families. This includes praying for the relationships between parents, children, and siblings and our families' overall well-being and happiness.

Scripture References

Psalm 133:1: "How good and pleasant it is when God's people live together in unity!"

Colossians 3:14: "And over all these virtues put on love, which binds them all together in perfect unity."

Ephesians 4:3: "Make every effort to keep the unity of the Spirit through the bond of peace."

Inspirational/Motivational Quotes

"The strength of a family, like the strength of an army, is in its loyalty to each other." - Mario Puzo

"The most important thing in the world is family and love." - John Wooden

"In every conceivable manner, the family is link to our past, bridge to our future." - Alex Haley

Prayer

Dear Lord,
Today, I pray for my family and ask for your blessings. I pray for unity and harmony in our relationships so that we may live together in love and peace, just as it is good and pleasing in your sight. I pray for the bond of love to hold us together and for the unity of the Spirit to keep us in perfect peace. I ask for understanding, compassion, and kindness to guide our interactions and deep appreciation and gratitude for the gifts each family member brings to the table.

I pray for our overall well-being, both physically and emotionally. I ask that you would grant us good health, joy, peace, and happiness. I pray that we will be a source of encouragement and support, lifting each other in times of need and rejoicing together in celebration.

Lord, I also pray for our future together. I ask that you would bless our family with longevity and that we would have many years to love and care for one another. I ask that we remain steadfast in our commitment to each other, even through the ups and downs of life, and that we will always be there for one another, no matter what.

I am thankful for the gift of family and the love and support we share. I pray that your love and grace will be evident in our lives and that we will shine as examples of your goodness to all those around us. Amen.

Ivon Valerie

Declaration

I declare that God's grace and guidance strengthen our family relationships. I believe our family can be an example of love, kindness, and unity to those around us, reflecting the love and unity of the Holy Trinity. I declare that we will be quick to forgive one another, show compassion, and extend grace to each other, just as God has extended grace to us. We will grow in love and understanding, always encouraging and building each other up in the faith.

We will celebrate our differences, recognizing each member's unique gifts and talents to our family dynamic. I declare that we will work together to overcome challenges and obstacles, knowing that we are stronger with God's help. I declare that I will be a peacemaker in my family, promoting unity and harmony and resolving conflicts that honor God.

I declare that I will pray for my family's physical and emotional health and that we will support one another in times of need. I know we will enjoy spending time together, creating memories, and building relationships that will last a lifetime. I declare that our love for each other will only grow stronger as we journey through life together.

I thank God for the gift of family and the opportunity to grow in love, unity, and harmony. I trust in His guidance and wisdom, knowing He will work all things for our good and His glory. I declare that I am lifting my family in prayer daily, asking for blessings of unity and harmony within our relationships.

Prayer Lifestyle

Ivon Valerie

Travel and Safety

Travel and safety are both essential components of life. Exploring new places can offer unique experiences that help us to learn, while the assurance of safety grants a sense of satisfaction and confidence. In this chapter, we will explore the value travel and security have in our lives, with prayers, declarations, and strategies laid out to aid readers in planning safe trips for themself or loved ones as well as finding peace on their adventures.

Prayer Lifestyle

Safe Travels

Traveling can be a wonderful experience filled with uncertainty and potential dangers. Praying for safe travels is a powerful way to ask for protection and guidance during our journeys.

Scripture References

Psalm 91:11: "For he will command his angels concerning you to guard you in all your ways."

Psalm 121:7-8: "The Lord will keep you from all harm—he will watch over your life; the Lord will watch over your coming and going both now and forevermore."

Proverbs 3:23: "Then you will go on your way in safety, and your foot will not stumble."

Inspirational/Motivational Quotes

"Travel is the only thing you can buy that makes you richer." - Unknown

"Traveling – it leaves you speechless, then turns you into a storyteller." - Ibn Battuta

"The world is a book, and those who do not travel read only one page." - Saint Augustine

Ivon Valerie

Prayer

Dear Lord,

I come to you in prayer for my upcoming travels. I humbly ask for your protection and guidance as I embark on this journey. I trust in your promise to command your angels to guard me in all my ways, to keep me from all harm, and to ensure my safe travels.

I pray for your hand of protection to be upon me and for your grace to cover me as I travel. I ask for wisdom to make wise decisions, discernment to recognize any danger that may come my way, and courage to face any challenges that may arise.

I pray for good health and strength to endure the journey, Lord. I ask that you would renew my body and mind so that I may have the energy and focus on completing my tasks with excellence.

I pray for your peace to calm any fears or worries that may arise. I ask that you give me rest and renew my spirit so I may serve you with joy and a clear mind.

Lord, I pray for your wisdom to guide me and your light to shine upon my path. I ask that you reveal any hidden dangers and give me the courage to face them head-on. Lord God, I pray for your protection and guidance as I lift my travels to you in prayer. I trust your promises and place my complete faith in you, knowing that you will never abandon or forsake me. Amen.

Declaration:

I declare my unwavering belief in the protection and guidance of our Lord and Savior, Jesus Christ. I lift my upcoming travels to Him, asking that He guide me every step of the way and keep me safe from all harm. I trust in His promise to command His angels to watch over me and keep me from stumbling, and I know He will protect me during my travels.

I declare that the hand of the Lord will be upon me, shielding me from danger and providing me with His peace and comfort. My mind and heart are filled with His presence, and I walk in His wisdom and make decisions that honor Him. I will be a shining light to all I encounter on my journey, reflecting God's love, grace, and mercy.

I declare that I will not be afraid, for the Lord is with me and will never leave nor forsake me. I declare that I am confident in His plan for my life and that my travels will bring Him glory and bring me closer to Him. I declare that I am a child of God and that His love and protection surround me always.

With each step I take, I will trust in the Lord, for I know He is my refuge, strength, and shield. I will call upon His name in every moment of need and trust in His goodness and grace. I will rest in the knowledge that He is always with me and that He has a plan for my life that is good and perfect.

I declare that my travels will be safe and my foot will not stumble. I declare that I am under the protection of the Lord and that He will guide me in all my ways. I declare that my faith and trust in God will never waver.

Ivon Valerie

Protection While Away From Home

Being away from home can be difficult and scary, but praying for protection can give us peace of mind and reassurance. Praying for protection while away from home is important for our physical and emotional safety.

Scripture References

Psalm 91:1-2: "He who dwells in the secret place of the Most High shall abide under the shadow of the Almighty. I will say of the Lord, "He is my refuge and my fortress; My God, in Him I will trust.""

Psalm 140:7: "O Lord, my Lord, the strength of my salvation, You have covered my head in the day of battle."

Psalm 121:5: "The Lord is your keeper; The Lord is your shade at your right hand."

Inspirational/Motivational Quotes

"Home is where the heart is, but it's nice to have a place to put it." - Unknown

Prayer Lifestyle

"Home is not where you live but where they understand you." - Christian Morgenstern

"Home is not a place, it's a feeling." - Cecelia Ahern

Prayer

Dear Lord,
I bring my time away from home to you in prayer. I lift my fears and worries and trust in your promise to be my refuge and fortress. I ask for your protection and guidance as I navigate this new experience and place my faith in your care. I pray for physical safety while away from home and for your hand of protection to cover me. I ask that you watch over me and keep me from all harm, especially in battle or danger. I pray for your wisdom and guidance in decision-making and the strength to face any challenges that may come my way.

I pray for emotional safety and peace of mind. I ask for your reassurance, comfort, and presence to fill my heart and soul. I pray for the confidence to trust in your care and the courage to step out in faith, knowing that you are always there to guide and support me. I pray for provision for my needs. I ask for your wisdom in managing my resources and for your blessings to flow into my life. I pray for your provision in every area of my life and for your hand of favor to be upon me.

Lord, I pray for your peace to calm any fears or worries that may arise. I ask that you give me rest and renew my spirit so I may serve you with joy and a clear mind. I pray for your comfort and peace to fill my heart and soul, especially during loneliness or difficulty.

I pray for your protection and guidance as I lift my time away from home to you in prayer. I pray I may glorify your name and bring honor to your kingdom through my time away from home. Amen.

Declaration

As I embark on this time away from home, I declare that my heart is lifted to the Lord, and I receive His hand of protection as my covering, especially in battle. I trust in His promise to be my refuge and fortress. I believe He is always with me, and His love and care will never fail me.

I declare that I will be protected physically and emotionally during this time away from home. I ask for wisdom, guidance in decision-making, and provision for all my needs. I pray for the peace of mind and reassurance, knowing God is always my keeper and my shade at my right hand.

I declare that I am a child of God and that His grace and mercy surround me always. I trust in His plan for my life, and I am confident that this time away from home is a part of that plan. I will not be afraid, for the Lord is with me, and I am confident in His power and protection.

I pray for the strength and courage to face any challenges that may come my way and for the wisdom to make decisions that honor God. I ask for the grace to trust in His timing and plans

Prayer Lifestyle

and for the peace to rest in His love and care. So, I declare this day that I am under the protection of the Lord and that He will be my refuge and fortress.

Ivon Valerie

Guidance in Travel Decisions

Traveling can be a wonderful experience filled with uncertainty and potential dangers. Praying for guidance in travel decisions is a powerful way to ask for protection and guidance during our journeys.

Scripture References

Proverbs 3:5-6: "Trust in the Lord with all your heart and lean not on your own understanding; in all your ways submit to him, and he will make your paths straight."

Psalm 32:8: "I will instruct you and teach you in the way you should go; I will counsel you with my loving eye on you."

James 1:5: "If any of you lacks wisdom, you should ask God, who gives generously to all without finding fault, and it will be given to you."

Inspirational/Motivational Quotes

"Travel is fatal to prejudice, bigotry, and narrow-mindedness." - Mark Twain

"The world is a book and those who do not travel read only one page." - Saint Augustine

Prayer Lifestyle

"Travel is not really about leaving our homes, but leaving our habits." - Pico Iyer

Prayer

Dear Lord,
I ask for your guidance and wisdom in my travel decisions. I trust your promise to instruct and teach me where I should go. I am confident you will always counsel and guide me with your loving eye and sure hand. I pray for wisdom as I consider where to travel. I ask that you show me the right path and guide me in making the best decision for my growth and well-being. I pray for clarity and for your guidance as I weigh the pros and cons of each option and make a decision that is in line with your will for my life.

Lord, I also pray for wisdom in deciding whom to travel with. I ask for your guidance in choosing the right companions for this journey and for your protection over any relationships that may form while I am away. I pray that I may be a positive influence on those around me and that I may build meaningful connections with those I meet.

I pray for your provision and protection during my travels. I ask for your hand of favor to be upon me and your blessings to follow me wherever I go. I pray for safety on the road, comfort during difficulties, and peace in uncertainty. I ask that you protect me from all harm and keep me from danger.

I pray my travels may be an opportunity for growth, and I ask that you open my eyes to new perspectives and experiences and that I may learn and grow in understanding and compassion because of this journey. I pray for your wisdom as I navigate new situations and for your comfort during any challenges. Amen.

Declaration

As I make travel plans, I lift my decisions to the Lord and ask for His wisdom and guidance in deciding where to go, whom to travel with, and when to embark on this journey.

I declare that I trust God's promise to instruct and counsel me. I know He is the source of all wisdom and will guide me in my path. I know He is my shepherd and will supply all my needs according to His riches in glory. I declare that His hand of protection is upon me, and His sufficient grace is always around me.

I declare that I am open to new experiences and perspectives and will grow in understanding and compassion because of my travels. I believe that my travels are a part of God's plan for my life and that He has a purpose for me everywhere I go. I declare that I am relying on the guidance and wisdom of the Lord in all my travel decisions.

Prayer Lifestyle

Provision During Travels

Traveling can be a wonderful experience filled with uncertainty and potential dangers. Praying for provision during travels is a powerful way to ask for resources, protection, and guidance.

Scripture References

Matthew 6:25-26: "Therefore I tell you, do not worry about your life, what you will eat or drink; or about your body, what you will wear. Is not life more than food, and the body more than clothes? Look at the birds of the air; they do not sow or reap or store away in barns, and yet your heavenly Father feeds them. Are you not much more valuable than they?"

Philippians 4:19: "And my God will meet all your needs according to the riches of his glory in Christ Jesus."

Psalm 34:10: "The young lions lack and suffer hunger; But those who seek the Lord shall not lack any good thing."

Inspirational/Motivational Quotes

"Travel is about creating memories, not just taking photographs." - Unknown

"Traveling – it leaves you speechless, then turns you into a storyteller." - Ibn Battuta

"Travel, in the younger sort, is a part of education; in the elder, a part of experience." - Francis Bacon

Prayer

Dear Lord,
I put my confidence in You for all my travels, trusting in Your promise to supply all my needs. I pray for your provision for all my physical needs. I ask that you provide me with food to nourish my body, a place to rest my head, and transportation to get me where I need to go. I pray that you will keep me healthy and strong and give me the energy I need to enjoy my travels and carry out the tasks you have set before me.

I also pray for your provision for my emotional and spiritual needs. I ask that you grant me peace in my heart, joy in my spirit, and understanding in my mind. I pray that I may be able to approach my travels with a positive attitude and with a heart of gratitude, knowing that all good things come from you.

I pray you will help me trust your provision and not worry about the future. I ask that you give me the courage to step out in faith, knowing that you are always with me and will never leave or forsake me. I pray that I may have peace of mind that passes all understanding and enjoy my travels to the fullest, knowing that you have everything under control.

Lord, I thank you for your provision and faithfulness in meeting all my needs. I will not be afraid or discouraged, no matter what the future may hold. I pray that I may bring honor and glory to your name through my travels and be a positive witness to those I meet along the way. Amen.

Declaration

I declare that I put all my trust in God's hands as I embark on this journey. I declare that I believe in His promise to provide for all my physical and emotional needs. I declare that I am lifting my travels in prayer, asking for His guidance and protection every step of the way.

I declare that I am not afraid of the unknown, for I know God is always with me. I declare that I will not worry about the future, for I know He has a plan for me. I declare that I will trust in His provision, no matter what may come my way. I declare that I will have peace in my heart, even in the midst of uncertainty, for I know that God is my peace.

I declare that I will have joy in my spirit, even in difficulties, for I know God is my joy. I declare that I will have understanding, even in confusion, for I know that God is my understanding. I declare I will not be discouraged, for I know God is my strength.

I am grateful for all God has done in my life, and I trust that He will continue to do great things. I will be a testimony to all I meet, showing them the love and provision of God in my life. I declare that I am confident in God's promises and will not be swayed by fear or doubt. I will trust in God's provision and will not be held back by worry or anxiety.

Ivon Valerie

Protection While Traveling With Loved Ones

Traveling with loved ones can be a wonderful experience with uncertainty and potential dangers. Praying for protection while traveling with loved ones is a powerful way to ask for protection and guidance during our journeys.

Scripture References

Psalm 91:11: "For he will command his angels concerning you to guard you in all your ways."

Psalm 121:7-8: "The Lord will keep you from all harm—he will watch over your life; the Lord will watch over your coming and going both now and forevermore."

Isaiah 54:17: "No weapon forged against you will prevail, and you will refute every tongue that accuses you. This is the heritage of the servants of the Lord, and this is their vindication from me," declares the Lord.

Inspirational/Motivational Quotes

"Wherever you go, go with all your heart." - Confucius

Prayer Lifestyle

"Traveling with a loved one is an opportunity to strengthen your bond and create unforgettable memories." - Unknown

"The greatest thing in family life is to take a hint when a hint is intended—and not to take a hint when a hint isn't intended." - Robert Frost

Prayer

Dear Lord,
As I embark on this journey with my loved ones, I pray to you, asking for your protection and guidance. I trust your promise to be our shield and defender, always watching over us and keeping us safe. I pray for the physical and emotional safety of each member of our group that we may all return home in good health and peace. I pray for unity and understanding within our group so that we may support and encourage each other as we navigate this journey together.

I ask for your wisdom and guidance as we make decisions and face challenges. I pray that we may be open to new experiences and perspectives and that our travels may bring us closer as a group and deepen our love for one another. I pray for your provision in all our physical and emotional needs that we may never lack for anything that brings us comfort and peace.

Lord, I ask that you would be with us always, guiding our steps and watching over us. I pray that you will use this time away from home to grow our understanding of you and our love for one another. Amen.

Declaration

I declare that I put my trust in God's hands as I embark on this journey with my loved ones. I declare that I believe in His promise to protect us and to watch over our lives. I declare that I am lifting our travels in prayer, asking for His guidance and protection every step of the way.

I declare we are not afraid of the unknown, for we know God is always with us. I declare that we will not worry about the future, for we know He has a plan for us. I declare that we will rely on His protection and guidance, no matter what may come our way. I declare that we will have peace in our hearts, even in the midst of uncertainty, for we know that God is our peace.

I declare that we will have joy in our spirits, even in difficulties, for we know God is our joy. I declare that we will have understanding, even in confusion, for we know that God is our understanding. I declare we will not be discouraged, for we know God is our strength.

I declare that we will be a testimony to all we meet, showing them the love and protection of God in our lives. I declare that we are confident in God's promises and will not be swayed by fear or doubt. I declare that we will rely on God's protection and will not be held back by worry or anxiety. I declare that we are filled with faith, hope, and love.

Ivon Valerie

Creativity and Arts

The power of creativity and the arts should not be underestimated. They provide a way to express ourselves, build relationships, and find joy and satisfaction in our lives. This chapter emphasizes how integral these elements are in our everyday life. Through prayers and declarations offered here, readers will discover ways to access their creative side, draw motivation from their surroundings, and amplify any special talents they possess artistically.

Prayer Lifestyle

Inspiration and Creativity

Creativity and inspiration are vital for those in the arts and anyone looking to bring new ideas and perspectives to the world. Praying for inspiration and creativity is a powerful way to ask for guidance and to tap into the well of ideas that comes from the divine.

Scripture References

Psalm 45:1: "My heart is stirred by a noble theme as I recite my verses for the king; my tongue is the pen of a skillful writer."

Isaiah 64:8: "Yet you, Lord, are our Father. We are the clay, you are the potter; we are all the work of your hand."

James 1:5: "If any of you lacks wisdom, you should ask God, who gives generously to all without finding fault, and it will be given to you."

Inspirational/Motivational Quotes

"You can't use up creativity. The more you use, the more you have." - Maya Angelou

"Creativity is intelligence having fun." - Albert Einstein

"Creativity is not a talent. It is a way of operating." - John Cleese

Prayer

Dear Lord,

I come to you today with a humble heart, seeking your inspiration and creativity for my artistic pursuits. I pray for your guidance and wisdom, I ask that you give me new ideas and perspectives that will allow me to grow and improve my craft. I know that you have promised to give generously to all who seek wisdom, so I trust in your generosity as I pray for an increase in my artistic talents.

I pray that you will give me a new vision for my work and that I may be able to see things in a way that I never have before. I ask that you open my mind and heart to new possibilities and give me the courage to explore uncharted territories in my creative journey.

I also pray for your protection and guidance as I navigate the challenges of pursuing my artistic passion. I know there will be obstacles and difficulties along the way. I ask that you would give me the strength and resilience to overcome any challenges that come my way and that I may continue to grow and improve in my artistic pursuits.

Lord, I thank you for the gifts and talents you have given me, and I pray that I may use them to bring joy, beauty, and inspiration to others. I ask that you grant me the wisdom and creativity to create works that reflect your love and grace. And as I continue on this journey, I pray that you will use me to bring hope and light to a world that desperately needs it. Amen.

Declaration

I trust that God will guide and give me wisdom as I seek new ideas and perspectives in my artistic pursuits. I know that with God, all things are possible and that I have the potential to bring my creative visions to life. I declare that I will not give up until my artistic talents reach their full potential. I believe God has given me the gifts and talents for a reason, and I am committed to using them to bring glory to His name.

I declare that I will not be discouraged by obstacles or setbacks in my journey as an artist. Instead, I will use them as opportunities to grow and learn and continue to trust in God's wisdom and guidance. I will persist in pursuing inspiration and creativity and will not settle for anything less than greatness.

I declare that I will be a light in the world of art and that I will use my talents to bring joy and beauty to those around me. I will be a positive influence in the lives of others, and I will inspire others to tap into their creativity and follow their dreams. I declare that I am fully committed to my artistic pursuits and will never give up. I am confident in my abilities and trust God's plan for my life. I am ready to take on the world and make a positive impact through my art.

Ivon Valerie

Success in the Arts

Success in the arts can mean different things for different people, but for many, it means achieving recognition and financial stability for their work. Praying for success in the arts is a powerful way to ask for guidance and provision in pursuing one's artistic goals.

Scripture References

Psalm 37:4: "Take delight in the Lord, and he will give you the desires of your heart."

Colossians 3:23: "Whatever you do, work at it with all your heart, as working for the Lord, not for human masters."

Proverbs 16:3: "Commit to the Lord whatever you do, and he will establish your plans."

Inspirational/Motivational Quotes

"Art is not what you see, but what you make others see." - Edgar Degas

"Success in the arts is a journey, not a destination." - Unknown

"The greatest glory in living lies not in never falling, but in rising every time we fall." - Nelson Mandela

Prayer

Dear Lord,
I know you have given me a passion and a talent for creating, and I ask that you guide me as I work toward my artistic goals. I ask for your provision and support as I strive to bring my artistic vision to life. I trust in your promise to give me the desires of my heart as I delight in you, and I pray that you will show me the path to success in my artistic pursuits.

I ask for the ability to work with all my heart as if working for you and for the wisdom and discernment to make good decisions in my art. I know there will be challenges along the way, but I ask for the strength to persevere and never give up on my dreams. I pray for the courage to take risks and to step out of my comfort zone and for the grace to handle both success and failure with humility and grace.

I ask that you grant me the wisdom to seek out opportunities that will allow me to grow and improve in my craft and the discernment to recognize and avoid situations that distract or detract from my artistic vision.

Lord, I ask that you grant me the ability to create beautiful and inspiring works that reflect your love and grace. I pray that my art will be a source of hope and light in a world that desperately needs it and that I may use my talents to bring glory to your name. Amen.

Ivon Valerie

Declaration

I declare that I am lifting my desire for success in the arts in prayer. I believe with all my heart that God will guide and bless me in my pursuit of success in the arts. I know He has a plan for my life.

I am determined to use my talents and gifts to glorify God. I declare that I will be a faithful steward of the resources and opportunities God provides, and I trust in Him to provide for all my needs as I pursue success in the arts. I will not be discouraged by obstacles or setbacks; instead.

I declare that I will be bold in sharing my art with the world and use my gifts to impact those around me positively. I will be disciplined and committed to my artistic pursuits. I will work hard to develop my skills and talents and always strive to improve and grow as an artist. I believe that with God's help, I will achieve greatness in the arts.

I will be grateful for every opportunity and resource God provides and use them wisely. I will be mindful of the needs of others, and I will use my success in the arts to bless and serve those around me.

Prayer Lifestyle

Wisdom and Guidance in Artistic Decisions

Making decisions in the arts can be challenging, and it's important to seek wisdom and guidance from a higher power. Praying for wisdom and guidance in artistic decisions is a powerful way to ask for clarity and direction as you navigate the creative process.

Scripture References

Proverbs 3:5-6: "Trust in the Lord with all your heart and lean not on your own understanding; in all your ways submit to him, and he will make your paths straight."

James 1:5: "If any of you lacks wisdom, you should ask God, who gives generously to all without finding fault, and it will be given to you."

Isaiah 30:21: "Whether you turn to the right or to the left, your ears will hear a voice behind you, saying, 'This is the way; walk in it.'"

Inspirational/Motivational Quotes

"The greatest mistake you can make in life is continually being afraid you will make one." - Elbert Hubbard

"Art is not a handicraft, it is the transmission of feeling the artist has experienced." - Leo Tolstoy

"The artist is a receptacle for emotions that come from all over the place: from the sky, from the earth, from a scrap of paper, from a passing shape, from a spider's web." - Pablo Picasso

Prayer

Dear Lord,
I humbly long for your wisdom, instruction, and guidance in my artistic decisions. As I navigate the creative process, I ask for your clarity, direction, and ability to hear your voice and obey. I trust in your promise to make my paths straight as I submit to you and put my trust in you, and I pray that you will give me the discernment to make good decisions in my art.

I ask that you help me see things from your perspective and give me the courage to take risks and not be afraid of making mistakes. I know the creative process can be uncertain and challenging, but I trust your faithfulness to lead me in the right direction. I pray that you would grant me the ability to listen to your voice and to follow your guidance, even when the path ahead is unclear.

Lord, I also pray for the courage to embrace the unknown and the confidence to take risks and try new things. I ask that you help me not be discouraged by failures or setbacks but that I may continue to grow and improve in my craft through your guidance and wisdom.

I ask that you help me see my art as a tool for your glory and that I may use it to bring joy, beauty, and inspiration to others. I pray that my art will reflect your love and grace to the world and that I may be a faithful steward of the gifts and talents that you have given me. Amen.

Declaration

I trust in God's promise to give me clarity and direction as I seek to create art that honors Him. When I seek His wisdom and guidance, I know He will give it generously. I will listen to His voice and follow His guidance in my art, even when it feels difficult or uncertain.

I declare that I will have the courage to take risks and not be afraid of making mistakes. I believe that with God's help, I can overcome any obstacle and that every mistake is an opportunity to learn and grow. I declare that God will use my unique artistic vision to create something beautiful and impactful.

I declare that I will be patient and persistent in my artistic pursuits. I will not give up when things get tough; I will trust in God's plan for my life. I will use my gifts to make a difference in the world and seek to bring joy and inspiration to others through my art.

I declare that I will be thankful for every opportunity and blessing God provides and use them wisely. I will not be afraid to seek help when I need it, and I will be grateful for the support of others. I will always strive to be a blessing to those around me and to use my art to make a positive impact.

Ivon Valerie

Increase in Artistic Talents

Everyone has a unique artistic talent, but it can be helpful to pray for an increase in those talents to help take your art to the next level. Praying for increased artistic talents is a powerful way to ask for growth and improvement in your craft.

Scripture References

Psalm 138:8: "The Lord will fulfill his purpose for me; your love, O Lord, endures forever—do not abandon the works of your hands."

Ephesians 2:10: "For we are God's handiwork, created in Christ Jesus to do good works, which God prepared in advance for us to do."

1 Corinthians 12:4-6: "There are different kinds of gifts, but the same Spirit distributes them. There are different kinds of service, but the same Lord. There are different kinds of working, but in all of them and in everyone it is the same God at work."

Inspirational/Motivational Quotes

"Art is not what you see, but what you make others see." - Edgar Degas

"The more you know, the more you can create." - Unknown

"The secret to getting ahead is getting started." - Mark Twain

Prayer

Dear Lord,
I come to you today with a deep desire to increase my artistic talents and grow and improve my craft. I ask that you guide and bless me as I create and share my art and help me see my art as a tool for your glory. I thank you for the passion you have placed in my heart for the arts and the joy and fulfillment it brings to my life. I pray that you will continue to use my talents and gifts for your purpose and lead me in the direction you have for me.

I trust in your promises, and I ask that you give me the grace and strength to persevere through any challenges or obstacles that may come my way. I pray that you will help me to see the beauty in the struggles and to learn and grow from them. I also pray for the ability to create and share my art in a way that honors you and inspires others.

Lord, I ask that you continue to guide and bless me as I seek to increase my artistic talents and glorify you in all I do. I pray that you will fulfill your purpose for me and that I may be a faithful steward of the gifts and talents you have given me. Amen.

Declaration

I declare that with God's help and guidance, I will reach new heights in my artistic abilities. I trust God's promise to bless and guide my artistic growth and improvement. I will seek to learn, grow, and refine my skills. I will not be afraid to challenge myself and try new things, knowing that God is with me every step of the way.

I declare that I will not be discouraged by setbacks or criticism; instead, I will trust in God's plan for my life. I will not compare myself to others but focus on my journey and growth. I will be grateful for God's gifts and use them to the best of my ability.

I declare that I am thankful for every opportunity and blessing God provides, and I will use them wisely. I will be grateful for the support of others. I will always strive to use my art to impact the world positively. Amen.

Prayer Lifestyle

Protection for Artists and Creators

Being an artist or creator can be challenging, and asking for protection and guidance along the way is important. Praying for protection for artists and creators is a powerful way to ask for spiritual and physical protection as you navigate the creative process.

Scripture References

Psalm 91:11: "For he will command his angels concerning you to guard you in all your ways."

Psalm 121:7-8: "The Lord will keep you from all harm—he will watch over your life; the Lord will watch over your coming and going both now and forevermore."

Psalm 5:11: "But let all who take refuge in you be glad; let them ever sing for joy. Spread your protection over them, that those who love your name may rejoice in you."

Inspirational/Motivational Quotes

"The only way to do great work is to love what you do." - Steve Jobs

Ivon Valerie

"Creativity is a wild mind and a disciplined eye." - Dorothy Parker

"Creativity is not a talent. It is a way of operating." - John Cleese

Prayer

Dear Lord,

I come to you today with a humble heart for protection. As an artist and creator, I know that the creative process can be a challenging journey filled with many obstacles and uncertainties. I ask for your divine protection as I navigate this path and face the trials that come my way.

I trust in your promise to guard me and watch over my life, and I pray for the ability to take refuge in you and to find joy and safety in your protection. I ask that you shield me from all harm and danger. I pray that your grace and peace will surround me, providing comfort and strength when I am weak.

I also pray for the ability to spread your protection over others in the creative community. I ask that you bless and protect those who use their gifts to bring beauty into the world. May they find comfort and strength in your love, and may their work bring joy and inspiration to all who experience it. Lord, I trust in your promise to be with me always, and I thank you for the gift of creativity. Amen.

Declaration

I declare that God is my shield and protector. I declare that God will protect me spiritually and physically as I navigate the creative process. I will trust God's promise to guard me and watch over my life. I will not be afraid of obstacles or challenges, knowing God is always with me and has my back.

I declare that I will take refuge in God and find joy and safety in his protection. I will seek His guidance and direction as I create and trust His love and care for me. I will not be intimidated and negatively affected by the opinions of others but will have the courage to be true to myself and my art.

I declare that I will spread God's protection over others in the creative community. I will be a source of encouragement and support for my fellow artists and creators. I will pray for their safety, their art, and their well-being. I believe we can positively impact the world through our art and creativity.

Ivon Valerie

Prayer Lifestyle

Ivon Valerie

World Peace and Justice

World peace and justice are fundamental components of global development. They have a considerable impact on everyone and the entire world, thus making them an integral part of our lives. This chapter presents prayers, declarations, and other spiritual guidance to help you become advocates for peace and justice throughout your life so that we can promote harmony worldwide.

Prayer Lifestyle

Peace in the World

Praying for peace in the world is a way to lift the ongoing struggles for peace and ask God to intervene. This can be a powerful way to support those affected by war and violence and to help bring about an end to conflicts.

Scripture References

Isaiah 2:4: "He will judge between the nations and will settle disputes for many peoples. They will beat their swords into plowshares and their spears into pruning hooks. Nation will not take up sword against nation, nor will they train for war anymore."

Psalm 29:11: "The Lord gives strength to his people; the Lord blesses his people with peace."

Matthew 5:9: "Blessed are the peacemakers, for they will be called children of God."

Inspirational/Motivational Quotes

"Peace is not something you wish for; It's something you make, something you do, something you are, and something you give away." - Robert Fulghum

Ivon Valerie

"The world will not be destroyed by those who do evil, but by those who watch them without doing anything." - Albert Einstein

"Peace begins with a smile." - Mother Teresa

Prayer

Dear Lord,
I come before you today asking for your peace and guidance. The world is filled with conflict and violence, and I pray you will end the wars ravaging many nations. I lift the innocent people affected by these atrocities and ask for your protection. Please give them the strength and courage they need to endure these difficult times.

I pray for justice to be served to the oppressed. Help them to find the justice they deserve and to feel your comfort and love in their struggles. I pray that their oppressors will repent and turn away from their wrongdoing. May they know the peace and love that can only come from you.

Lord, I ask for your wisdom and guidance in my own life. Help me to be a peacemaker, spreading your love and grace wherever I go. May my actions and words bring hope and comfort to those around me, and may I be an example of your love and grace to the world.

I also pray for our nations' leaders to have your wisdom and guidance as they make decisions that affect the lives of so many people. May they seek discernment, peace, and justice and be guided by your love and grace as they lead.

Prayer Lifestyle

Lord, thank you for your promise to bring peace and settle disputes between nations. I trust in your goodness and mercy and know that you will end the conflicts and wars that ravage the world. Amen.

Declaration

I declare that the world will be filled with the peace of God. I trust that God will intervene to end conflicts and wars worldwide. I am dedicated to being a peacemaker in my own life and in the world around me. I understand that peace begins with me, and I am committed to spreading peace in my life, community, and world. I am not afraid to stand for what is right, for the safety of those affected by violence, and for justice for the oppressed.

I am a peacemaker and will do everything I can to promote peace in the world. I will spread love and kindness wherever I go and speak up for those who cannot speak for themselves. I will not allow fear or hate to control my heart or actions. Instead, I will walk in love and be a light in the world. I know peace is possible, and I will not give up on this goal.

Ivon Valerie

Peace in War-Torn Countries

Praying for peace in war-torn countries is a way to lift those affected by ongoing conflict and violence and ask God to intervene and end the fighting. This can be a powerful way to support those suffering and bring about change in countries ravaged by war.

Scripture References

Isaiah 60:18: "Violence will no longer be heard in your land, nor ruin or destruction within your borders, but you will call your walls Salvation and your gates Praise."

Psalm 34:14: "Turn from evil and do good; seek peace and pursue it."

Matthew 5:9: "Blessed are the peacemakers, for they will be called children of God."

Inspirational/Motivational Quotes

"Peace cannot be kept by force; it can only be achieved by understanding." - Albert Einstein

"Peace is not the absence of conflict, but the ability to handle conflict by peaceful means." - Ronald Reagan

Prayer

Dear Lord,

I come before you today with sorrow and concern for the world's war-torn countries. I pray for an end to the violence and destruction that has claimed the lives of so many and left countless others homeless and afraid. I pray for the safety of those caught in the crossfire and for justice for those who have suffered at the hands of oppressors.

I know you have a heart for peace, and I trust your promise to end the disputes and conflicts ravaging these nations. I pray that your love and grace will cover these lands, bringing hope and healing to all who live there. May they know that they are not alone and that you are with them every step of the way. I also pray for the leaders of these nations that they would have your wisdom and guidance as they make decisions affecting the lives of many. May they seek peace and justice and be guided by your love and grace as they lead. Please help them to put aside their differences and work together for the good of their people.

As I pray for these war-torn countries, I also ask for your guidance and wisdom in my own life. Help me to be a peacemaker, spreading your love and grace wherever I go. May my actions and words bring hope and comfort to those around me, and may I be a shining example of your love and grace to the world. I pray that I will have the strength to stand up for what is right, even when it is difficult. Please grant me the courage to speak out against oppression and violence and work toward peace and justice in my life and the world around me. Amen.

Ivon Valerie

Declaration

I believe and trust that God will intervene to end conflicts and wars ravaging war-torn nations. I am a peacemaker doing my part in bringing peace to the world. I understand that peace is a process, and it begins with me. I will take responsibility for promoting peace in my own life and in the world around me. I believe in God's promise to bring peace and settle disputes between nations, and I trust that this promise will come to pass. I am not afraid to stand up for what is right, advocate for the safety of those affected by violence, and for justice for the oppressed in war-torn countries.

I will not allow the atrocities of war to cloud my judgment or to fill my heart with anger and hate. Instead, I will choose to walk in love and be an example of peace in the world. I will pray for peace and take action toward it becoming a reality. I will speak up for those who cannot speak for themselves and fight for the safety and well-being of all people in war-torn countries.

Prayer Lifestyle

Justice for the Oppressed

Praying for justice for the oppressed is a way to lift marginalized and mistreated people and ask God to intervene and bring about change. This can be a powerful way to support those suffering and bring about righteousness.

Scripture References

Isaiah 1:17: "Learn to do right; seek justice. Defend the oppressed. Take up the cause of the fatherless; plead the case of the widow."

Psalm 82:3-4: "Defend the weak and the fatherless; uphold the cause of the poor and the oppressed. Rescue the weak and the needy; deliver them from the hand of the wicked."

James 2:12-13: "Speak and act as those who are going to be judged by the law that gives freedom, because judgment without mercy will be shown to anyone who has not been merciful. Mercy triumphs over judgment."

Inspirational/Motivational Quotes

"The true measure of any society can be found in how it treats its most vulnerable members." - Mahatma Gandhi

"To sin by silence when they should protest makes cowards of men." - Abraham Lincoln

Prayer

Dear Lord,

I come before you today with a heavy heart for the oppressed and marginalized people in the world. I pray to end the mistreatment and marginalization that so many have suffered for far too long. I lift the vulnerable and the forgotten, asking for your justice and righteousness to be their portion.

I pray for wisdom and guidance for those in positions of power that they would make decisions that bring about fairness and equality for all people, regardless of their background or circumstances. May they be guided by your love and grace as they lead, and may they use their power to bring justice and righteousness to the oppressed.

Lord, I ask for the strength and courage to stand up for the oppressed and to be a voice for those who cannot speak for themselves. Please help me to see the needs of the vulnerable and to work for their good. Please give me the boldness to speak out against injustice and to fight for what is right, even when it is difficult.

Father, I thank you for your promise to defend the weak and the fatherless and to bring justice for all. I trust your goodness and mercy and know that you will not forget the oppressed and marginalized. May they find comfort and hope in your love and know they are not alone. Amen.

Declaration

I declare that I am a champion for the oppressed and a voice for justice. I pray for justice for those who have been marginalized and discriminated against. I believe in God's promise to defend the weak and the fatherless and bring justice to all. I am committed to being a voice for justice and standing up for those who cannot speak for themselves.

I believe the fight for justice is a noble cause, and I am willing to sacrifice my time, comfort, and convenience for this cause if this is required of me. I will not be discouraged by the challenges that come with this fight for justice, but instead, I will be inspired by the possibility of a world where all individuals are treated with dignity and respect. I will relentlessly pursue justice and will not stop until it is a reality for all.

I declare I will be a voice of justice for the oppressed and work towards a world of fairness and righteousness. I declare that I will stand up for those who cannot speak for themselves and fight for justice in all areas of life. I declare that I will not be complacent in the face of oppression but will be a passionate advocate for change. I am a defender of justice and will bring about a world of fairness and equality.

Ivon Valerie

Safety for Humanitarian Workers

Praying for the safety of humanitarian workers is a way to lift those who put themselves in dangerous situations to help others. This can be a powerful way to support those making a difference and ensure their safety as they work to bring about change.

Scripture References

Psalm 91:11: "For he will command his angels concerning you to guard you in all your ways"

Psalm 121:7-8: "The Lord will keep you from all harm— he will watch over your life; the Lord will watch over your coming and going both now and forevermore."

Isaiah 41:10: "So do not fear, for I am with you; do not be dismayed, for I am your God. I will strengthen you and help you; I will uphold you with my righteous right hand."

Inspirational/Motivational Quotes

"The best way to find yourself is to lose yourself in the service of others." - Mahatma Gandhi

"The purpose of human life is to serve, and to show compassion and the will to help others." - Albert Schweitzer

Prayer

Dear Lord,
I come to you today asking that you watch over and bless the humanitarian workers who selflessly serve others in difficult and dangerous situations. I lift them in prayer, asking for your protection and safety to always be with them. I pray for wisdom and guidance for their decisions and actions to be led by your hand as they serve those in need. I ask for provisions for their needs, so they have the resources and support to continue their important work.

I ask for the strength and courage to serve and help others in my own life. Please help me to see the needs of those around me and to have the bravery to step out of my comfort zone to serve them. May I have the compassion and generosity to put the needs of others before my own and to make a positive impact in the world through my actions. Thank you for the selfless example set by these humanitarian workers. May they know they are appreciated and valued, and may they continue to inspire all. Amen.

Declaration

I am committed to being a voice for humanitarian workers and a source of support and encouragement for their incredible work. I believe that every person deserves access to basic human needs, such as food, shelter, and medical care, and that it is the duty of all of us to work towards this goal. I declare that I will support humanitarian workers in any way I can and advocate for their safety and well-being.

I also believe in God's promise to always be with humanitarian workers, watch over them, and protect them from harm. I declare that God will give them strength, wisdom, and courage to face any obstacle that comes their way. And I know that God will be their refuge and strength, a present help in times of trouble. I will pray for them and work towards a world where they are safe and able to impact the lives of those they serve positively. I believe humanitarian workers are heroes, and will do everything I can to support and uplift them.

Prayer Lifestyle

End to Human Trafficking

Praying for an end to human trafficking is a way to lift those who are being exploited and abused and to ask God to intervene and bring about change. This can be a powerful way to support those suffering and to bring about an end to this form of modern-day slavery.

Scripture References

Isaiah 61:1: "The Spirit of the Sovereign Lord is on me, because the Lord has anointed me to proclaim good news to the poor. He has sent me to bind up the brokenhearted, to proclaim freedom for the captives and release from darkness for the prisoners,"

Psalm 72:4: "May he defend the cause of the poor of the people, give deliverance to the children of the needy, and crush the oppressor."

Jeremiah 22:3: "This is what the Lord says: Do what is just and right. Rescue from the hand of the oppressor the one who has been robbed. Do no wrong or violence to the foreigner, the fatherless or the widow, and do not shed innocent blood in this place."

Inspirational/Motivational Quotes

"Human trafficking is a crime against humanity. We must unite our efforts to free victims and stop this abuse." - Antonio Guterres

"It is not enough to be compassionate. You must act." - Dalai Lama

Prayer

Dear Lord,

I come before you humbly lifting all those exploited and abused through human trafficking. I pray for your intervention that you would bring an end to this form of modern-day slavery. I ask for your protection and provision for those suffering, so they will know your love and care for them in their time of need.

I pray for wisdom and guidance for those working to bring about change, that your Spirit would empower them to make a difference in this world. I ask for courage to speak out against this injustice and to stand up for the oppressed and marginalized. I pray that my voice would be a voice for those who cannot speak for themselves and that I would be a light in the darkness, shining your truth and love.

Lord, please give me the strength, boldness, and determination to advocate for those trafficked and to work toward a world where all people are treated with dignity and respect. I pray that you would awaken the hearts of those in positions of power and influence, that they would take action to end human trafficking, and that your wisdom and justice would guide them. I trust in your unfailing love and believe that all things are possible with you. Amen.

Declaration

I declare an end to this modern-day slavery we know as human trafficking. I know we can bring about real change and hope for those suffering from human trafficking. I believe that prayer has the power to protect and provide for those who have been subjected to this horrific injustice, so I am committed to using my voice and actions to work toward a world where all individuals are treated with dignity and respect.

As a person of faith, I know that God is always with us, and I trust in His promise to defend the weak and the oppressed. I will stand in solidarity with those who have been affected by human trafficking and work towards bringing an end to this atrocity. I will not be silent in the face of this injustice. I believe that through collaboration and teamwork, we can work towards creating a world where human trafficking is abolished and where all individuals are free to live their lives with dignity and respect.

I will not be discouraged by the challenges ahead; instead, I will be inspired by the possibility of a better world for all. I will continue to lift those affected by human trafficking in prayer and will not stop working towards a world where they are free from this modern-day slavery. I will champion the case of the oppressed and do all I can to bring an end to this modern-day slavery.

Ivon Valerie

Prayer Lifestyle

Ivon Valerie

Natural Disasters and Relief Efforts

Natural Disasters and Relief Efforts are a very real part of our lives. They can bring heartache and destruction yet inspire us to help those in need. This chapter focuses on the power that Natural Disasters and Relief Efforts have in our everyday existence. We will find prayers and declarations so that one may pray for those affected by disasters and discover ways to assist them through their trying time, along with how we can support disaster relief efforts worldwide.

Prayer Lifestyle

Safety During Natural Disasters

Natural disasters can be devastating and can cause great harm to individuals and communities. It is important to pray for the safety of those affected by these events and protect their homes and properties.

Scripture References

Psalm 46:1-3: "God is our refuge and strength, an ever-present help in trouble. Therefore we will not fear, though the earth give way and the mountains fall into the heart of the sea, though its waters roar and foam and the mountains quake with their surging."

Isaiah 43:2: "When you pass through the waters, I will be with you; and when you pass through the rivers, they will not sweep over you. When you walk through the fire, you will not be burned; the flames will not set you ablaze."

Matthew 7:25: "The rain came down, the streams rose, and the winds blew and beat against that house; yet it did not fall, because it had its foundation on the rock."

Inspirational/Motivational Quotes:

"Nature is not a place to visit. It is home." - Gary Snyder

Ivon Valerie

"In every walk with nature, one receives far more than he seeks." - John Muir

Prayer

Dear Lord,

I come to you today in humility and with a heart full of gratitude. I am aware of the natural disasters affecting people worldwide, and I am grateful for your protection and provision. As I pray for the safety of those affected by these disasters, I also ask for your protection and provision for me. I ask that you keep me safe from harm and bless me with your provision so that I may continue to serve and help those in need.

I pray for wisdom for crisis management leaders and guidance for those on the ground providing relief efforts. I ask that you give them the courage and determination to carry out their duties with compassion and kindness. I also pray for their families that you may give them peace and comfort during these trying times.

I know you are in control and will always protect and provide for your children. I pray that you continue to bless me and all those affected by these disasters so that we may have the strength and resilience to overcome the challenges that lie ahead. Amen.

Declaration

I trust in God's sovereignty, knowing He controls all things, including natural disasters. I believe He has a plan and purpose for every person affected by these events and will use these experiences to bring about good in their lives. I declare my faith in God's provision for those affected by natural disasters, and I know He is a God of abundance and has the resources to provide for all of our needs, including those impacted by these events.

I am grateful for the opportunities given to me to pray for and support those affected by natural disasters, and I take this opportunity seriously. My prayers and actions can make a difference in their lives, bringing hope and healing in the aftermath of the crisis, so I stand with those affected by natural disasters, declaring my faith and commitment to them in this time of need. I believe that together, through prayer and action, we can positively impact the lives of those impacted by these events.

Ivon Valerie

Protection of Homes and Properties

Natural disasters can cause significant damage to homes and properties, leaving individuals and families without a safe place to live. It is important to pray for the protection of these homes and properties during times of crisis.

Scripture References

Psalm 127:1: "Unless the Lord builds the house, the builders labor in vain. Unless the Lord watches over the city, the guards stand watch in vain."

Psalm 91:9-11: "If you make the Most High your dwelling— even the Lord, who is my refuge— then no harm will befall you, no disaster will come near your tent. For he will command his angels concerning you to guard you in all your ways."

Proverbs 24:3-4: "By wisdom a house is built, and through understanding it is established; through knowledge its rooms are filled with rare and beautiful treasures."

Inspirational/Motivational Quotes

"A house is made of walls and beams; a home is built with love and dreams." - Unknown

Prayer Lifestyle

"Home is where love resides, memories are created, friends always belong, and laughter never ends." - Unknown

Prayer

Dear Lord,

I come to you today with a heavy heart as I lift those affected by natural disasters. I pray for their safety and well-being and the protection and provision of their homes and properties.

I understand the pain and suffering of losing a home, and I pray that you will be with those without a safe place to live. I ask that you provide them with shelter and comfort and bless them with your peace and grace.

I pray for wisdom for those responsible for rebuilding homes and properties. I ask that you give them the knowledge and resources they need to do so effectively and efficiently. I also pray for the means to rebuild and the generosity of those who can contribute to these efforts.

Lord, I trust in your sovereignty and provision in all things. I know you are always with us and will never leave or forsake us. I pray that you continue to bless those affected by natural disasters so that they may have the strength and resilience to overcome the challenges that lie ahead. Amen.

Ivon Valerie

Declaration

I declare that I will not turn a blind eye to the plight of those whose homes and properties have been affected by natural disasters. I declare that I am committed to lifting these individuals in prayer, asking for God's protection and provision for all their needs.

I declare that I trust in God's sovereignty, knowing He controls all things and will provide for those in need. I will be a voice for struggling people, calling attention to their needs and advocating for their well-being. I declare that I will provide comfort and support, offering a listening ear and a shoulder to lean on to those hurting.

I declare that I will not be swayed by fear or doubt but will always trust God's love and grace. I declare that I will remain steadfast in my commitment to those affected by natural disasters, offering my prayers and support no matter what the future may bring. I am a champion for those suffering and will continue to be a source of hope and comfort for all those in crisis.

Prayer Lifestyle

Provision During Times of Crisis

Natural disasters can leave individuals and families needing necessities such as food, water, and shelter. It is important to pray for provision during these times of crisis.

Scripture References

Psalm 23:1: "The Lord is my shepherd, I shall not be in want."

Matthew 6:25-26: "Therefore I tell you, do not worry about your life, what you will eat or drink; or about your body, what you will wear. Is not life more than food, and the body more than clothes? Look at the birds of the air; they do not sow or reap or store away in barns, and yet your heavenly Father feeds them. Are you not much more valuable than they?"

Isaiah 41:10: "So do not fear, for I am with you; do not be dismayed, for I am your God. I will strengthen you and help you; I will uphold you with my righteous right hand."

Inspirational/Motivational Quotes

"In times of crisis, we must not forget to ask for help, not just from others, but from the Lord." - Unknown

"God's provision is not limited by our crisis, but rather it's multiplied in it." - Unknown

Ivon Valerie

"When we bring our fears and worries to God, He replaces them with His peace and provision." - Unknown

Prayer

Dear Lord,
I come to you today with a heart full of concern for those in need of provision during times of crisis. I lift those struggling to meet their basic needs, whether due to natural disasters or other circumstances.

I pray for your provision in their lives, and I ask that you bless them with food, water, and shelter and meet all their needs according to your glorious riches in Christ Jesus. I pray that you give them the strength and courage to face each day with hope and joy.

Lord, I need your wisdom in directing aid and relief efforts, and I pray that those responsible for providing aid and relief will be guided by your hand and be able to reach those in need with love and compassion. I also pray for the generosity of those who can contribute to these efforts, that they may have a heart full of kindness and love.

Father, I trust your faithfulness to provide for your children, and I am sure that you are always with us and will never leave or forsake us. I pray that you continue to bless those in need. Amen.

Declaration

I stand with those in need of provision during times of crisis, declaring my faith and commitment to them in their time of need. I believe that together, through prayer and action, we can bring hope and provision to those struggling during these difficult times.

I declare my commitment to supporting those in need through my prayers and actions. I believe that it is our responsibility as believers to come alongside those struggling, offering encouragement, support, and practical help in any way we can.

I trust in the faithfulness of God, knowing that He is always present with us, especially during times of crisis. I believe He has a plan and purpose for every person in need and will use these experiences to bring about good in their lives.

I am grateful for the opportunities given to me to pray for and support those in need during times of crisis. My prayers and actions can make a difference in their lives, bringing hope and stability to their struggles.

Ivon Valerie

Guidance in Disaster Relief Efforts

Knowing how to help and where to start helping can be difficult in times of crisis. We can always start by lifting those in charge of disaster relief efforts in prayer, asking for God's guidance and wisdom in their decisions and actions.

Scripture References

Isaiah 30:21: "Whether you turn to the right or to the left, your ears will hear a voice behind you, saying, "This is the way; walk in it."

Proverbs 3:5-6: "Trust in the Lord with all your heart and lean not on your own understanding; in all your ways submit to him, and he will make your paths straight."

James 1:5: "If any of you lacks wisdom, you should ask God, who gives generously to all without finding fault, and it will be given to you."

Inspirational/Motivational Quotes

"In the chaos of a disaster, it is important to trust in God's guidance to bring hope and restoration." - Unknown

Prayer Lifestyle

"When we pray for guidance in disaster relief efforts, we are partnering with God to bring about His will and bring hope to those in need." - Unknown

Prayer

Dear Lord,
I come to you today with a heart full of compassion for those affected by crises and natural disasters. I lift those in charge of disaster relief efforts and pray for your guidance and wisdom in their decisions and actions.

I ask that you bless those in charge of disaster relief with the knowledge and resources they need to respond to the crisis effectively. I pray for their safety and well-being and for protecting all those involved in the relief efforts. I ask that you give them the strength and courage to face each day with hope and grace.

I also lift those affected by the crisis. I pray for your provision and protection and for the comfort of your presence in their lives. I ask that you bless them with hope and restoration and bring peace and healing to their hearts during this difficult time. Amen.

Declaration

I declare that we are working tirelessly to bring hope and restoration in times of crisis. I declare my commitment to supporting disaster relief through my prayers and actions. I trust in God's ability to bring hope and restoration in crisis, knowing He is the source of all comfort and peace. I believe He has a plan and purpose for every disaster and will use these experiences to bring about good in the lives of those affected.

I am grateful for the opportunity to pray for and support disaster relief efforts. My prayers and actions can make a difference in the lives of those affected by the crisis, bringing hope and restoration in the aftermath of a disaster.

I stand with those in charge of disaster relief efforts, declaring my faith and commitment to them in their important work. I believe we can partner with God to bring about His will in times of crisis, bringing hope and restoration to those in need.

Prayer Lifestyle

Wisdom for Leaders in Times of Crisis

Leaders play a crucial role in guiding and directing disaster relief efforts, and it is important to lift them in prayer, asking for God's wisdom and guidance.

Scripture References

Proverbs 11:14 - "For lack of guidance a nation falls, but many advisers make victory sure."

Proverbs 2:6-7 - "For the Lord gives wisdom; from his mouth come knowledge and understanding. He holds victory in store for the upright, he is a shield to those whose walk is blameless,"

Isaiah 33:6 - "He will be the sure foundation for your times, a rich store of salvation and wisdom and knowledge; the fear of the Lord is the key to this treasure."

Inspirational/Motivational Quotes

"Wisdom for leaders in times of crisis is not found in their understanding, but in seeking the guidance of the Lord." - Unknown

Ivon Valerie

"When leaders turn to God for wisdom in times of crisis, they become a sure foundation for the people they lead." - Unknown

"Leaders who fear the Lord and seek His wisdom will be able to navigate crisis with the knowledge and understanding that comes from God." - Unknown

Prayer

Dear Lord,
I humbly pray before You today for leaders facing a crisis. I seek Your divine intervention and direction to steer them through these difficult times. Let the reverential fear of the Lord possess their hearts and guide all they do so that their decisions may align with Your will. May compassion fill our leaders as they lead us through hardship; let them become an embodiment of your love and grace unto salvation for those who follow them.

God, I wholeheartedly rely on Your compassionate care and shielding for those in such a crisis. Bestow them with calming serenity and peace while providing hope and restoration to their lives. Furthermore, may our leaders be guided by Your divine knowledge so they can act out of sympathy rather than wisdom as they work towards bettering this situation.

Lord, I implore that you be present with our leaders as they face the hard times ahead. Grant them strength and resilience to overcome whatever difficult obstacles lay in their way, allowing them to become a beacon of hope for those around them. Amen.

Declaration

I declare that God will grant guidance and wisdom to leaders during times of crisis. I believe that when leaders turn to God for wisdom, they become a sure foundation for the people they lead, offering hope and stability in the midst of uncertainty.

I declare my commitment to lifting leaders in crisis through prayer and support. I believe it is our responsibility as believers to come alongside those leading in difficult times, offering our prayers and encouragement for their journey.

I trust in God's provision and protection for those affected by the crisis, knowing He is always present with us, especially during times of difficulty. I declare my faith in the fear of the Lord as a guiding principle for leaders during times of crisis. When leaders turn to God for wisdom and guidance, they are empowered to bring about salvation for the people they lead, bringing hope and stability to those in need.

The End

www.ingramcontent.com/pod-product-compliance
Lightning Source LLC
Chambersburg PA
CBHW070714160426
43192CB00009B/1181